T0302731

ACOSTA

First published by O-Books, 2010
O Books is an imprint of John Hunt Publishing Ltd., The Bothy, Deershot Lodge, Park Lane, Ropley, Hants, SO24 0BE, UK
office1@o-books.net
www.o-books.com

Distribution in:

UK and Europe
Orca Book Services Ltd
Home trade orders
tradeorders@orcabookservices.co.uk
Tel: 01235 465521
Fax: 01235 465555

Export orders
exportorders@orcabookservices.co.uk
Tel: 01235 465516 or 01235 465517
Fax: 01235 465555

USA and Canada
NBN
custserv@nbnbooks.com
Tel: 1 800 462 6420 Fax: 1 800 338 4550

Australia and New Zealand
Brumby Books
sales@brumbybooks.com.au
Tel: 61 3 9761 5535 Fax: 61 3 9761 7095

Far East (offices in Singapore, Thailand, Hong Kong, Taiwan)
Pansing Distribution Pte Ltd
kemal@pansing.com
Tel: 65 6319 9939 Fax: 65 6462 5761

South Africa
Stephan Phillips (pty) Ltd
Email: orders@stephanphillips.com
Tel: 27 21 4489839 Telefax: 27 21 4479879

ISBN: 978 1 84694 333 1

Design: Stuart Davies

A CIP catalogue record for this book is available from the British Library.

Printed by Digital Book Print

O Books operates a distinctive and ethical publishing philosophy in all areas of its business, from its global network of authors to production and worldwide distribution.

ACOSTA

Yolanda Acosta

BOOKS

Winchester, UK
Washington, USA

Chapter One

Our Worst Hour

Like most other buildings in the Old Town area, the interior of Hotel Albuquerque is an accurate reflection of days gone by: polished brick floors; elaborate Spanish furniture; vigas overhead; ristras on the walls; area carpets featuring Indian designs in earth tones. The hotel's Q bar, however, looks more like a club you might find in Miami than a lounge in the heart of the wild west. There are several seating areas, and the sofas in all of them are upholstered in pink or purple or purplish-pink. The walls are salmon colored; the ceilings are rose tinted; the overhead chandeliers are huge, modern, elaborate. Unlike the angular Indian designs on the carpeting in the lobby, the carpeting in the Q bar consists of lighter and darker pink swirls on a pink background.

But I can describe the Q bar only because I have been there many times. On the night of April 19, 2006, I did not notice the pinkness of the place — or anything else for that matter.

We had just arrived, myself and my friend Darla, and we had only just ordered our drinks when my cell phone rang.

"Where are you?" my daughter Leah Dawn asked casually.

I told her.

"Stay there for a while. I'm coming out there."

She might have fooled me, because her voice was so breezy, the tone you would expect from an adult daughter who had nothing more in mind than seizing an opportunity to have a drink with her mother on a Wednesday night. But then some impulse made her say more: "I have some bad news, something I have to tell you."

Whatever her news was, it wasn't just bad; it was devastating.

I knew that immediately. Her effort to conceal it initially only confirmed that it would be worse than I could possibly imagine. I stopped breathing. The faces of my loved ones began to flash across my mind: my son Brandon, my mother, my sister....

"It's Uncle Oscar," Leah Dawn continued, now unable to stop herself.

That was impossible. Oscar was in the Dominican, managing the New York Yankee's Gulf Coast League. "You stop," I screamed into the phone. "Don't you tell me that."

"He was in a car accident," Leah Dawn said.

"You shut up," I screamed. "Don't you tell me that. You shut up right now."

"He died."

She was screeching herself now, half talking, half crying.

"Shut up, shut up. Don't tell me this!"

I could feel as much as see that people were moving towards me, pressing into me, making it harder to breathe: the bartender, the managers, the waiting staff, Darla....

"My brother is dead!" I cried, the phone still open in my hand.

I turned to Darla. "Call Steinbrenner," I demanded. She worked for the governor's office at the time; she could get a hold of someone who could get a hold of Steinbrenner if she tried. "You tell him I want my brother back now."

Leah Dawn's voice was coming from somewhere. "Mom, I'm coming. I'm coming right over."

Someone was holding a glass of water to my lips. I could feel the liquid trickling down the side of my chin. Darla had her own phone out now. I could hear enough of the conversation to know that she wasn't calling Steinbrenner; she was calling Sandra, her aunt, my friend, a woman I had worked for some years ago.

Sandra and her husband Tony and Ralph and I had spent a lot of time together. We had traveled together. Ralph had died in 1998 but I was still mourning him. My father had died in 1986 and I was still mourning him too. I refused to believe that Oscar was gone as well.

Later I believed, but only because I could see no way around it.

We were all at my house, Leah Dawn and her friend Heather and Brandon and Darla and Sandra. They were helping me to pack for my trip to Portales, where my mother lived. "What else?" asked Sandra, looking around the room.

"Go through the drawers. Throw in anything black. Everything black."

When I worked for her, Sandra had owned a dress shop. She would know what to pack. Watching her slide hangers across the rack in my closet, I thought I felt calm enough to call my mother.

"Oh, mi hija, estoy sentada con tu tía. Volvé de Mexico. No puedo estar lejos. Nos estamos preparando para ir a la cama."

She was sitting with my Aunt Victoria. She'd gone to Mexico to visit her but she had felt uneasy about being away. When she spoke to Oscar on Easter Sunday, just a few days earlier, she'd told him that she felt closer to him when she was home in Portales. I'd spoken to my mother only the day before and she had remarked that Oscar had sounded so happy on the phone.

"Tengo deseos de ir a hacer una visita," I told her now. *I feel like coming down for a visit.*

It would be a four hour drive. My heart was broken, but my voice hadn't broken yet, so I continued, telling her to go to bed, it would be after midnight before I got there. I hoped she would fall asleep right away, because I knew that never ever again would she have the opportunity for a few hours of sound sleep.

The suitcase was almost full. Staring at the black bundle it occurred to me that I had never looked into a suitcase before and seen only black. I was mesmerized for a moment. Then I was flying around the apartment, frantically searching for pictures of Oscar, pulling them down from walls, from the surfaces of furniture. There was a poster-sized picture of Oscar that I knew I would want displayed at the funeral. Oscar was everywhere —

in my house, in my mother's house, in my sister Carol's house. Images of Oscar were more prevalent than those of all of the other men we'd known collectively. The closet door was still open, and my eye fell on the hat box where I kept some photos and also the gold coins that Ralph had given me years ago. I took it down from the shelf and showed the coins to Leah Dawn. "If anything happens to me, these are for you and your brother," I told her.

The drive from Albuquerque to Portales was all moon and sky. The moon was larger than I had ever seen it, a silver beacon guiding us to our destination. While Leah Dawn drove, she talked to Naomi, her cousin, Carol's daughter, on her cell phone. The facts Leah Dawn got from Naomi helped us to piece together the story.

Oscar had not died alone. He had been with Humberto Trejo, a field coordinator for the Yankees. They had been in the car together. As far as anyone knew, they both died instantly. The Yankees were going to take care of getting Oscar's body out of the Dominican and back to the States. Humberto's body would be returned to his home somewhere in Venezuela.

Carol had gotten the call hours ago, Leah Dawn said, from Kathy, Oscar's wife, who lived in Tampa. Kathy had known better than to give the news to Carol directly, so when Carol answered the phone, she asked if Cheto, Carol's husband, was at home. Carol said he was but she refused to put him on the line. "What is it?" she demanded. "What happened? Why do you want him?"

So Kathy told her, and Carol immediately dropped the phone and ran outside screaming. Naomi said that she lost her mind and began to roll in the dirt. Her husband tried to pull her up, but she continued to throw herself down again. So Cheto called Naomi, and by the time Naomi got there and they calmed her down and got her inside, a good two hours had passed.

All of this meant that by the time Naomi called Leah Dawn and Leah Dawn called me, everyone knew that Oscar Acosta was dead. The news would have been on the Internet, on the ESPN site, on all the sports channels.

When Carol had calmed down enough, we learned from Naomi, she was inspired to call the local hospital and request that an ambulance be sent to our mother's house in advance of giving her the news. This would have happened sometime after I'd called my mother to say that I was coming down; so she wouldn't have gotten her couple of hours of peaceful sleep anyway. Then Carol and her family drove to Mother's house and waited until the ambulance arrived to go in. Our Auntie opened the door. Mother was already asleep, and as Carol was incapable of giving her the news herself, it was Naomi who woke her gently to tell her that her baby was gone. Mother got out of bed and immediately collapsed, and thanks to Carol's foresight, the EMT was there to help her.

When we rushed in some hours later, Mother was seated on the sofa, already dressed in black, fixed in a stupor of rocking and crying from which she would not emerge for several days.

"Mi niño chiquito. Tú fuiste una estrella desde el día que naciste.¿Cómo puede ser? ¿Cómo puede ser?" I went right to her and collapsed in her arms. "Mi hijo, mi hijo," she cried into my neck.

We cried together, Mother and Carol and I and the others, bundled as carelessly as the black clothes in my suitcase. At some point I moved away to give her some air. "¿Dónde estás tú, hijo mío?" she asked me.

The events that followed played out in a kind of parallel reality, in which even the most familiar objects and voices seemed strange and at a distance. We cried all night. Then morning came, and with it a non-stop parade of visitors arrived bearing food, flowers, and memories. We cried with everyone. All through the house people were caressing, stroking, wailing....

Men came, many of whom had been Oscar's classmates, but

unlike Oscar, they had not gone off to live the lives they had dreamed about. They were still here, ranching, farming, tending to the ongoing needs of heavy equipment. Jim Bob Nuchols came and cried with Mother for a long time. He had been a surrogate father to Oscar. He had taught him how to be a cowboy, as well as how to box and how to play baseball. In all his 49 years, Oscar had never tried to deny the cowboy in him. He had always come back to Portales. And when he was back, he got up at three in the morning and worked 18-hour days like any other man on any other ranch.

When Jim Bob finally stood up, Mother said, "Usted, usted será uno de los portadores del féretro." *You, you will be one of the pallbearers.* She nudged me. "Dígale, dígale, Yolanda." *Tell him, tell him, Yolanda.* And so I told Jim Bob in English and of course he said he was honored, and he sank to his knees at Mother's feet so that she would understand.

As the morning went on, Mother designated more and more men to be pallbearers, and everyone she asked agreed to do it. Everyone wanted to carry Oscar Acosta's body to its final resting place.

At some point it dawned on me that she had more commitments than were necessary, but as the process gave her a focus for her grief, I said nothing. She wouldn't have allowed it anyway.

By noon we had more food than could be kept refrigerated, but only some of our guests were able to eat. The rest of us were sick to the stomach with wretchedness. "Mi hijo, mi hijo," Mother continued to cry.

"Maybe a tranquilizer for her," someone suggested.

Mother heard and quickly responded, "No voy a tomar ninguna píldora. Deseo estar despierta cuando vuelva Oscar. Deseo recordarlo todo." *I'm not taking any pill. I want to be awake when Oscar returns. I want to remember everything.*

We had another brother, an older brother from the time before Mother came up from Mexico and met Daddy, and he still lived there, in Juarez. Even though he had stayed in Mexico and Oscar had been raised in New Mexico, they had loved each other very much. I called John to let him know.

Because I was involved in politics, I knew who to call at the governor's office to begin the process that would allow John and his family to cross the border to attend the funeral. The people at the governor's office helped me to reach Customs in El Paso. The supervisor at Customs knew who Oscar was. A few more calls and the arrangements were made.

We spoke to Kathy many times during the day. Mostly she told us how people there in Tampa were doing and we told her how we were doing in Portales. In that sense, we mourned together at first. During one conversation, I mentioned that I would get a hold of Father Tobin, Oscar's dear friend and the pastor of the Catholic Church in Portales. I thought he should be the one to preside over the funeral. That's when Kathy said, "There won't be a funeral. I'm having Oscar cremated."

"You can't do that," I cried. "What about Mother? She has to see him again!"

"This is about me and Oscar," Kathy replied. "Oscar wanted cremation. We talked about it many times."

I did not give this information to my mother right away. Her grief was so great and I couldn't bring myself to add to it. Nor did I speak to Kathy again throughout the ordeal. If we wanted to pass on information, there were plenty of other people to do it for us, such as our daughters. The Yankees had arranged to have a memorial in Tampa, as soon as Oscar's body was returned. Until then, there was no point arguing with Kathy.

Again we did not sleep, or at least we did not go to bed. If we dozed, we dozed together, piled on the sofa, clinging to one another like survivors on a life raft.

The second morning was like the first: people, food, embraces, more tears. We learned from Amanda, Oscar and Kathy's 28-year-old daughter, that Kathy had been notified that

Oscar's body had been returned from the Dominican. But then not long after, she was contacted again and told that in fact it was Humberto Trejo's body that had been sent to Tampa. Oscar's body had been flown to Venezuela, and poor Mrs Trejo had been the one to realize the mistake when she went to see her husband and found my brother instead. "Éste no es mi marido! Éste no es mi marido!" she had cried. *This is not my husband!* She contacted one of the Yankee reps. Of course they promised to take care of the matter as quickly as possible, but all I could think was that the Venezuelan president, Hugo Chavez, might want to keep my brother there, to be used as a hostage for political reasons.

After everything else, I just couldn't handle the fact that Oscar had been sent to the wrong country. I went outside and cried to God, "Why? For what possible reason?"

I had googled the newspapers in the Dominican to learn as much as I could, and what I found out was that Oscar's car was clipped by another car and then hit by an SUV. Both Oscar and Humberto were killed instantly. The SUV driver was fine, except for a broken leg. Apparently Oscar and Humberto had just left the baseball field. Some officials from the Yankees had arrived in Santo Domingo and were driving behind them — and so they were there to identify the bodies. The U.S. State Department warns American citizens continually that if they are going to drive in the Dominican Republic, they need to watch for erratic drivers. Many times a two lane highway can suddenly turn into six lanes. Usually the manager and other baseball officials are assigned drivers in foreign countries. I did not understand why Oscar had not had a driver assigned to him. I did not understand why Oscar had been in the Dominican in the first place. If he hadn't been bilingual, they never could have sent him there. He would have been managing a team in Tampa.

Anxiety overtook me and I pulled a large branch down from one of the trees in the yard and beat the tree with it until virtually every leaf was gone. Exhausted, I sat down on the grass. Brandon pulled up with his friend Sylvia, and as they got out of the car, I heard Sylvia ask him how I was holding up. There was silence for a moment. I suppose they were taking in the broken tree limb, the leafless tree, me sitting cross-legged staring at nothing.... "That's my mom," I heard Brandon whisper.

Even though there was no body yet, Carol and I felt that we could no longer put off the task of getting Kathy to change her mind about the funeral. But, in fact, now that there would be a delay in getting Oscar back, Kathy was in even more of a hurry to make the cremation arrangements. She had been told that in the Dominican the embalming methods left something to be desired. Carol begged her. "Even if the casket is closed," she said, "it's better than no casket — no Oscar — at all." But as she would not concede, we were forced to conclude that it was time to tell Mother, who was still making plans for a grand funeral with more pallbearers than any funeral had ever seen before.

"¡Ahí van a quemar a mi hijo!" she screamed when we told her. *They're going to burn my son!* "No, no," she insisted. "Ellos no lo pueden quemar. Yo deseo que lo envuelvan como a Jesús en una sábana blanca." *They can't burn him. I want him wrapped like Jesus in a white sheet.*

It took us awhile to convince her that the matter was out of our hands. When she finally began to understand, her grief shifted; now it was grief mixed with outrage. It was what Oscar told Kathy he wanted, I reminded her, but she was not buying it.

Meanwhile, and even though Oscar had not been returned yet, the Yankees had a memorial service for both Oscar and Humberto, in Tampa, at Legend's field. The stadium was filled with baseball greats from around the country as well as with young men from the Dominican who had flown over to be part of the service.

Carol and I, and our families, stayed with Mother in Portales, making plans for our own service.

We were still waiting to hear that Oscar's body had been

returned when the heavy rain started. Then later, when the rain began to abate, Carol called me out to the front porch. She spread her arms. "Look, Yolie," she said, "Oscar is in heaven." And sure enough when I looked I saw not one but several vivid rainbows glowing against a still darkened sky. Carol hugged me and whispered, "Happy Birthday." I had all but forgotten. We stayed outside, where the sun was shining in some places and rain was falling in others, for a long time.

Hours later Kathy spoke to Carol again. Oscar had finally been returned to Tampa, and Kathy had gone to see him and reported that he was unrecognizable.

Afterwards, I called the funeral home in Tampa. "This is Yolanda Acosta," I told the director, a woman with a kind voice. "Has there been a cremation yet?"

"No," she answered. "We went to Miami to get the body and brought him back."

It took all the courage I could muster to keep my voice from cracking. "Can you tell me what he was wearing?" I asked. "Was he wearing street clothes or his baseball uniform?"

"His uniform, dear. His face was fine; the trauma was all in his chest, though they don't embalm there the way we do here. Your sister-in-law came earlier, with her daughter. She didn't think Amanda could handle it, so she went in alone. She had flowers and pictures to put in the casket. Now he's in the crematorium."

"Thank you, thank you," I whispered. "And please, don't mention to Kathy that I called."

We organized a Rosary service in Portales a few days later. I called all the papers, not only in Portales but up in Albuquerque and other areas where Oscar had made many friends. We hung up pictures of him in the front of the little church. Even though it was short notice, people came from all over the state and beyond. Our relatives came from both Mexico and Colorado. Some of the Yankees came, even though most had already attended the first service in Tampa. Some of the Cubs came too. Jakie and Maureen

Howard, local musicians whom Oscar adored, played the violin.

Once, when Kathy and Oscar had separated and we were sharing an apartment in Corrales, I asked Oscar who was the one who had really been responsible for setting him on the path that would lead him into the world of sports, and he said it was Jakie; Jakie had taught him how to pitch.

After the Rosary, people took turns telling their stories about Oscar. When it was my turn, I read a story that had been written about him in the *Daily Herald Times* out of Chicago. And then I put the newspaper aside and told the congregation my own story.

My story of Oscar Acosta cannot be contained by a casket; you can move it from a small country on an island in the West Indies to Venezuela and back to the States again without the slightest bit of decomposition. It does not burn. The story of Oscar Acosta is very much a family story; it is the story of a man and woman who endured a great struggle to see their children thrive in the land of opportunity. And as such, it is a universal story that has been told many times by many people all over the world. And it is also a unique story, because Oscar Acosta is the unique manifestation of the dream that immigrants share.

Chapter Two

Where It Started

Zacatecas has a rich history, and like so many other places where the story of the past is lavish, it proceeds from a fusion of minerals and blood.

Of the minerals, silver was the most abundant, and once the rich vein that harbored it was discovered in 1546, many peoples came to the heart of Mexico to participate in the silver rush, including the Spanish under Philip II. In fact, it was Zacatecas silver that financed the wars fought by his Spanish Empire.

As for the blood, it flowed more or less continuously. In 1914 Zacatecas witnessed the bloodiest battle of the entire Mexican Revolution. But even before that it had earned a reputation for bloodletting. One famous event was the result of a revolt by Mexican Federalists in 1835. The Federalists opposed the president, the infamous Antonio Lopez de Santa Anna, because he had suspended the constitution and established a dictatorship to take its place. The Federalists were easily crushed, and thereafter, to reward his soldiers for their good work, Santa Anna granted them the freedom to spend two full days raping and pillaging in Zacatecas.

A land that receives the blood from such violence must also retain some vestige of the events themselves, some undercurrent that drives people to cling to customs that the outside world would term barbaric.

My mother was born in Ojo de Agua, a village in Zacatecas. In Ojo de Agua the prickly pear cacti grew as large as trees; everyone who lived there knew how to carefully pull the outer layers off the fruit, the pear (which is really more like a fig), so as not to allow the tiny spines to penetrate their skin.

Ojo de Agua was surrounded by beautiful mountains, and though the land was mostly dry, there was a stream that flowed through the center of the village. Back when my mother was a girl, the women toweled their heads against the constant pounding of the sun and gathered along the banks to scrub their laundry on the rocks and hang it on tree branches to dry.

My mother's father, Jesus Salazar, had land and cattle. He was not what we here in the United States would call a wealthy man, but in Ojo de Agua, he was certainly not considered poor. He was tall and handsome, something of an icon in his large ornate sombrero. Many people saw in him a resemblance to General Emiliano Zapata. He rode all the time, either horses or mules, and his feet, in their leather *huaraches,* were always callused. He was known to everyone, and as a gesture of respect, most people called him "el comisionario," *the commissioner.*

There were five children in the family and they were all kept busy working in some way or other on the ranch. My mother's job each day was to take the corn kernels from the plants they grew to the mill. Once the corn was ground and made into dough, she would bring it back home and help her mother to prepare tortillas. There was no stove. The tortillas were slapped into shape by hand and placed on a kind of ceramic grate in the fireplace. The kitchen was black with all the wood smoke that had accumulated over the years.

My mother was 15 years old — and weighed less than 100 pounds — the morning she met Jeronimo. She had seen him before — perhaps they had even exchanged a few smiles — but they had never formally met. On this particular morning, however, a romance was about to blossom. It happened like this: As my mother was walking to the corn mill, Jeronimo appeared, as he often did, at some distance on his horse. But this time he was not alone. Several of his friends rode at his side, which could only mean one thing in that place at that time. My mother was about to be stolen.

The scene unfolded in a flash. With Jeronimo in the lead, the men began to gallop. As soon as he was close enough, and without slowing down his horse, Jeronimo bent from the waist and wrapped one strong arm around Mother's waist and heaved her up onto the horse with him. And away they rode.

"This is rape!" I said to my mother once when she told me the story. "Así es la costumbre," she insisted. *No, no, it is custom.*

When a man liked a girl, she explained, he rode out with his friends at his side and simply stole her. Once he had taken her away, his friends remained, to make sure the girl's brothers (my mother had three) did not follow the couple and try to get her back.

In my mother's case, the gossip about the daughter of el comisionario spread like wildfire: "¿Oh, oyó usted? Conchita fue robada ayer por la noche." *Oh, did you hear? Conchita was stolen last night.* Later, maybe a few days later, the couple would reappear and visit the girl's family to ask forgiveness. But again, this was all a formality. There was nothing to be gained by refusing forgiveness because by then the couple was already married — or at the least, they had already been to bed.

My mother and Jeronimo set up a home of their own in a small house only a short distance away from Mother's family. Life was hard. Jeronimo didn't have any land. His profession was playing cards, and while he seemed to be quite good at it, like most gamblers, he was also a womanizer. Was she happy back then? I don't know. She says she loved him very much; yet when she recounts her memories of their time together, she always moves directly from the story of the day he stole her to the story of the day he died, some six years later.

They had children by then. Juan had been born before the end of their first year together. He was very dark skinned, like his father, and my mother's family accepted him reluctantly, especially when his uncles were there with their children, who were said to be almost white by comparison. Mother's mother,

Sara, would taunt her, dancing around with her lighter skinned grandchildren until Mother showed her anger and announced that she was leaving. Only then would Sara exclaim, "Oh, no seas así. Déjame acariciarlo a él también." *Oh, don't be that way. Let me caress him too.* But by then the point had been made. Felicitas, who was also dark skinned, came along three years later.

My mother was alone much of the time. Like other Mexicans who needed money, Jeronimo made extended trips *para el norte,* to Texas and New Mexico, to find work when he had to. Probably he worked on ranches. Surely he gambled as well.

But even when he was not away, he was seldom at home — and he was always full of surprises. Mother likes to tell the story of how she awoke one morning to the voice of her Godmother, who was banging at the front door. When she opened the door, she found the other woman loaded down with her best dishes and a cage of chickens. Jeronimo had spent the night playing poker with her husband, the woman explained, and her husband had lost. She had been sent over to deliver Jeronimo's winnings. Mother sent the woman, who was as poor as she was, back home with her possessions.

Mother spent the night before Jeronimo's death alone. She and her two children were asleep in their tiny house when suddenly Mother was awakened by a ferocious banging on the door and a man's voice yelling, "¡Usted es un hijo de su chingada madre! ¿Dónde está usted? Lo encontraré pronto!" *You son of a bitch! Where are you? I'll find you soon.*

This must have been par for the course to some extent, for Mother only screamed back that Jeronimo was not in, and then for good measure she put a board across the door and went back to bed. But later, just after dawn, there was pounding on the door again, and this time she heard the voices of her mother, Sara, and her sister, Victoria.

"Qué sucedió? Qué sucedió?" Mother cried when she opened the door and saw the gravity in their expressions *What happened?*.

Baby Felicitas woke up and began to cry, and Victoria went to her. "Get dressed," Sara told Mother. Jeronimo was outside, in the back of a pickup truck. He was hurt and they needed to get him to a hospital.

While Mother rushed to dress herself, Sara offered the details she knew: Jeronimo had been with another woman. That woman's husband had come after him and found him just before dawn as he was riding home on his horse. He shot him, and later some other people went by on the road and saw him lying there in the dirt and went immediately to tell Mother's family, as no one wanted to go to Mother herself with such news.

While Sara and Victoria comforted the children, both of whom were awake by now, Mother ran out to the waiting pickup. The three men who had found Jeronimo sat in the cab in the front. Jeronimo was stretched out in the bed of the truck. Mother put one foot up on the wheel well and hauled herself up and climbed in beside him. She adjusted his head so that it lay in her lap. She could see right away that his condition was worse than Sara had prepared her for. Even with the blood rising and spreading over his body like some kind of ghastly film in the early morning light, she could count six distinct wounds in his chest.

When he saw her there, Jeronimo whispered, "Conchita, tú seguías diciéndome que permaneciera lejos de esta mala vida. Nunca te escuché a ti." *You kept telling me to stay away from this bad life. I never listened to you.* She whispered back that he shouldn't talk; he should lie still and not worry and everything would be fine. But she knew that everything would not be fine; there were too many holes in his chest. Too much blood was pouring out of him.

He never made it to the hospital. He died in her arms.

The women brought Jeronimo back to the house and cleared the long table where the family usually took their meals and placed his body on it. They cleaned him up and dressed him in his best clothes. Then someone ran to the church to begin the tolling of the bells. In places like Ojo de Agua the ringing of church bells is an art form. The people who listen can easily determine whether the tolling indicates a wedding or a warning, a celebration or a loss. Everyone heard the bells that day, and they quickly dropped whatever work they were doing and changed into their best black clothes and followed the crowds to my mother's home to pay their respects. And there they saw Jeronimo, the man who had stolen a beautiful 15-year-old girl to be his bride, lying on a wooden table in a room with white-washed walls and a dirt floor, surrounded by people holding candles and rosaries and mumbling prayers, and my mother, crying for her unbearable loss.

The mourners were so intent on their grief that poor little five-year old Juan managed several times that day to jump up on the table before anyone could grab him. Each time he climbed onto his father's midriff and began to rock wildly, yelling, "Mi caballo, mi caballo!" *My horse! My horse!*

This confirmation of Juan's love for his father only made the mourners cry harder.

The following morning Jeronimo's body was taken to the church and Mass was said for him. Then he was buried. Not surprisingly, Mother refused an offer to settle with her two small dark skinned children on her parents' ranch now that she was a widow. Instead she accepted another offer, from Aurelia, Jeronimo's mother, who was also a widow. Aurelia had family in Ciudad Juarez. Now that Jeronimo was gone, she saw no reason not to return to them. In Juarez, she promised Mother, her children would have cousins and aunts and uncles who would love them.

There are few bonds as strong as grief. Only Aurelia understood the extent of Mother's suffering; and only Mother, having children herself, understood Aurelia's loss. Through their shared love for Jeronimo they had come to love each other, and the story of their bond and their journey is not unlike the Biblical story of

Naomi and Ruth, who, having lost everything, decided to travel together to the older woman's home.

But before they could actually leave, there was one more devastating loss to come.

Having given up her small house, Mother was staying with her parents until she and Aurelia and the children could go. And one night as she lay in her childhood bed, she dreamed of Jeronimo. In the dream he said to her, as clearly as if he were at her side and whispering into her ear, "Ahora voy al norte, a los Estados Unidos, y voy a llevar a Felicitas conmigo, pero voy a dejar a Juan contigo." *I'm going north now, to the United States, and I'm going to take Felicitas with me, but I'm going to leave Juan with you.* Then, perhaps in a gesture meant to comfort her, he touched her face, and the cold from his cold dead hand continued to tingle on her cheek even as she woke up and began to scream.

Sara came rushing in to her and Mother told her what had transpired. Sara tried to comfort her, telling her that it was only a dream and Felicitas was fine. But a few days later, Felicitas got sick, with a fever and diarrhea. It might have been nothing, the sort of virus all children get from time to time, but instead of getting better, it got worse, and eight days after Mother's dream, Felicitas was dead. Only then did Sara admit that she knew this about dreams: When someone already dead comes to you to let you know he is taking another with him somewhere, you can believe him.

Soon afterward, Mother and Aurelia and Juan boarded the first of a succession of buses that would take them from Ojo de Agua to Ciudad Jaurez. Once they arrived they moved into the tiny apartment that Aurelia's relatives had secured for them. Juarez was a big city, and had not Mother already lost almost everything she loved in life, it might have been frightening to her. But she was numb to pain now, and so she went out into this new world crowded with strangers and found a job in a small restaurant making tortillas. It stood to reason that if she was working, Juan would spend more time with his grandmother than with her, but it hurt her to come home and see the special relationship they were forming. In fact, it seemed to her that Aurelia was purposely cultivating an alliance with Juan that excluded her. Juan was all she had now; she did not think she could stand it to lose him as well.

Mother did not make very much money shaping tortillas, and the working conditions in the tiny restaurant left something to be desired. It was always so hot in that kitchen, always so oppressive. And the hours were far too long. But sometimes she got to chat with the customers, and in this way she came to know an Anglo couple, a doctor and a nurse, who were traveling through Mexico and had taken note of how hard Mother worked, how sincerely she seemed to want to please. "Why don't you think about coming home with us, to Roswell in New Mexico?" the woman asked one day. "We can give you room and board and three times the amount of money you're making now."

That evening Mother told Aurelia about the offer the Anglo woman had made. Aurelia, of course, thought it was the best possible idea. No one in their right mind would turn down an offer to go to the United States. And she was there to take care of Juan, as if he were her own, until Mother was in a position to send for him. And as for getting across the border, Aurelia had a niece who had documents that she could surely use.

And so another chapter in my mother's life began. She was still only a very young woman, and having suffered so much, some part of her was glad to have the opportunity to experience such an adventure. On the other hand, she was brokenhearted to have to leave her son behind. But she imagined all the opportunities that he would have as he got older, because of the money that she would be able to send. And one day, he would come to her, or she would come back to him, and all the suffering and loss of the past would dissolve.

Her big adventure in the United States did not turn out to be as exciting as it was challenging. The doctor and nurse seemed to think that she was a machine that could work from morning until night. Not only was she responsible for taking care of every detail of their large home, she also did their laundry and starched and ironed the uniforms they wore to work each day.

The doctor and nurse had no children, and the house was too quiet. The room they had promised her was large enough, but it was located in the basement. Like spiders and rodents and other subterranean creatures, she lived with little light — at least when she was not upstairs working. And as for nourishment, since the couple took most of their meals at the hospital, there was very little food in the house at any given time. Mostly she subsisted on bread.

But they kept to their word about the money, and little though it was, it was more than she had ever had before. She sent home virtually every penny, and the letters of gratitude she received from Aurelia confirmed that young Juan was thriving, that the money would continue to ensure that he had everything he needed to live comfortably there in Juarez.

But Mother was lonely. Though the doctor and his wife knew her language, they had no reason to speak it in their home, unless of course they needed to direct her in some way. Each Sunday she was permitted four hours of freedom so that she could go to church, and after Mass each week she walked to a small Mexican restaurant. There she got to know the owners and the staff. Their conversations meant the world to her and they became her only friends.

For all that she had been through — and as small as she was — she had energy, enthusiasm and she knew how to work hard. Before long, the owners of the restaurant asked her to leave the Anglo couple and come to work for them. They promised to give her more than the doctor had been paying her, enough so that she could find an apartment and still send money home for her son. It was an offer she could not refuse.

In no time Mother had established herself in a tiny apartment and started her new job. She helped in the kitchen, on the floor, wherever she was needed. She got to know the regulars, one of whom was a very handsome young man who also happened to be a big tipper. As he seemed to have a lot of girlfriends — one in particular accompanied him often — she tried not to give him too much thought. But he was a sweet-talking man with a sense of humor, and not thinking about him at all proved impossible.

One day he came in with the young woman he seemed to favor and mentioned that he and his friend were going to a shoe store after they had had something to eat. He asked my mother if she wanted to come along. By then he knew her schedule, and he knew she would be getting off work in a short time. As my mother had not bought herself a pair of shoes in a very long time, she agreed to go with them.

Mother found a pair of shoes she thought would do very nicely. But just as she was about to pay for them, the handsome man appeared at the cash register saying he wouldn't hear of it; he would pay for the shoes. My mother stood her ground. She had her own money, she told him, money she had earned, and she would pay for her new shoes herself. He gave up, but he must have liked this side of her because the next time Daddy appeared in the restaurant — and whenever he came in after that — he was alone.

Chapter Three

The Making of Men

Daddy was a cowboy, a hardworking cowboy who got up before the sun each morning and did what cowboys do — cattle running, branding, breaking, butchering, fence mending, welding — whatever needed his attention on Jim Williamson's ranch. He lived on the ranch as well, in a small cottage beside the main ranch house, and naturally he wanted Mother to live there too. That's when she explained that she was not alone; she had a son, and as soon as she had the opportunity, she was going to Juarez to get him. If Daddy couldn't accept the fact that she'd already been married, that she'd had children with another man, then there was no point in any further discussion. But Daddy insisted that he didn't care. He said he would adopt her son and love him as if he were his own.

Even back then Mother had an inkling that Daddy could not be trusted 100 percent. She'd learned, for instance, that the girl he'd been seeing just before he started seeing her — the one he'd brought to the shoe store that day — had only broken it off with him because she was married to a soldier, and her soldier husband was on his way home from wherever he had been stationed. For all Mother knew, Daddy had a wife back in Mexico. Lots of men traveled from Mexico to the United States for work, and they often wound up with wives and children in both places. Daddy swore up and down that he'd never been married. But Mother insisted on confirmation. Accordingly, he provided her with the contact information for his mother back in Chihuahua, and Mother promptly wrote a letter introducing herself, explaining about her sordid past, and inquiring about Daddy's. Before long she had a letter back. As far as anyone knew, it stated,

Daddy had never been married. But then Daddy had been gone for over eight years and his family had heard nothing from him. They were thrilled to know he was alive and well.

There were other complications to be addressed. When Jim Williamson learned that Mother had come to the States illegally, he explained that he did not care to risk having her living on the premises. He did, however, kindly offer to help her to obtain papers. Daddy already had his papers because he had come over on the Bracero Program, a guest worker program that began in the early 1900s as a way to acquire cheap labor to work on farms. By the time Daddy came to the U.S., the program was sponsoring border crossings so that Mexicans could lay and maintain rails for the country's expanding system of railroads.

Not long after their talk with Jim Williamson, the three of them, Mother and Daddy and Jim, drove to the Border Patrol in El Paso, and Jim explained the situation to Immigration. Immigration in turn explained that before Mother could even apply for papers, Daddy and Mother would have to be married. They took care of the matter while they were there, in El Paso. With Jim's help, they found a Justice of the Peace and two Customs Patrol officers who would act as witnesses. And so Mother was married for the second time in her short life.

It took three months longer for Mother's papers to come through. In the meantime, Mother and Daddy traveled to Mexico and Daddy met Juan, my half brother, and told him that as soon as they could arrange for his papers, he would come and live with them. Then they went to Chihuahua, where Daddy was reunited with his family. Daddy's father was a baker. The family owned no land. They were not very well off. They were glad to hear that Daddy was doing well in America, making decent pay doing something he loved. But his adoring sisters wasted no time in letting Mother know that they would have been happier if she had been a virgin, that their brother could have done better in that department. Still, Mother and Daddy had now made their commitment to each other both legally and publicly, and they happily began their new life together.

Although he was nothing like Mother's first husband, Daddy was known to disappear when it suited him, and he was not around when my sister Carol was ready to be born in 1954. Carol was delivered by a midwife in nearby Clovis. She was so beautiful that Veda Pruitt, a wealthy rancher who knew my parents, wanted to adopt her, and in fact, Veda was the one who named her Carol Ann. More than anything else in the world, Mother and Daddy had wanted a son, a baby brother for Juan when he arrived. But Carol quickly became my parents' pride and joy…in spite of her sex.

Some eleven months later, however, when mother was ready to give birth to her second child with Daddy, he made it very clear that while one girl was acceptable, he didn't think he could handle the disappointment of another. Mother told him not to worry; she was certain that this time they would have a son.

It was Veda Pruitt who drove Mother to the hospital in Brownfield, TX, to have her next baby. Daddy stayed behind to work and to take care of little Carol. The following day, he left Carol in the care of another ranch hand's wife and came to the hospital early to see how Mother was doing. When he learned that she'd already given birth and that the child was a girl, he cried, "¡Oh, otra mujer!" *Oh, another woman!* and promptly left the hospital in a state of disgust. Mattie, Veda's sister, had to come and pick us up.

Mother recalls our return to the ranch to this day. Although she was upset that Daddy had abandoned us in the hospital, she was pleased to see that all Carol's diapers were out on the line, almost as clean as she would have gotten them herself, fluttering in the wind like the wings of snow geese. Ranchers came by that day and the next and the one after that, to see the second child of Conchita and Juan Acosta. Each time someone approached, Daddy would throw the end of my blanket over my face and cry,

"No la miren a ella. Ella es fea. Ella es flaca. Aquí está la Linda." *Don't look at her. She's ugly. She's skinny. Here's the pretty one...*and he would point them in Carol's direction. Of course he didn't really think I was that ugly, but it was a convenient way to turn his disappointment into a joke. That was his nature.

The next pregnancy did not come until two years later. In between, when I was about six months old, Mother received a telegram saying that her mother was seriously ill. She set off for Ojo de Agua, but by the time she arrived, Sara, who was only 40, had already been buried. Mother took her death very hard.

Mother and Daddy were so busy wishing for a boy with the next pregnancy that perhaps they forgot to wish that things would go smoothly. Mother's labor went on and on, day after day, for more than three full days. The doctor wasn't sure that he was hearing a baby's heartbeat anymore at some point, and he could only conclude, after all that time, that the baby might have died in the womb. There was only one way to find out. He called Daddy into the room and explained the situation. "You may have to make a decision," he told him. "I'll have to operate, but in the event that I can only save one, I have to know who you want me to save." Although Daddy's heart was broken at the prospect of losing this baby, whom he was sure would be a boy this time around, he replied, "Tengo dos muchachas pequeñas en la casa. Necesitan una madre." *I have two little girls at home. They need a mother.*

Even though Mother had been anaesthetized before the Cesarean surgery, she was awake enough to hear the shrill cry of her child when it came. And just after, she heard the words that she and Daddy had dreamed of: "It's a boy!"

Her heart flooded with joy as she drifted back into a much needed deep sleep. The operation had been an intense one, one that would leave horrible scarring. To this day Mother appears to have ten belly buttons along her cut line. But Mother survived it. And Daddy was beside himself. Not only did he still have his wife, but the son he had longed for had finally come into the world. Although Daddy despised weakness in men, he broke down and cried. For joy. For Oscar.

Given his great desire to have a son, you would think that Daddy would have taken the lead in Oscar's parenting, but that was not his way. Daddy was not much for little children, male or female. He loved us all of course, but he worked long hours, and he loved the company of adults when he had free time, and there were always plenty of them around on the Williamson ranch and from the ranches nearby. And when my parents didn't have company, Daddy was content to sit at the end of the work day, by the heater when it was cold, in his overalls and work boots, as he waited for dinner to appear on the table. His plan was to let Mother raise us, and when the time came and Oscar was old enough, he would jump in and teach him the one thing he knew inside and out: how to be a man.

How to be a man: It was a mantra in our house. Daddy was a real cowboy, a real man, and he never let anyone forget it. All of the men he knew were the same. In his mind, Oscar could be no different.

In the meantime, Oscar was just a baby — one who had three adoring mothers. Sometimes when he slept, Mother would place her hand lightly over his mouth to make sure he was still breathing. When he gasped for air, she would know he was alive and relax again. Once, she and Daddy took him on a trip to buy groceries. On the way home, Mother noticed that his little hands looked purple and she began to scream and insist that Daddy drive directly to the hospital. She was so shaken by the time they arrived that she could hardly tell the nurse what she had witnessed. The nurse took his hands in hers — and declared that nothing was wrong with them, or him. She suggested that it was the lighting, the street lights, that had made his hands seem purple in the car. Daddy could only shake his head in amazement.

Carol and I were as anxious about him as Mother was. We watched him all the time. We taught him his good manners and his first words in English. In keeping with our desire to be the best possible surrogate parents, one day when he was about 18 months old and Carol and I were six and four years old respectively, we decided to take him to the grocery store, as any good mother would. We found our mother and informed her of our intention. We sat down at the table, where she was magically transforming used flour sacks into new clothes for us on her old black pedal sewing machine, and wrote out a list of items that she agreed we were short on. Then off we went, three young children, one wagon, and one bike. Oscar of course sat in the wagon, and Carol and I alternated between pulling him and riding the bike.

The store was about five miles away, and to get there, you needed to travel along the freeway for some distance. We'd been traveling for quite some time but were only just approaching the highway when we heard the screech of tires and turned to see a cloud of dust rising up in the air. The truck Mother drove belonged to Jim Williamson. Mother did not have a license, but she drove in the fields when she had to, and when she had been unable to find us anywhere at the ranch, she had jumped into the pickup and taken off like a bat out of hell. Now she threw the vehicle into park and leapt out and ran in our direction, her small frame a wad of fury.

As soon as she reached us, she spanked Carol and me. The spanking was as surprising as it was painful, because, after all, we *had* told her what we were doing. She had given us no indication that she thought we were only "playing" grocery shopping. She lifted Oscar from the wagon and put him in the cab while Carol and I climbed into the bed, and we took off for home at a speed that confirmed the intensity of her anger.

Mother sang to Oscar all day long, bouncing him on her knee in between her many domestic obligations. "Sugar in the morning, sugar in the evening," she would croon in English, but as she did not know any of the other words to the McGuire Sisters' song, she would fill in the blanks with a series of la la las to go with the tune. Her love for Oscar was reflected in his little white shirts and diapers, which she scrubbed in a tub of steaming hot water until they were so white they looked blue when he wore them out in the sun. He had our father's light complexion. His eyes were light brown and his hair was almost gold. Mother, who had suffered ridicule from her own family over the dark complexion of her first son, encountered no such taunting now. In fact, she became the taunter, often setting little Oscar down on the ground in the midst of the darker skinned children of the other ranch hands, where their differences became unmistakable. "Mire lo hermoso que es nuestro bebé," she would say to Daddy. *Look how beautiful our baby is.* And while he took pride in Oscar's beauty as well, he would admonish her for her arrogance. She couldn't help herself. Oscar was her star. He was our star.

My half brother Juan, whom we called John, was 12 when he finally came to live with us. Carol was eleven, I was nine, and Oscar was seven. We were living in a two-bedroom house in Elida, New Mexico by then, and Daddy was still ranching, although he no longer worked exclusively for Jim Williamson. He went wherever the work was.

While Mother stressed the importance of a good education and made sure we did our homework, we saw right away that John was a different kind of smart than the older kids that Mother insisted we emulate; he was street smart. Although he'd grown up without a father in Juarez, he'd had plenty of older cousins to teach him survival tactics.

John wasn't crazy about school in the United States, but his teachers liked him, and between his classes and his three bilingual half siblings, he learned to speak English very quickly. And because he'd made his money in Juarez selling burritos on the street, his math was far better than ours. But if he was a good student, he was an even better teacher, and he taught Oscar a number of enterprising activities. He showed him how to make a top, from whittled wood, with a nail hammered through and a string attached. He taught Oscar how to make a slingshot. They spent hours together in the late afternoons and on weekends, whittling wood from branches, cutting rubber pockets from old bike tires. And he taught him that a stone the right size and the right shape propelled hard enough at the phone wires would make the wires sing, assuming you could hit them. And John could. And amazingly, so could little Oscar. Our dark skinned brother was like a magician to us, especially to Oscar.

But for all that we worshipped John, his heart remained in Juarez. He had spent his formative years with Aurelia, Jeronimo's mother, his grandmother, and although she had passed on not long before John came to Elida, he continued to think of her as his only real parent. While he was always respectful to Mother, he let her know in little ways that she would never be able to take Aurelia's place. And he turned the tables when he could, telling Mother that he didn't feel that she loved him as much as the rest of her children. He told her he didn't like Elida, where, he said, there was nothing to do; he didn't like New Mexico; he didn't like the United States. How Mother would cry when he expressed his desire to return to Juarez.

If John wasn't outside with us, demonstrating skills like using a slingshot to make a lizard spin in the air like a dancer before it fell down dead, he was inside talking to Mother. Their conversations were endless, and while they both seemed to crave having them, they appeared exhausted and less than happy when they were over. The only other activity John put so much time into was riding a bike. He could be gone for hours once he set off, riding through rural areas that he professed to dislike after his life in the city. He was restless.

By this time Daddy had already made some effort to teach

little Oscar how to be a cowboy and a man. But like Mother's long and often emotional conversations with John, not much good ever came of it. Daddy didn't have patience with Oscar. He wanted him to know the lesson before it was even taught. Daddy complained that Oscar didn't have it in him; he wasn't cut out for the hard stuff. Little Oscar complained that he couldn't learn from Daddy. Strangely enough, even though John hated the rural life and wanted nothing to do with ranching, Daddy conceded that he, at least, was a real man. They would sit and talk like two old friends for hours in the evenings, while Oscar, sitting between Carol and me, looked on in silence.

John's big break came as a result of a disaster — a train wreck in Elida. The wreck was bad and there was a lot of damage. People were hired on the spot to help clean up. John was glad to have the work. When he came home the first night after working all day at the site, he told my father that as soon as he had the money, he was heading back to Mexico. My father patted him on the back. He loved him and didn't want to lose him, but he understood John's compulsion to find a purpose for his manhood, and he didn't try to discourage him. Mother, of course, was brokenhearted. After he left, Daddy seemed to be even harder on Oscar.

Oscar learned all his ranching skills from other men, other ranchers. These men, old enough to be considered father figures, became Oscar's best friends. By the time Oscar was 12, he could butcher and wrap as well as any professional. He could work with horses and he could even ride bareback. He could drive a tractor. He could weld. He worked every day after school for these ranchers, as well as on the weekends. And they paid him. In a very short time he was in a position to buy his own clothes. Since Daddy didn't make a lot of money, this was an enormous help to the family. It benefited Mother too, as she was still sewing all of our clothes. Yet Daddy refused to acknowledge that Oscar must be doing a pretty good job to be in such high demand among the ranchers.

The irony of Daddy's relationship with Oscar was that Oscar quickly became the cowboy Daddy had dreamed he'd become, but Daddy never saw it. In his mind, whatever Oscar did fell short of perfection, and perfection was the only acceptable standard where Oscar was concerned. And Oscar sought perfection too, probably for the sole purpose of finally pleasing Daddy. It was sad to see him trying so hard to achieve the impossible — not perfection, because that he did achieve, but getting Daddy's attention and approval.

While Daddy was in a state of constant denial where Oscar was concerned, he didn't seem to care what Carol and I were up to, as long as we obeyed one firm and unalterable rule: no boys. This wasn't a big problem when we were younger because we had Oscar, and then, later, John, and who could have wanted more in the way of male companionship? But as we got older, it became a major dilemma. The closer we got to the age where most girls had boyfriends, the more Daddy, who had always liked a drink or two on the weekends, got closer to becoming a weekend drunk. And when Daddy was drunk, he would sometimes become violent.

Sometimes he and Mother would argue, and as she was not one to back down and retract any statement she believed to be true, Daddy would feel compelled to hit her. Sometimes he would grab her by her hair and threaten to burn down the house. Mostly we kids were safe as long as we didn't get in the way. But when things got too rough, one of us would get between them, and then we would get hurt too.

Daddy simply could not handle the fact that we were growing up, and a lot of their arguments arose out of Mother's desire to defend our right to have social lives. There were plenty of times when he would chase us out of the house and we would wind up sleeping at the homes of friends or cousins.

Once, when Oscar was still quite young, he retrieved Daddy's (unloaded) hunting rifle from under the bed and told him that if he didn't stop his ranting and raving he was going to have to shoot him. Oscar had seen one too many "Bonanza" episodes, and he fancied himself as Little Joe, responsible for saving the women folk from peril. Upon seeing the gun in his hand, Mother broke out of battle mode to admonish him: "Alright, stop it," she told him. "Pon eso lejos ahora mismo." *Put that away right now.*

Not all the arguments were this bad though. Sometimes they just consisted of a lot of cursing. It was almost funny to hear Daddy curse because while we spoke Spanish exclusively in the house, when Daddy was angry, he cursed in English. He had learned the words back on Jim Williamson's ranch. "Sorry son of a bitch," he would say. Mother would cuss in Spanish, and since she, at least, knew what she was saying, her profanity could be a lot crueler.

Often their arguments were more a result of Daddy's exhaustion than any real difference of opinion. For the most part, Mother and Daddy were devoted to each other. They didn't show much affection in front of us kids — in fact, Mother seemed to think it was taboo to kiss in front of us — but she laughed at all Daddy's jokes, even when they were at her expense. And the smiles they shared when things were good — when Daddy wasn't drinking — spoke volumes about their feelings. If it were not for the drinking, we could have been a model family. Certainly we all tried. And out of all of us, Oscar probably tried the hardest.

There was a small Catholic church in Elida. But the priest who had been assigned to it had assignments elsewhere as well, and he only showed up once a month. From the time we were very small, Mother would dress us up, Carol and me with lace mantillas on our heads, and we would attend his services with a few other families. During the summers, we would attend Bible school at the Baptist Church. The pastor there, Brother McDonald, spoke of heaven and hell with passion, and something about his discourse — and maybe Mrs Lambirth's beautiful piano playing of old gospel songs — touched Oscar deeply, and at the age of 11, he accepted the Lord through Baptism in the Baptist Church. He did this all on his own, without the encouragement of our parents or anyone else.

At the time, Daddy was working part time at a feed store. His boss, a man by the name of Tot Saddler, was also a practicing Baptist, and he didn't miss an opportunity to remind Daddy that his son had accepted Jesus and that it might be a good idea for him to do so too. "Oscar wants to talk to you about going to church," he would say. And Daddy would reply, "Oh, yeah! Oh hell, yeah!" ("Oh hell, yeah" was yet another English phrase Daddy had learned working on the Williamson ranch.) "Will you come then?" Tot Saddler would continue. "Oh, yeah, oh hell yeah." "Because Christ died for our sins, yours and mine." "Oh hell yeah. God almighty! Hell yeah."

And so it came to pass that Daddy quit drinking and he and Mother were both baptized in the Baptist church, in the traditional Baptist manner, which is to say, they were submerged in a tank of water and cleansed of their sins. Carol and I began going to the Baptist church as well. Strangely enough, once he got the rest of us going, Oscar drifted away. But Daddy became sort of a fixture there on Sundays, so much so that at the end of each service Brother MacDonald would ask him to lead the congregation in the final prayer. Even though there were only a handful of Spanish-speaking people in the congregation, Daddy would never try to do the prayer in English. He would do it his way, in Spanish. Although he stayed with the church, Daddy did go back to drinking after a time.

Just as Oscar had taken the initiative in leading us all in religious practice, he took the initiative in leading us in acts of kindness outside the church. Oscar had a heart of gold and always wanted to help those who had less. Sometimes in his travels he would meet up with people who had crossed the border from Mexico and he would never fail to bring them home. Then Mother would take over, making sure they had a good meal, a good night's sleep, and some clean clothes before they set out to look for work. And then it was Daddy's turn, taking them from ranch to ranch to see who might want to hire them.

Although my family functioned as a complete support team for strangers from Mexico who came our way, it was Oscar who got attached to them. He wasn't satisfied to help them with food and clothes and other practicalities: he wanted to become their friend. He wanted to know all about them.

There was one man in particular he became very attached to. And when the man decided to give it up and return to Mexico, Oscar wanted to go back with him. Mother explained that the man had his own family, that Oscar wouldn't be helping him by putting him in a position of having yet another mouth to feed.

About the time that Daddy reached the next level in binge drinking, we received a letter from John saying that he had met a girl, Ernestine, back in Juarez, and they were going to get married. He was all of 18. But he was a serious guy, and if that was what he wanted to do, none of us doubted that he could make it work. He had found a good job in El Paso, driving a delivery truck for the Coca Cola Company. And in addition to Ernestine, he had fallen in love with wrestling. Sometimes, he told us, he even made money at it.

While John was discovering wrestling in Mexico, Oscar was learning to play baseball in Elida. Some of the same older men who were teaching him to be a remarkable cowboy were coaching him in Little League. What they all concluded early on was that Oscar had a good arm...a very good arm: Oscar was a fantastic pitcher. When he could, Oscar would watch the pros play on our black and white TV. Sometimes he would ask Carol or me to go outside and move the antenna around until he yelled that the picture was clear. He also started buying bubble gum so that he could collect the baseball cards that came with it. His heroes were Mickey Mantle, Babe Ruth, Willie Mays....

Daddy didn't see the point of anyone spending so much time consumed with something like baseball. In his mind, all those Little League games could only deflect a real man from his true purpose. When Oscar returned from the games, all sweaty and wearing clothes streaked with grass and mud, Daddy would say, "¿Ganó usted?" *Did you win?* And if Oscar answered no, Daddy would make a howling sound like a lobo —"oowwwoooww" — and add that he was going to have to feed the team some skunk steaks.

But the field the kids played on was so close to our house that the floodlights illuminated our rooms in the evenings, and even Daddy's ears perked up when the horns started honking and the chanting began: "Let's go, OSCAR! Let's go!" And then, "OSCAR! OSCAR! OSCAR!"

Chapter Four

The Making of Dreams

One summer, when Oscar and Carol and I were 13, 16, and 15, Daddy had an opportunity to go to Denver and work construction for several weeks. It had come his way via our cousins who lived there, one of whom owned the construction company. They had enough room for all of us, they said.

Oscar, being male, had the freedom to come and go more or less as he liked. Carol and I were dying for an adventure, and Denver seemed to have some potential. We left Elida filled with enthusiasm, ready to invite into our lives whatever little bit of excitement might be made available to us. But weeks went by, and soon enough Denver began to feel like a more populous version of our home in Elida.

In fact, we began to miss the square dances the old-timers held at the post office, when Maureen and Jakie Howard would play the violin and guitar respectively, and someone else would play the piano, and people would dance to the "Orange Blossom Special" or Hank Williams Sr.'s "Your Cheating Heart." We never went in — we stood with Mother and watched from the door — but once we got home, Mother would teach us how to do the polka and the other dances we'd seen. That was fun at least, and so were Sunday nights when friends from other ranches would come to our house and Mother would make banana ice cream — Carol and Oscar and I would take turns cranking the handle of the wooden ice cream maker — and sit outside on the porch talking against a backdrop of crickets until late into the night.

One night towards the end of our stay in Denver, we got the chance we had been waiting for. Among the relatives we were living with were cousins our age, and since they were permitted to go to dances and parties, Daddy got bullied into allowing us to go to one as well, with the stipulation that Mother chaperone every inch of the way. He was not a bit happy about it though. Back in Elida, if he so much as saw a strange car in the neighborhood — and he considered any car that wasn't a pickup to be strange — he made the assumption that it belonged to a young man who'd come to track us down. Then he'd fly into a rage, and if he was drinking at the time, he'd take it out on Mother, calling her a *madrota*, a madam. So the night of the dance, our hope was to keep a low profile and not make any mistakes that might eventually reach Daddy's ears. The number of people leaving the house — Mother, Carol, all of our cousins and me— must have made Daddy feel more secure because he didn't change his mind at the last second as we had feared. We were so excited we could hardly stand it. The band that would be playing that evening was none other than Ramon Ayala y Los Bravos del Norte. Ayala is a Grammy-winning accordion superstar who is well known to anyone who loves Norteño music.

No sooner had we arrived and settled ourselves in one corner of the huge dance hall when a handsome man in his late 20s left the woman he had been with and approached my sister. It was clear to those of us who witnessed their greeting that they had met before. Carol, it seemed, had a secret life — which was of course the only kind one could have in our household. So intent was I on watching my sister move out onto the dance floor with this older stranger that I did not see the young man coming my way. He tapped me lightly on the shoulder and invited me to dance as well — and off we went. We were enjoying our dance together very much when I happened to notice Mother, whose arms were stretched high in the air, her fingers outspread in what could only be an effort to get my attention. I apologized to my partner and hurried back to see what was wrong. It became clear soon enough. As I pushed my way through the sea of people, I saw the woman — the one who had been with the man who my sister apparently knew — trying to beat Carol with her fists, and Carol attempting to deflect her blows. Arms were flying everywhere.

The band finished their song and the great Ramon Ayala cried into the microphone, "¡No se peleen, no se peleen!" *Don't fight! Don't fight!* Everyone turned to see what was happening. Mother, meanwhile, was yelling, "Usted es una mujer vieja. ¿Por qué pelea con mi hija? Ella es solo una niña." *You're an old woman. Why are you fighting with my daughter? She's only a girl.* Perhaps it was just as well that that was the only dance we ever got to go to the whole time we were in Denver.

The next three weeks passed quietly, and then it was late August and time to return to Elida to prepare for the school year. No one, of course, had told Daddy about the scene at the dance hall, and so there was no reason for him to suspect that Carol had met the man of her dreams.

All the morning of our last hours in Denver, Carol was right there with Oscar and me, folding clothes, carrying bags out to the truck, making everything secure. But then, just as we were saying goodbye to our cousins and thanking them for all that they'd done for us, we realized that Carol had disappeared! We looked everywhere for her. The only thing we could conclude was that she had been abducted. By the time night fell we were sure that she was dead. Mother was beside herself with grief. So were father and Oscar and I. Finally one of the cousins reached the point where she could no longer stand to see us in such a state. She admitted that she knew Carol was alive, and probably well enough, with Octavio, the man from the dance. They had run away together.

Our grief changed immediately to red hot anger. Mother wanted to find her right away and shake some answers out of her. Oscar had let Carol borrow his good leather belt a day earlier, and now he realized that she had absconded with it — and he was furious. I was too. How could she do this to our family? How could she disgrace our father in this way? Daddy's reaction was to head to the nearest bar.

We were thinking that things couldn't get any worse that night when we got a call saying Daddy had been in an car accident. Along with our cousins, we rushed out to the emergency room where we found him sobering up and feeling ashamed. Since the hospital decided that his cuts and scrapes were mostly superficial, he was released to us. But in fact, he had hurt his back, and while nothing was actually broken, he was in no condition to make the trip back to Elida. Mother wouldn't have left anyway without Carol. But as the school year loomed ahead, arrangements were made for Oscar and me to return to Elida alone — via Greyhound — to stay with our neighbors, Mary and George Lee, until our parents and sister, hopefully, could follow.

After all the craziness of our time in Denver, it was good to be back in Elida, a place where one day flowed into the next almost uninterrupted. It was also good to stay with the Lees. Their children were grown, and their house was so quiet you could hear yourself breathe.

Mary was an old, hard-working, strictly Christian, pioneer woman. Even though she (an Anglo) spoke little Spanish, and Mother spoke little English, they had become good friends over the years. In the summers they spent hours and hours together outdoors, picking string beans in the fields belonging to the Lees, Mary wearing an old-fashioned bonnet that belonged to another era. To Oscar and me, she seemed to be the wisest and most resourceful woman in the world.

During our time with her she taught us many things, including how to make soap from lye and lard. The components had to be stirred with a wooden paddle over an open fire for hours, until the consistency was just right. The repetitiveness of the work made a perfect background for casual conversation, and for the Bible stories Mary enjoyed reading to us. When she could, she liked to compare the people from the stories to people we knew. The woman that King Lemuel's mother prophesized that he would marry, for instance, was just like our mother: a virtuous woman who would endure any hardship to give her family whatever they needed. Mary Lee never tired of reminding us of how hard our mother worked to put food on the table, to make sure we had warm clothing, and so on. When her thoughts turned to our father, though, we could see the change in her temperament flicker across her brow. "Alleluia!" she would cry. "John has accepted the Lord." Then she would lower her voice and tell us that no matter what our daddy did, he would always come back. "If he's going to stray, he's going to stray," she would say, shaking her head with some certainty. "But like the little lost lamb, Jesus will always find him and bring him back." It gave us great comfort to hear this good news.

Soon enough our parents returned, with Carol and Octavio in tow. Oscar and I would never learn all the details involved in Carol's recovery, but we were happy to have our sister, who was already pregnant, back with us, and we welcomed Octavio, who was now her husband, into our home. Daddy helped him to find work with local ranchers, and before long he had begun to save money so that he and Carol could one day buy a house of their own. In the meantime, my niece, Naomi, was born in our house, and as soon as Carol was on her feet again, our mother insisted that she return to school and complete her high school education. She offered to take care of the baby until Carol got her degree. Carol fought her on this; she did not feel like a high school girl anymore and she was sure she would be ridiculed. But Mother would not relent. And so Carol returned to school, and in the end she had to admit that it wasn't as bad as she had anticipated. Everyone, including her teachers, was kind to her. No one made her feel ashamed. In 1973, Carol and I graduated high school together, the only two Hispanics in our small graduating class.

Although I had done well in school, I never had the hope of

going to college. For years, Daddy had claimed that only *putas*, whores, went to college, and there was always some young woman from the community that he could point to as an example of a woman who had come to a bad end as a result of her so-called higher education. Really, there was no hope for any of us. Even though Carol must have experienced a flare of liberation by eloping with Octavio, in some ways she had merely committed herself to the very tradition she had hoped to escape.

Though Oscar was still in school, he had no hope either. He was a brilliant athlete, but there was no reason for him to dream that he would ever make a living at anything but ranching. Nor could he even aspire to have a ranch of his own. Families that came from Mexico worked on other people's ranches all their lives, and were happy to have the work, or so our father said.

Still, Oscar, like Carol, did his best to rebel against the confines of his prospects for the future. When he got his driver's license, he used the money he'd made working so hard for so many years to buy a yellow Charger with mag wheels and a hemi exhaust. The car was like biting his nose to spite his face because you could hear it all over town, especially when he was at the nearby park doing wheelies, and it would get him into trouble every time. "There he goes again," Mother would exclaim, and she would set off at a fast clip to find him. Since her years with Jeronimo back in Mexico, Mother had always liked to wear a tight belt around her small waist. Over time she had learned to whip that belt off in a split second. "I'm coming home, I'm coming home," Oscar would cry when he saw her rushing toward him, her belt flying in her hand.

Mother had three modes of dealing with our bad behavior. In addition to the belt mode, she had "heart attack" mode, which was when she would pretend that our shenanigans were causing her to have a heart attack. Once, for instance, when we were smaller, Oscar, who had been chasing me, reached into a bucket of apples, found a really rotten one, and hit me smack in the back with it. It burst all over my shirt and I made a big deal about it. Mother came running out of the house to hit him, but he was already running as fast as he could in the opposite direction. So, she went into heart attack mode, and rather than waste her energy, she called him to her, crying, "Oscar, Oscar, I can't breathe. I'm having a heart attack." And with her bent over like that, panting, her palms on her knees, who was to say that this time she was not, in fact? "I'm going to die," she moaned. Oscar stopped running and considered the possibility for one horrified moment. Then he went to her. As soon as he was within striking distance, she straightened up and whipped out the belt.

We all conceded very quickly when the belt came off, because we knew from experience that she was not afraid to use it. The third mode was simply to make us kneel in the kitchen. We couldn't bend forward or sit back; we had to kneel perfectly upright until we "learned to behave." Daddy, on the other hand, never scolded us at all…unless, of course, he'd been drinking.

Even though Oscar did his best to accentuate his rebellious side, the side of him that sought Daddy's approval was always evident too. One Fourth of July, for instance, Oscar signed up to ride a bronco in a local rodeo. As soon as Mother and Carol and I heard about it, we begged him to call it off. Any number of things could happen. We'd seen plenty of rodeos before and lots of cowboys got hurt badly, especially young ones. Oscar paid no attention to us. When Daddy heard, he said, "This I've got to see. He's going to be a man, let's see what kind of man he's going to be."

We sat on the hood of our pickup for vantage viewing the day of the event. Mother and Carol and I held our breath when the gate opened for Oscar, but it was immediately clear that the bronco they'd put him on was not a bucking one. And Oscar, already so tall by 16, practically scraped the ground with his feet on that small horse. He tried kicking the horse to get him to buck, but the horse only twitched a little, as if an annoying bird had inconveniently landed on his back. Mother and Carol and I took a collective breath: while Oscar was as ready as a cowboy could be, the horse was not going to participate. How Daddy laughed at Oscar's performance.

One of Oscar's older cowboy friends, Jim Bob Nuchols, had taught Oscar to box some years earlier, and before he was even out of high school, Oscar had won a Golden Gloves event in Muleshoe, Texas. Actually he'd won it by default, because his opponent hadn't shown up. Nevertheless, a continued effort in the ring was yet another way for Oscar to assert his manhood — and get Daddy's attention.

One day he informed us that he was going to Roswell to fight Michael Spinks. Mike Spinks was not yet the famous "Spinks Jinx" that he would later become, but he was already well known for his amazing amateur boxing record. We all went of course, Carol and Mother and I moaning all the way, "Oh, why does he have to do this to us? Why is he putting us through this? Why? Why? Why?"

Our stomachs were in knots imagining the terrible things that could happen to our beautiful Oscar, to his beautiful face. We honestly didn't think he *could* box. We knew his Golden Gloves award had been a fluke, and now he was to fight in a title championship with someone already well known for his accomplishments.

We found seats on the bleachers and sat tight together and hoped and prayed for the best. Before we knew it, the fight had begun and Spinks was coming after him relentlessly, one punch, then another, then another. Unable to breathe, I watched the punches come. I felt like I was the one taking each shot. Oscar was taking a beating. When I couldn't stand it anymore, I bent down so low in the bleachers that I could not see past the person in front of me. When the bell rang, I emerged to join Carol and Mother in screaming, "Throw in the towel! Throw in the towel!" Daddy, meanwhile, was yelling, "Don't give up! Give it to him!

Give it to him!" The bell rang and I hid again.

This was the story, round after round. Oscar had just enough left at the sound of each bell to propel himself forward and take more of a beating. When the final blow came, Oscar seemed to hang in the air, a stunned look lingering on his face for a long moment before he finally went down. Mother and Carol and I flew to our feet. "Don't get up! Don't get up!" we shouted. And he didn't. Oscar had lost by a knockout.

Looking back it seems as if worrying myself sick about Oscar was as much a part of my identity as the fact that I wasn't allowed to date and that I was forbidden to go to college. It was simply who I was. Carol and Mother would likely say the same. Oscar wasn't afraid of anything, and so, it seemed, there were a million ways that he might possibly hurt himself. As if the ranch work wasn't enough to keep him in shape, he worked out constantly, pummeling punching bags he'd hung in the garage. If I were out there with him, he'd lie on the floor and have me stand on his stomach and throw a leather ball down on his chest. Then he'd more or less bench press me, lifting me up and down, sometimes with one hand, as if my 112-pound frame was nothing. And when it was time for the martial arts portion of his workout, he'd get his nun chucks off the shelf and begin a session that Bruce Lee would have envied.

In his last year of high school, Oscar began to let his hair grow long. He also bought a pair of plaid hip hugger pants, bell bottoms, like the hippies wore. Daddy didn't like those pants one bit. Daddy didn't like to see any man in anything that wasn't denim. "What are you, a woman?" he would ask. "¿Un maricón?" *A fag*.

Oscar couldn't wear his plaid bells when Daddy was around. It just wasn't worth the tongue-lashing he would receive. So he wore them when Daddy wasn't around. He could easily leave the house before Daddy got home from work, and when he returned later in the night, he would knock lightly on the window and

Mother, who would be watching for him, would indicate with hand gestures that Daddy was asleep and it was safe to slip in.

One morning Oscar made the mistake of leaving the plaid pants on the bedroom floor, and Daddy noticed them when he passed by. A while later Daddy marched into the kitchen and asked Mother whether she had trash for the burn bin. Mother knew right away that something was going on, because *she* was the one who always brought the trash to the bin. But she gave him what she had, and he added the pants to the mix and went outdoors to start the fire. When Oscar came into the kitchen for breakfast, Mother explained that Daddy had burned his pants. We never saw Oscar in anything other than cowboy clothes after that.

Before Oscar was out of school, I was married. I felt I had to go about my marriage in a way that would bring honor to my father. Leo came from a well respected Catholic family in Portales. He was five years older than me. I'd met him when I was still a junior in high school. Just like Oscar and Carol, I'd figured out by then that it was necessary to have a secret life. I'd tried out for cheerleader in my junior year. And I was one of the girls who was picked to cheer for our basketball team. Still, it took a succession of intercessions from other parents to get Daddy to allow me to be on the team. The parents who came to advocate on my behalf had to promise to drive me back and forth to the games and watch my every move.

Leo came to the games. Then he began to come to my school during lunch hour. He would drive there from the factory where he worked in Portales, and arrive with burgers and shakes he'd pick up along the way. Sometimes I would still be lingering in history, my favorite class, talking to my teacher when he arrived. Mr Egan, who taught me to love politics, would see him from the window before I would. Mr Egan knew my father; he knew how things were for me. "Go," he would say. "Your friend is here. Go have some lunch."

I also met Leo at the park sometimes, the same park where Oscar got in trouble for doing wheelies when he should have been at home studying. But if Mother had shown signs of being all riled up because she knew I was in the park with a young man instead of at the store or down the road at a friend's house as I'd said, Daddy would have hit the roof. So she would send Oscar out to bring me back. Oscar had a extraordinarily loud whistle. Leo and I would hear him right away. When he caught up to us, he'd say, "Mother is mad at you. You'd better get home NOW."

I would return to find her pacing the floor. "Don't do this to me," she'd say. "Your Daddy is upset." But other times I would rush in to find Mother cooking or doing laundry, apparently not even aware that I had been gone. I'd know then that Oscar had come after me on his own, for no other reason than that he was just like Daddy when it came to me having boyfriends. He simply didn't think it should be permitted.

In my senior year there was a rumor afloat that I would be nominated to be homecoming queen. I told my friends that wasn't what I wanted. Daddy would have misinterpreted what that distinction meant. And even if more parents interceded on my behalf, my parents didn't have the money for the dress I would have had to buy. Instead, I ran for class president. It made better sense anyway. Homecoming was one night — albeit a Cinderella-like one. As class president, my picture would hang in the gym with all the other former class presidents for years to come. And so it does.

Leo proposed at the end of my senior year, when my sense of hopelessness regarding the future had reached its peak. We broke the news to Daddy in increments. First we had mutual friends come by to drop hints that there was a man, a very nice man, who wanted my hand in marriage. Our objective was to make sure that Daddy didn't blow Leo's head off the first time they met. Then we arranged for Mr and Mrs Montoya, Leo's parents, to come from Portales for dinner. After the meal, Mr Montoya read a letter that he and his wife had composed together, explaining their son's desire to marry me. Daddy liked this approach, and permission was granted.

We married a year later in the Catholic Church the Montoyas attended. The place was packed. The Montoyas had lots of friends and lots of relatives. Daddy was proud to walk me down the aisle. Three weeks before the wedding, Mother had taken me to the doctor's to get birth control. This time everything had gone the way it was supposed to.

Before Leo and I left the reception hall, we knelt for my parents' blessing. What a strange feeling it was to know I would not be going home with them. When Leo and I arrived at our bridal suite, I was already crying for my mother. Leo called her at home for me, and she was crying too. She said my father was in the bathroom crying as well.

Oscar had come to the wedding, but he didn't come to the party afterwards. Instead he went to a rodeo. He was restless. He didn't even know if he wanted to stay in school for his senior year. And after working since the age of 12, he didn't really want to ranch anymore either. He decided to spend the summer in Juarez with John, and if he liked it, maybe stay there. Mother protested that he'd better be back in time for school in September. But Daddy said, "Let him go. Let him learn to be a man."

Just as living in Elida, New Mexico had been culture shock for John, Oscar experienced enough culture shock living in Juarez to return early with an alternative plan. Now he decided he would go up to Denver and work for our cousins in the construction business, as Daddy had done previously. He had thought construction would be easier than ranching, but when he called home, he complained that our cousin woke him at five in the morning, handed him his packed lunch, and sent him off to the site. It got old fast. Daddy came home one day to say that he'd seen some bum walking on the road, in the direction of the house. Mother flew out the door. And there was Oscar, ready to return to school.

Oscar was smart and his grades had always been good, but in his senior year, his grade in conduct fell sharply. The boys in his class, Rod and Timothy and Joe, were pranksters, and the lot of them were getting into trouble on a regular basis. Oscar and his friends spent more time in the principal's office than they did in class. Even though Oscar had been elected Best Dressed, Homecoming King, and Athlete of the Year, his graduation day was as nerve-wracking for Mother and me as his boxing and rodeo competitions. He got drunk early in the day and insisted that when his time came to accept his diploma, he was going to pop the president of the school board in the face. Mother and I admonished him. We made him eat some food and poured cup after cup of coffee down his throat to sober him up. When the big moment came, he shook Mr Burris' hand, moved his tassel to the other side of his cap, and walked off the stage just like any other graduate. Mother and I took a deep breath from our seats in the gym.

Now that graduation was over, Oscar wouldn't have to schedule his ranching work to coincide with school hours. It was time for his life as a cowboy and a hand working on other people's ranches to begin in earnest.

As children, we had not been taught to dream. We'd been brought up to know how to take the reins and do what needed to be done, whether it was "manly" work, as in Oscar's case, or domestic tasks for Carol and me. We simply didn't have the time or the encouragement to learn the *knack* of imagining alternative lives for ourselves. So it was natural that when a door opened and something that could be construed as an opportunity appeared, we jumped right in, no questions asked.

Oscar had never imagined a life that did not feature ranching in Elida. He wanted one, desperately, but he never imagined what one would be like — until one day that summer when a man by the name of Larry Hays, the baseball director of Lubbock Christian College, came by and offered to help him to get a scholarship to play baseball at Dallas Baptist College, with which he was also affiliated.

Oscar had always been a great athlete. His room was full of trophies, for both baseball and basketball. I'd once watched him on the court sink 75 baskets in a row. The school teams he played with won championships. So he shouldn't have been surprised to be singled out for a sports scholarship, to have been "found" in the small, dusty, mostly Anglo ranching community of Elida, New Mexico. But he was. We all were.

In fact, there was a lot of athletic talent in little Elida. But it all went to the rodeo. Kids like Oscar, like his friend and fellow Little Leaguer Jimmy Dale Ward, aspired to rope and ride as well as any Charles Good or Sonny Davis. And they knew how to take care of their wounds as well. Oscar was once bucked by a horse and had his shoulder thrown out of joint. Jim Bob Nuchols took a look at it and said it would need surgery. But Oscar worked that shoulder an hour a day until it was completely mended.

When he heard about the scholarship, Jim Bob was one of the first to tell Oscar to jump on the opportunity. "Don't ever come back to Elida," he told him. "There are no jobs here." But not everyone felt that way. Both our parents were very upset. Mother simply did not want Oscar to live far away, like John did.

As for Daddy, he thought Oscar was a fool to accept the scholarship. "You won't make a living playing games," he told him. "You need cattle." Daddy was still working for other ranchers, but he had also recently managed to get some cattle of his own. Since he didn't have land, he leased the property to graze them.

Mother worked at his side, getting up early to break the ice in the winter so that the cattle could drink, feeding the newborns with a bottle in the spring. This was more than Daddy had ever hoped for. This was as good as it got for a man and a woman who had migrated from Mexico with nothing more than the shirts on their backs and a desire to get by.

Daddy wanted Oscar to see the beauty of the foundation that he had laid for him. And Oscar might have. But as quickly as Mr Hays had opened the door, Oscar had, in fact, learned how to dream.

Chapter Five

Irreparable Damage

Although Oscar spent his break time in Elida, and Carol and I were living only 20 miles away in Portales, now that we were all out of the house, our parents were beginning to get their first taste of the "empty nest." Mother, who remembered Jesus in good times and bad, turned one of the now empty bedrooms into a prayer room. She cleared off the top of a dresser and replaced various bedroom items with pictures of Christ, both the Sacred Heart and the Infant Savior, and candles, one of which was always lit.

And prayers would be needed, as it turned out.

Mother, who had gotten her driver's license, made a trip to Denver to retrieve Carol, who'd gone there with Octavio but was now arguing with him. As soon as I knew she was home, I drove down to see her. It was a Saturday. Mother was in her room, getting dressed, when she called me to her to check out a lump that she had noticed on her breast. I placed my hand on it and discovered that it was the size of an egg and as hard as a rock. "Why didn't you tell anyone? How long have you had this?" I shrieked. She shrugged. She said it was nothing. It had only come up in the last few weeks and she thought it would disappear as quickly. I could hardly wait for Monday to arrive so that I could set up an appointment with Dr Miller, the same Portales doctor who had delivered Oscar. The soonest he could see us was the following Friday. But based on the information I had given him, he agreed to do a biopsy in his office at that time. Mother was in such pain after the biopsy that Leo and I decided to bring her to his mother's house, where Mrs Montoya and I could care for her together, rather than let her go home. We were afraid that Daddy, who had a low threshold for other family members' pain, wouldn't know what to do to help her. And we were right.

The following week when the news came that she had cancer and would have to have her entire breast removed along with surrounding nerves, muscles, and lymphoid, Daddy was unable to take in this information because he was preoccupied with one of his cattle. One of his steers had somehow swallowed some wire while eating hay and was now swollen and in great pain.

Mother's operation took six hours and she had to stay in the hospital for several days afterward. And all the time that she was hospitalized, Daddy fretted about his steer. He would come to see Mother of course, but then he would leave to check on the steer. At some point during her stay, he loaded the steer up on a trailer and hauled him to a vet for x-rays (which confirmed the wire's presence) and took him back to the field.

Precious hours that he could have spent at Mother's bedside were wasted. I found myself furious with him, though I held my tongue. He watched the steer scrupulously for signs that he would pass the wire and recover. But when it was clear that he would not, he loaded the animal up once again and brought him to a barn sale and sold him to be butchered.

In this way, he survived Mother's ordeal.

Before Mother was discharged, Carol and I went to the hospital to learn how to change the dressings. It took my breath away to see her ribs protruding through her skin where her breast used to be. Perhaps I was more like Daddy than I imagined. Carol moved in with Mother for a time and nursed her back to health.

Daddy, meanwhile, was working harder than ever, and finally getting ahead financially by splitting his time between his increasingly larger numbers of cattle and hogs and his job at the local feed store. But then he had an accident — one that would ultimately change his life in ways no one could imagine. He was riding shotgun in the feed store's delivery semi when the truck overturned. He spent a week in the hospital and many weeks more in therapy, but the end result was that his back would never be the same.

The feed store's insurance company (which had paid for Mother's medical bills) compensated him for the loss of his job with a lump sum such as he had never seen before. Not only did he now have some money, but he also had more time than ever, since he had only his animals to concern himself with. But while he loved his cattle and hogs, they were not enough for a man who had left home by the age of 14 and found his way into the U.S. by the age of 16, and worked ever after from morning until night at any job that came his way. And now his kids were gone too.

For the first time in his life, Daddy had too much time on his hands.

He might not have been able to lift anymore — at least not without pain — but Daddy was too much of a man to allow his situation to dampen his spirits. He remained as outgoing as he had ever been. And he continued to look for ways to ensure that when the insurance money ran out, he would still have the extra income he needed to expand his head of cattle.

One day three men came into Elida, up from Mexico. They were looking to purchase used tractors, Caterpillars, that they could bring back and resell. Since Daddy knew every rancher in the area, he was able to negotiate a few deals on their behalf, and before long, Daddy and the three men saw the potential for some kind of business relationship.

Daddy traveled with his new partners to Namiquipa, in the state of Chihuahua. He was impressed with what his partners had there in Mexico. He was impressed too with the many business opportunities they told him about. He made a decision; he would take the risk and make an investment. When he returned from Namiquipa, he told Mother that he had used some of the insurance money to buy land in Mexico, and apple trees to plant on it. "Why would you want to invest your money in Mexico?" she asked him. "What has Mexico ever done for you?"

I was working at a bank in Fortales at this time, and one day Daddy came in with one of his new partners, a man called Grajeda. Daddy and Grajeda had about $10,000 in small bills, fives and tens and twenties, and they wanted it cashed out for hundreds. I handled the transaction for them. Later, one of the older bankers, a man named Charles, pulled me aside. "Don't you find it a little strange," he asked, "that they would have so much money in such small denominations?" I hadn't really thought about it. "They're business partners," I explained. "They're taking that money down to Mexico for investments." "Why hundreds?" he persisted. "Why not a wire transfer?" I wasn't sure what the old banker was implying, but as my father had never had a shortage of integrity in his public dealings, I didn't give it another thought.

In the meantime, on one of his trips home, Oscar announced that he had met a woman who played on the basketball team at Dallas Baptist. She was tall, pretty, and Anglo. Her name was Kathy and he seemed to really care about her. Nevertheless, he had decided that he wanted to leave Dallas Baptist and instead play — and study — at Lubbock Christian College, where his mentor Larry Hays was coaching. He contacted Larry, and in no time Larry had managed to get him the scholarship he needed to make the transfer. Already he was a golden boy; no one in the sports world, it seemed, would deny him what he needed. By this time his fast ball — which had started at 83 mph — was up to 92 mph, and it was looking like he would be a contender for the professional leagues once he was done with school.

Oscar did great things in Lubbock right from the start. We learned that at one particular game, three athletes from the opposing team laughed at him, because he had such a high kick when he pitched, his leg practically going up over his head.

When each of them got up to bat, Oscar promptly struck them out, and no one on that team laughed at him again. As for *his* team, he took them right to the championships. He was an NAIA honorable mention, the "newcomer of the year," and an "all area" award winner, the "area" designating seven states.

One semester break Oscar came home and said he wanted to bring Kathy to the house to meet our family. "Of course," Daddy said, "bring her home." Once he had Daddy's permission, Oscar asked Mother if she could do something about the bathroom. Mother in turn called me, and I came over and we looked at the bathroom together, as if through Oscar's eyes. As soon as he had gone back to school we picked out some wallpaper and a new paint color and got to work. Oscar was so happy to be going to school, to be playing ball, to be making new friends and falling in love. If remodeling the bathroom could add to his happiness, Mother and I were all for it.

We had been very nervous about meeting Kathy the first time, but we saw right away that she was kind and considerate. Her family, she said, were Baptists, and very strict, to the point of being priggish. But it was clear that she opposed their rigidity and felt at home with our more casual lifestyle. And it was not hard to see that she was madly in love with Oscar — and he with her. When he went out to visit his old buddies and help out on their ranches, she went with him. When he went out in the evenings to play a game of pool or have a beer, she was by his side.

One day well into his time at Lubbock, his team was playing Wayland Baptist University, from San Antonio. One of the players was someone Oscar knew from Portales, a cocky guy who never had a kind word for anyone. On the day of the game, he spoke condescendingly to Oscar, and when he came up to bat, Oscar made a mistake, probably the biggest mistake of his career: He threw before he was ready; and he threw as hard as he could. Right away he felt something shift in his shoulder. He kept pitching, but the pain did not go away.

Except for me, he didn't tell anyone about his injury at first, but the scouts figured it out anyway. The scouts had long been impressed with him and they had been watching him closely. The consensus seemed to be that he would need rehab, but that a talent like his was worth taking a chance on, injured or not. Oscar believed his arm would get better too. In 1978, Phillies scout Doug Gassaway signed him up to play for their minor league team in Helena, Montana.

That same year Oscar called to say that he wanted to marry Kathy. Our family was thrilled, but we learned that when Kathy told her family, they were not only *not* thrilled, they were absolutely appalled. They did not want their daughter marrying a Mexican. However, they didn't want her to disgrace them by eloping either. So when they couldn't talk her out of her decision, they agreed that she would have the wedding she had always dreamed of and that they would do their best to accept Oscar as part of the family.

Kathy's mistake was in telling Oscar all this, and Oscar's mistake was in telling us. My father flatly refused to go to the wedding. He was hurt and upset. "If they can't accept my son," he said, "I have no business with them."

Mother and Carol and I were going, of course. "If this is what he wants," Mother said firmly, "Iré a los extremos de la tierra para dárselo." *I will go to the ends of the earth to give it to him.*

We had a wedding shower for Kathy in the hall of the Baptist Church in Elida. All Oscar's classmates showed up for the event, and all the ranchers we knew and our many friends in the area. Of course Kathy's family — who lived outside Dallas — didn't come.

I had had my first child by then. And since Leah Dawn was only six months old, Leo and I decided that she would be best off at home with him during the wedding. Carol's children, Naomi and Noel (Noel had come along two years after his sister), had been invited by Kathy to participate. Naomi would be the flower girl and Noel the ring bearer. The day before the wedding, we piled into one car, Carol and Mother and I and Carol's kids. Before we pulled out of the driveway, Daddy came outside and walked to the window. "Adiós, tontos," he said, laughing. *Goodbye fools.* As for him, he was spending the weekend in Mexico, seeing to his apple orchard.

Almost all the way to Dallas we repeated our familiar refrain. "Oh, why is Oscar putting us through this?" "Why couldn't he just elope?" The last thing we wanted to do was be the only Hispanics at a wedding where we knew Hispanics were not wanted. Nor did we want to have to pretend that we didn't know we were disliked and that we were actually happy to be there. "Why?" we lamented. "Why? Why? Why?"

Dan Howard was one of Oscar's best friends from Elida. He was the son of Jakie Howard, the man who had taught Oscar to ranch and also got him interested in Little League years earlier. Dan met us at our hotel in Dallas. As soon as we saw him, we ran to him crying, "Oh, Dan, why didn't they just run away?" Dan was Anglo, but he understood our concerns. "I don't know," he answered. "This is what he wants. It's what Kathy wants."

That evening as we dressed in our hotel room in preparation for the wedding rehearsal, I began to sing "Viva Chihuahua" at the top of my lungs. "Viva Chihuahua" is a traditional Mexican song that expresses the joy of being Mexican. At first Mother and Carol looked at me as if I'd gone nuts, but then they laughed and joined in. "Let's go out and get sombreros," I suggested when we were hoarse from singing the verses over and over again. "Let's all go into the church wearing them."

How we laughed imagining it. But by the time we left the hotel for the church, we were quite somber again. No amount of singing would change the facts. Knowing that these people felt superior to us should have made us bold and angry, like Daddy. Instead we allowed ourselves to feel inferior. It took great courage to open the door to the church hall and walk in.

My first impression was that the gathering seemed more like one you'd expect to find at a funeral than a wedding rehearsal. The only other Hispanic there was someone Oscar knew from baseball. Moving in a group, we introduced ourselves to Kathy's family. They introduced us to others. Everyone was very cordial. Some people even went out of their way to talk to us.

The next day, the day of the wedding, Oscar wore a white suit, which highlighted his physique and his beautiful tawny complexion. His smile was radiant, as was Kathy's. I had the feeling that nothing would ever stand in Oscar's way of getting what he wanted in life. Certainly Mother and Carol and I would always be there to support him. We cried like babies all through the ceremony, and when it was over, Carol and I told Mother that she would have to go stand in the receiving line, just like Kathy's parents. We had to give her a little nudge to get her going in the right direction, but once she got there, she was fine. "How do you do? Pleased to meet you," she said to everyone in her best English.

Instead of taking a honeymoon, Oscar and Kathy went straight to Montana. Mother and Carol and I, meanwhile, returned to Elida. Daddy was already back from Mexico when we got home. "So," he said to Mother, "¿Enviaste a tu hijo al infierno?" *Did you send your son to hell?"* "No siree," Mother answered. "Cumplí con mi obligación." *I fulfilled my obligation.*

Just as Daddy had refused to attend the wedding, Oscar told Kathy that he would never set foot in her parents' house. She could go whenever she wanted of course, but she would have to go alone. He was proud, and he was not going to forget how difficult they had made things for him. So Kathy visited when she felt the need, though her visits were always brief. But during the off season, Oscar and Kathy returned to Elida and stayed with Mother and Daddy. My parents loved Kathy, and she loved them. She took to calling my father Daddy John. And of course she remained entirely devoted to Oscar.

Oscar had already been to rehab in Dallas, with the same physical therapists who worked on the Dallas Cowboys, but his arm still hurt and it would not function the way it once had. He didn't complain. He seemed to think that if he kept meeting with different therapists, at some point someone would put him back together again. And with this in mind, he began his pitching career with the minors.

Almost immediately, Oscar became the best of friends with his fellow rookie teammate and future Hall-of-Famer, Ryne Sandberg. When they were at the clubhouse, they ate their meals together, and they spent time together away from the clubhouse as well. Oscar said a number of times that he had the greatest respect for Ryne because even though he was a superb athlete, he never thought himself to be any better than the 25th man on the team.

Ryne said about Oscar, "All you had to do to be on his good side was play hard and do things right." Like Oscar, Ryne wore his uniform proudly. For players like them, baseball was a badge of honor, and they would not stand to see it slandered in any way. Pete Rose was in his prime at the time, playing for the Phillies' major team in Philadelphia. I loved watching Pete on TV, because he could hit the ball and he could run like lightning. Oscar didn't admire him as much. He said he was cocky and he thought too much of himself. He didn't see him as the kind of player he knew Ryne to be. Oscar's biggest mentor during this time was Larry Rojas, who constantly taught love and respect for the game. Oscar said during spring training Larry would work from 7:30 in the morning until 5:30 at night with everybody from the major league ballplayers to rookies.

Oscar went 0-1 with a 9.00 ERA in five appearances that first year. The following year he pitched for the Peninsula Pilots and managed a 10-7, 3.04 season. He finished ninth in the Carolina League in ERA. The year after that, he only pitched in nine games, going 2-0 with a 3.55 ERA, two saves and a shutout. All the while he was moving from minor league to Double A to Triple A, he kept the dream of playing for the majors out in front of him, where he could see it, where it felt almost tangible. But it was not to be. When the time came for him to move on, the majors chose not to draft him. Ever since his injury, his arm had not been the same.

Mother and Carol and I prayed all the time that Oscar would get what he wanted. We prayed for Oscar's arm. With the exception of the big money, we did not necessarily see how being a major league player could be that enticing, but as that was Oscar's dream, that was what we prayed for. When he came home, we reminded him that there were other things that he could do, including ranching. But he remained determined to have a career in baseball. He'd decided that he would become a free agent. He would find a team and he would negotiate a contract on his own and he would play. "I can do this," he told us. "I can make this work."

In the meantime, Oscar got work hauling rodeo stock (bulls and calves) from a ranch in Elida to cities where rodeos were being held. In order to do this, he had to participate in team roping. In team roping, there are two mounted cowboys. The "header" is the one who ropes the designated steer first, usually around the horns. Then the "heeler" ropes the steer by its hind feet, and the animal is quickly restrained. Oscar was always the header. He was fast and he was good and he loved the work.

In 1982 Oscar landed a contract with a baseball team in Mexico, the Plataneros de Tabasco. At the time, Kathy was pregnant with their first child. Although she did not like to be away from him, the decision was made that Kathy would stay with Mother and Daddy, and Oscar would go to Mexico alone.

Kathy's doctor was in Clovis. Sometimes she went on her appointments by herself, but more often Mother went along with her. When she went into labor, both Mother and Daddy accompanied her to the hospital, and they were prepared to stay for as long as it took. When the news came that she would need a Caesarian, it was Daddy who signed the release papers for the operation.

Oscar, meanwhile, was not happy on the Mexican league. He didn't like the team and he definitely didn't like the fans. He told Mother and Daddy on the phone that when you pitched badly in Mexico, the spectators were not satisfied to boo you. Instead they pissed in their beer cans and threw them down at you. If they didn't have beer cans, they used paper cups, whatever they could find. Even when you pitched well, if the team lost the game, they blamed it on the pitcher and the end result was the same. Mother had wanted him to come home from the get-go, but Oscar had always been a man of his word and he was reluctant to break his contract. Mother urged him even more once Melissa was born.

"When you break a contract here," Oscar explained, "they beat you up and drag you off like a slaughtered lamb. If I break my contract, they'll break my legs." Once Mother understood how serious the consequences could be, she stopped trying to get him to come home, but by this time she had planted the seed in his head, and more than anything, he wanted to be with his newborn daughter. And sure enough, one night he made up his mind.

He called Mother and told her to send a telegram saying that there was a family emergency and that he was needed right away. Drawing on the dramatic skills that she had perfected back when we were naughty children, Mother wrote that she had had a heart attack, that she was dying in fact, and that Oscar was needed immediately. Carol and I came to stay with her the night of the day that she sent the telegram. We lit the candles on the altar in the spare bedroom and prayed. "Please let Oscar get home without having his legs broken," we begged. "Please bring him back to us, and to his wife and baby, safely." All night long we prayed. Oscar's team was headquartered deep in the heart of

Mexico, and it would take him hours by bus to get to the border. And until we knew he had crossed it, we could not risk ending our supplications.

Oscar returned safely and stayed on at the house with Kathy and the baby. There was plenty of work for him in Elida, with various ranchers, including handling the rodeo stock as he had before he'd signed with the Mexican team. While the future of his baseball career was uncertain, he was networking with various teams, and he felt confident that things would unfold as they should. In the meantime, he was happy to be with Kathy and his new daughter.

In fact, it was a magical time for our entire family. Even with my father's many trips to Namiquipa, when he was home, he and Mother worked with the cattle together at a pace that made it seem more like fun than work. They were spending more time together than they had ever — and the fact that they had survived their respective tests, her cancer and his accident, seemed to strengthen their bond.

As for me, I had my daughter and Leo and we were happy and doing well. And Carol had just had her twins, Danny and Donny. "Bueno, no es a diario que una yegua pare dos potros," Daddy teased when he went to see Carol in the hospital. *It's not every day that a mare gives birth to two foals.* Like most twins, Danny and Donny were on the scrawny side at first. "Put them in the back where no one can see them," Daddy joked with the nurses. But no amount of kidding around could conceal how much Daddy loved his grandchildren. Perhaps a man who works as hard as Daddy did when he was younger appreciates children even more intensely when he finally finds himself with time. He had already bought calves for the older grandchildren — so that they could experience the joy of caring for a small animal, the joy of ranching — and he couldn't wait for the babies to grow old enough so that he could get calves for them too.

I had quit my job at the bank, where I'd worked for five years after high school, back when I was pregnant with Leah Dawn. It was a difficult pregnancy and it was necessary for me to stay off my feet. But I had never been one to sit around idly. And one day after the Sunday service at the Catholic Church I attended each week with Leo, I took the first step along a path that would lead me into politics. I was quite big by this time with my second child, my son Brandon, and after commenting on how fast my baby was growing inside me, a woman I saw each week at church shook her head and asked me if I had heard about the baby right there in Roosevelt County who had been aborted in the eleventh hour. I hadn't; I didn't even know that a baby could be aborted late in the last term. The woman explained it to me: A needle was inserted through the mother's abdomen to remove all the amniotic fluid. Then a strong salt solution was injected, which poisoned the fetus, and in the process badly burned its lungs and skin. The child was delivered — stillborn, of course — some 24 hours later. "Why would anyone do such a thing?" I asked her. This was incomprehensible to me. The woman went on, telling me who the abortionist was, and how several pro-life advocates were going to protest in front of the hospital where he worked later that week. There would be no violence of any kind, she explained, just a few pro-lifers carrying their Bibles and praying that this would not happen again.

I went to the protest with them, and then I began going to political meetings to learn more about the different parties. Toney Anaya was running for governor of New Mexico at the time, and when he came to Portales, I went to hear him speak. But as I sat in the ballroom at the hotel wanting to like Anaya (because, if elected, he would be the country's highest ranking Hispanic, and because his story — he had raised himself up out of rock bottom poverty — was so familiar to me and so much the same as the stories of the people I loved best in the world), I could not find any space in my heart for him. I sensed that he was lying. And his truths, when I could discern them, made no sense to me. How could he be for abortion yet against the death penalty? I thought of what I had learned years ago from Mary Lee about the messages in Deuteronomy: "Any man who causes a woman to lose a child forfeits his life also." And regarding the death penalty, "Forfeit life if you take a life" was also from the Bible. For me, everything came back to the Bible. I wanted to support people who thought the same way I did. So when I left that night, I found out everything I could about John Irick, who was running against Anaya. And then I jumped in and helped with his campaign.

We lost by a landslide. But I was hooked by then, and when I was invited to become the president of the Republican women's organization for Roosevelt County, I accepted readily. With a small child at home and one on the way, I couldn't devote myself full time, but I oversaw the meetings and helped build the agendas that got things done. When I was asked by State Senator Mickey Barnett to serve on the platform committee for Reagan's second-term campaign, I also agreed. I had no idea what might be involved, but I was glad to have the chance to represent my state, and also to represent the Hispanic population. In August I went to Dallas for the convention. I was 29, and though by then I was a political force locally, it was an amazing experience to find myself surrounded with people like Bob Dole and Jesse Helms and Jack Kemp and Henry Hyde. Kemp, in fact, sat next to me. At one point in this week-long affair, Kemp left, via a helicopter that had landed on the roof of the convention center, to attend a football game. I thought it was outrageous behavior on his part — until I learned that he had been a player himself for many years, a quarterback for both the San Diego Chargers and the Buffalo Bills. At home, Leo watched many of the convention debate sessions on TV; "You're doing fine," he said each time I called.

My family was proud of me too, especially Daddy, who kept my "President of Republican Women" business card in his wallet where he could produce it quickly, along with pictures of his grandchildren. Mind you, he didn't like politics or politicians himself. "Those people you think so highly of," he would say to me, "are nothing but crooks. They just know how to hide it better. You'll find out one day."

Oscar was home with Mother and Daddy for only a short time after his return from Mexico. He called his old mentor Larry Hays and Larry offered him the job of assistant coach at Lubbock Christian College. Oscar knew this marked the end of his dream of being a major league pitcher, and he was greatly disappointed. He was only in his 20s, but because he could not pitch for a living, he felt like an old man. But just as Mother had rallied after her cancer and Daddy had persevered after his accident, Oscar accepted his new situation with grace — perhaps in the literal sense of the word. "If this is what God wants for me," he said, "who am I to question it?" So he and Kathy moved away to Lubbock, and Oscar turned his attention to the young athletes at Lubbock Christian College.

Not long after he started, the players began to complain that he was too tough, but they also conceded that he got them to do their very best. "He can really get a guy going," Hays said in interviews. "That's why the pros like him." Oscar didn't care whether the players liked him or not; he only cared about how they performed. He was determined that he would be the best assistant pitching coach he could possibly be.

In the meantime, Daddy's trips to Namiquipa were becoming more and more frequent. At one point he sold off some of his cattle because he needed a thousand heaters to keep his apple trees from freezing over the winter. Then he sold off more cattle, to pay for other orchard-related expenses. He seemed to be increasingly more concerned with his apple trees than he was with the cattle that had paid for them. As a result, the work of caring for the animals, what was left of them, fell more and more to Mother.

Looking back, my parents' moment of great happiness seemed to be as fortuitous as finding the exact point of balance on a seesaw. It had taken years to achieve it, and there was no way to extend it. Once it was gone, it was gone.

Daddy had taken a partner in Namiquipa, someone to oversee the orchard when he was not there — which was seldom lately. He justified this partnership by saying that you had to be a citizen of Mexico to own an apple orchard, and as he was not, he had no choice but to find someone who was. We knew his partner only as "Lalo." Daddy answered evasively whenever we tried to find out more about him.

Mother, Leo and I realized at some point, was getting more and more withdrawn, and one day when we went to check on her, we found her sick in bed. Daddy was in Mexico at the time. She told us that he had bought a house there, and that during his last visit to Elida, he had found a buyer for their house. The cattle were all gone by then — he'd sold every last one of them — so there was no point, he'd said to Mother, in staying on. He had left with instructions for where she was to go to sign the papers to complete the transaction, and, she told us, she had signed them. Then she took to bed. Perhaps she was waiting for the new owners to arrive and cast her out.

We could hardly believe this news. Daddy could not for a moment have thought she would follow him to Mexico. Mother would never go that far from her children. Anyone who knew her knew we were her life. "Where's the money from the sale of the house?" we asked her. She said it had been sent directly to Daddy in Mexico. "And what about you? How much money do you have?" "Cinco mil dólares" she answered. *Five thousand dollars.* "Don't give it to him," I told her. "Don't you even tell him about it."

Leo and I took Mother to Portales, where we lived, and where Carol and Octavio also had a home, and we found her a small house and used her $5,000 as a deposit, making the purchase in our names as we had good credit and she had no credit. The little bit of support we extended in getting her resettled motivated her. She cast her mantle of depression aside and quickly became again the strong woman she had always been, the one who had not been afraid to cross the border to live in a country where she didn't know the language, to leave a job when her employers became abusive, to survive cancer, to find her way in the world.

Mother began cleaning houses. Carol and I knew a lot of folks in Portales, and we were able to get her good jobs with influential people who could pay her fairly for her hard work. And she would have been fine except she began getting calls around this time. Where was her husband? strange men wanted to know. Some of the callers said that Daddy owed them money. One even became threatening. He said, "Tell us where your husband is; if you don't, we know where your son is, and we'll kill him right there on the ball field." "Usted es un hijo de su chingada madre," mother answered. *You son of a bitch.* "You come here right now," she growled at the stranger. Mother had a gun — she had acquired it years ago, and it had accompanied us on every trip we'd ever made to Mexico — and she wouldn't have thought twice about using it.

Daddy called from Namiquipa to tell Mother that he was coming up to Portales to see her and to give her some money. She told him right away that while she loved him, while she would always love him, if he was involved in anything illegal, then he shouldn't come around. "Prefiero limpiar casas y lavar pisos," she said. *I would rather clean houses and wash floors.* She did not want a red cent from any crooked dealings. So Daddy stayed away longer. But the calls from strangers kept on coming.

On the night that Daddy finally did show up in Portales, we all went to Mother's new house to see him. He hated the house. "Why did she buy here in the city?" he asked us. "Why didn't she buy a ranch?" This should have been the time to remind him that he'd sold the house in Elida out from under her, that the money had disappeared and that if she hadn't had a few dollars of her own stashed away and we hadn't signed for her, she wouldn't have any home at all.

But what we wanted more than anything was for Daddy to break his ties in Mexico and come back to us. That was our only objective. So I answered him, saying, "If you want a ranch, Daddy, we'll find one. We'll make it happen." But he didn't have time to consider it, because he had to get back to Namiquipa.

On another occasion Daddy came to visit while Oscar was there visiting as well. While Oscar knew that Daddy's behavior had resulted in Mother selling the house and moving to Portales, we had never told him about the bad men who were calling, about our suspicion that Daddy was involved, at least peripherally, in illegal activities. Part of the reason was that we felt that Oscar had enough challenges to deal with; he didn't need to know. The other part was that it just wasn't possible that Daddy, of all men, could have gotten himself into any real trouble. We were biding our time, waiting for the explanation to present itself, waiting for something to change.

It was Oscar who got up from the table to open the door for Daddy that evening. "Come on in, Daddy," he said. "Mama's got this house here for you, so you're home."

Mother had made it clear years ago, when we were all babies, that she would never tolerate any criticism of Daddy from any of us for any reason. If there was a problem, we were to go to her, and if she saw fit, she would go to Daddy. We were taught to show nothing but respect where he was concerned. "One day he'll be gone," she would warn us, "and if you belittle him in any way, that's what you'll remember." Consequently, none of the three of us had ever raised our voices to Daddy. And though Oscar didn't raise his now, we could hear something in his tone that confirmed his displeasure with Daddy's behavior. Surely Daddy heard it too.

Daddy was gone again just a few days later. And not long after, we learned that his brother had died. His family called Mother, thinking she would know how to get in touch with him, but she didn't. So the family had the funeral without him, and they reported back to Mother afterwards that it was just as well that he hadn't come, because some very bad men had been there waiting for him to show up.

At one point Daddy came to Portales to say that he was ready to move in and be a husband to Mother again. But the calls had still been coming, and this time Mother told him that she didn't want him — not as long as he was still involved with bad men. How much money did he actually owe to these bad guys? Leo and I wanted to know. We felt certain that if we all made an effort, we could pay off Daddy's debt. But he only said that he had gotten himself into this mess and he would get himself out. "But in the meantime," I told him, "you're bringing this poison to your wife, to your grandchildren. You were so strict with us. How is it possible now for you to be involved in these bad things?"

He only repeated that he would find a way out, and then he left for Mexico once again.

Chapter Six

Shattered Dreams

Oscar liked working with Larry Hays; he liked working with the young players; and he liked the college itself. Lubbock Christian, as the name implies, was a place where God came first. Bible classes were offered to the students, and discussion of spiritual matters was always encouraged. Prayers were said before each of the games. There was no drinking permitted on campus. The philosophy at Lubbock was God first, then family, then job. It was a perfect environment for Oscar as he strove to settle down into a career that felt like a consolation prize.

Although he was tough, his young pitchers respected him. He knew the mechanics of the game inside out. He watched his pitchers like a mother hen, and he took them off the mound at just the right moment. He knew better than anyone that there is nothing more important for a pitcher than a healthy arm, and he made sure his players stayed in shape. Also, he recognized real talent when he saw it, and he knew how to work with the individual players to develop it.

When he came home to Portales to see us, Oscar didn't say that he was devastated not to be pitching himself, but he was and we all knew it. Kathy told us that he would start reading the newspaper at the kitchen table, but when he got to the sports pages and began reading about the rookie players who had made it to the top teams, he would leave the paper open on the table and retreat to another room. It was Kathy who folded over the pages and removed the newspaper from the table time after time.

Amanda was born, Oscar and Kathy's second daughter. With her brown eyes and dark hair, she looked just like Mother's side of the family, a Salazar. Oscar seemed happier for a while — he loved his little girls and he was a wonderful father — but his disappointment in himself cast a shadow even on his love for his family, and he and Kathy began to argue.

They were still visiting frequently, staying with Mother in Portales, and Mother was privy to plenty of their disagreements. One particular Saturday night, she said, Oscar came out of the bedroom "bien perfumado," *all perfumed up*. He was wearing a starched white shirt and starched Wranglers. Kathy, who had had a long hard day with the babies and was in her pajamas, asked him where he thought he was going. He said he was going out. She said she wanted him to stay in and help her get the kids to bed.

Mother left them to figure out a solution on their own. She went into the kitchen, where there were dishes in the sink that needed washing, and she turned on the faucet and got to work. The next thing she knew, there was a commotion going on outside that was so loud that she could hear it over the running water. She dried her hands and ran out to see what was happening. Oscar was in his pickup, trying to pull out of the driveway, and Kathy, who was crying hysterically, was clinging to the opened passenger door, insisting that Oscar stay home with her and the kids.

"What are you doing?" Mother screamed.

"I just want to go out," Oscar shouted over Kathy's sobs.

Mother hesitated for a moment and then charged in his direction. "No," she shouted. "You're married now. You should have thought about this before."

To the amazement of both Kathy and Oscar, she threw open the driver's door, and just like in the old days, in a flash she had loosened her belt from around her waist and was using it to strike out at Oscar's legs (as best she could, given that he was still in the truck). "You quit making a scandal," she screamed. By now Kathy had let go of the passenger door and was up in the truck bed, spread out across the back window, still sobbing her heart out. Oscar was surrounded. He got out of the truck slowly, slammed the door, and turned toward the house. He didn't look at Mother as he passed her. He just marched into the house and retreated into the bedroom.

So, yes, most of it was his frustration. And surely part of it was Daddy's departure from our family. Not a day went by that we didn't fully expect that he and Mother would resolve their problems and that he would be back. We were his life and we knew it. But in the meantime, he wasn't with us. And as a result, we all went about our business with long faces and heavy hearts. And maybe part of the problem was simply that Kathy and Oscar were from two different worlds. Certainly the way Oscar handled things — by going out without her, by drinking — had to be different than the model Kathy had seen in her father's behavior when she was growing up.

Kathy tried her best to keep the marriage together, but it was too much work. And the harder she tried, the more Oscar felt that she was suffocating him. More and more often he came to visit us without her. And after the season finished up at Lubbock Christian College, he moved back to Portales alone.

We all hoped he was home to do some ranching during the off season, that come autumn he would return to his family and his job. But that's not what happened. When fall came, he was still there. He made Mother's home his headquarters but stayed just as often with his friends in Elida, with Jimmy Dale Ward and Jim Bob Nuckols. Or if he was in Portales, he would hang out with Jerry Stroud.

Jerry Stroud was street smart, like our brother John. But unlike John, who had settled down to a marriage and a decent job, Jerry continued to make his living playing cards, shooting pool and tossing dice. He had been something of a mentor to Oscar when Oscar was still in high school, during his senior year when he had been a troublemaker. When Oscar graduated, Jerry told him not to follow in his footsteps; instead he advised him to get an education and make a life for himself. "There's no future for you here," he'd said. But now they were back together again.

Jerry had a lifelong feud going with another man from Portales, Kenny Smith. Once Kenny had bitten into Jerry's cheek during a fight, almost taking it clear off his face. The gash turned into a nasty and permanent scar that you could lose your fist in. Oscar admired Jerry's fearlessness and his quick wit. He could beat people — at pool, at cards, at dice — not just because he was good at games but because he was an earnest student of human nature and he knew how to beat people psychologically.

Some months before Oscar's return to Portales, Daddy had asked him if he knew anyone with a tractor to sell. Daddy was still looking for tractors to buy in New Mexico and bring down to Namiquipa. At the time, Oscar happened to know that his friend Rod Lambirth had a tractor he planned to replace, and Oscar negotiated the deal for Daddy. When Oscar moved back in with Mother, he learned that Daddy had never paid Rod a single penny; he had taken the tractor with the promise of making payments in installments, and Rod had never heard another word about it.

Mother was appalled when she learned that Daddy had let this happen. We all were. But no one was as upset as Oscar. "I'm going down to find him and get the tractor back," he said. "I'll come with you," Mother volunteered. "No," Oscar said. "I'll get Rod and we'll take care of it."

Not long after Rod and Oscar left for Mexico in Rod's shiny new red pickup truck. At the border Oscar acknowledged a sign that said "No Guns Allowed" by taking out his gun and waving it in the air. "Oh, is that right?" he asked an invisible authority, and Rod, a rodeo big-timer who was as tough as Oscar, laughed. Oscar and Rod had been cutups together in high school, and this trip was partly steeped in intense frustration and partly an occasion to act like cutups once again.

Oscar and Rod located the apple orchard in Namiquipa.

Neither Daddy nor anyone else was there at the time, but the tractor was, and they quickly loaded it up onto Rod's trailer and turned for home. Hours later they reached the border. The border guard, who was certainly used to finding reasons to extract bribes, said that while the truck could move across the border, there was no permit for the tractor and they could not haul it across.

There was no point in wasting time trying to explain that they were only retrieving the tractor because the man who had taken it had never made payments. So Oscar readied the trailer and backed the tractor down off of it. "You're not going to let me through?" he asked the border guard, giving him one last chance to do what was in everyone's best interest. The guard shook his head; he wasn't prepared to budge. But instead of driving the tractor off to the side of the road as the guard must have thought he would, Oscar drove it right up to the concrete barrier blocks that marked either side of the crossing area. He moved one, then backed up and put the tractor in gear and came forward and moved another. "All right, all right," the guard conceded. "You're going to have to pay a fine. Then take that thing and get the hell out of here."

After hours on the road and the delay at the border crossing, Oscar and Rod were too tired to continue the trip home. They found a hotel in the border town of Columbus, New Mexico, which was made famous in 1916 when Francisco "Pancho" Villa attacked it with his army of 500 Villistas. Columbus, New Mexico was still a cowboy town where anything could happen. And so while Oscar snored the night away in their hotel room, Rod sat at the window, keeping his eye on his truck, and his tractor on the trailer behind it. After everything else that had happened, it seemed perfectly reasonable that if he went to sleep, he'd awake in the morning to find the whole rig gone.

"If we have nothing else," Mother said to Oscar when he got home the next day and confirmed that Rod had his tractor back, "we have our word." But what about Daddy's word? What had happened to that? Oscar wanted to know.

The time had come for them to have a talk. Mother explained that it was possible that Daddy was involved "in things." He was always on the move it seemed, getting rides from Namiquipa to Portales, and then taking buses from Portales to Albuquerque to meet up with his various "partners." Who knows where they went from there? She'd been down to see John in Juarez on several occasions, and John had confirmed that Daddy had been acting strange when he saw him too, visiting without notice and then, subsequent to a series of horn beeps from outside, leaving in the middle of the night. Mother told Oscar too about the men who had been calling, though the calls were less frequent now than they had been.

Oscar internalized all this information the way he did everything else. He went to work each day — ranching, working with rodeo stock, welding fences, steel working, whatever was available — and he came back to Mother's at night and had his supper with her (and with Naomi, Carol's oldest, who stayed with Mother much of the time), and called Kathy to check on his kids and went out with his friends...and he never said much more about it. But when Daddy appeared out of nowhere one day, dropped off by some of his "business associates" and planning to take a bus to Albuquerque in the morning and catch up with them, Oscar took him aside before he even had a chance to call Carol and me and let us know he was in town. "Daddy," he said, "I love you. But if you're involved in bad things, things worse than not paying your debts, then you have to pack up whatever clothes or possessions you have here in Mother's house and leave. I'll drive you to the bus stop." No one was more surprised than Oscar when Daddy went into the other room and returned with a small suitcase. He had never taken the bulk of his possessions from the house in Elida, and so they had been packed and moved along with everything else to the house in

Portales. And he did not take them now. But he packed what he could and Oscar took him to the bus stop. When Oscar returned, Mother told me later, his eyes were flooded with tears.

How I prayed during this time, sometimes with Mother and Carol at Mother's altar but often alone. "Please protect my Daddy, Lord," I begged over and over again. Sometimes I prayed on my knees, focused on my petition. Other times my prayers slipped into ordinary moments when I had just the second before been thinking about something else. There had been a news story about a man in Nogales. He had come to owe the Mexican mafia money, and one day they came after him — although by then they wanted more than the money he owed. He was sitting in a restaurant having a meal when they appeared. First they shot him and then they dragged his bleeding body outdoors where passersby could see it and poured some gas on it and lit a match and let him burn. Then they stood back from the fire with their arms folded, admiring their handiwork.

Perhaps there had always been stories of such atrocities concerning the Mexican mafia, but now I seemed to hear them all the time. I could not turn on the TV news or even the radio to listen for a local weather update without hearing of such abominations. The unidentified body of a man — replete with bullet wounds — was found in Albuquerque, and I could not rest until I learned that they had finally identified him and he was someone other than my Daddy. "Please, Lord, let my Daddy not die a horrible death like that," I prayed. "Please keep your hand on him."

Daddy was traveling everywhere these days. We didn't know what he did exactly, but we knew he went to Bernalillo, to Santa Fe, even up into Colorado, and who knew where else. In my wild imaginings, it occurred to me that if anything awful did happen, Oscar would most definitely go after the culprits, and then something horrible would happen to Oscar too. Such violence was a cycle that would not end.

I was working at the Portales City Hall during this time, as the administrative assistant to the city manager. Because of my position, I played a supporting role when the construction of an ethanol plant began in Portales. Part of the "support" included helping the ethanol people to secure a $30 million dollar grant. The plant owner was impressed with my work and with my connections, both political and with the local farmers they would need to work with to make the ethanol plant a success, and before long he offered me a job at the plant. It was better money than I was making, so I agreed.

Every new job offers the potential for fulfillment, but it was clear after a short time at the ethanol plant that that was not going to happen. The problem was, like Oscar, there were too many aspects of my life that felt out of sync to me. And just as Oscar had taken his frustration with life out on Kathy, I took mine out on Leo. I felt restless. I only knew that I didn't want to be with Leo anymore. I wanted my babies but not him.

Leo took it well when I told him. He even agreed that we could manage a divorce without our children knowing about it if we worked it out just so. As it was, they were always with me at my mother's house on the weekends. So the plan was that they would stay at home with their father and I would come and go during the week, and on weekends they would be with me. It seemed like a workable solution. "Don't you want any monetary compensation out of this?" my attorney asked when I got that far along. "No," I told him. Other than my children, and my father, there was nothing in life that I craved.

At the same time that Leo and I were working out the preliminaries for our divorce, Kathy was having divorce papers prepared for her and Oscar. Oscar didn't want any part of it; what he wanted now was one last chance.

"I don't want this divorce," he told Mother and me. Then he asked us if we would drive to Lubbock and talk to Kathy and try to get her to change her mind. Mother and I were as quick to leave for Lubbock as we had been once to renovate the bathroom in preparation for Kathy's first visit. Anything for Oscar. But this time Mother and I were less successful in our mission. Kathy heard us out politely and then said no, she just couldn't do it. She would go forward with the preparation of the papers. And we were left to return to Portales with the bad news.

If things had been different, perhaps Oscar and I could have comforted each other regarding our respective failed marriages. But we didn't get that chance. Not long after Mother and I returned from Kathy's, Mother got a call from a state sheriff in Utah saying that Daddy had been arrested. Apparently, Daddy had been with some men and they had been pulled over for a traffic violation. Nothing illegal was found in the car, but when they did an identity check on Daddy, they learned that there was a warrant for his arrest.... "For drugs?" Mother asked, and the officer confirmed her worst fears.

The whole world sank for our family that day. We had already come to terms with the fact that Daddy was involved with people who were involved with drugs, but we would not let ourselves believe that Daddy was involved directly. We told ourselves that he would never do that. Yet, even while we were all devastated, we could see the hand of God in the way things had turned out: he hadn't been found lying in an arroyo somewhere; he hadn't been shot or burned or beaten. He hadn't been captured by a federal agency and locked away in a penitentiary in another state. He would be extradited to Portales the very next day. Our Daddy was coming home, and we would find the way to make sure he stayed now.

The county jail is right in the center of Portales, in the courthouse in the town square. I had to pass the building a few times the next day, coming and going from work, and each time I wondered how it was possible that my Daddy, who had worked so hard and taught us to be so hard on ourselves, could have come to this end.

It only took a few days to get him out on bail. Leo and I had already made calls. We had found an excellent attorney and we couldn't wait to sit Daddy down in Mother's kitchen and tell him about the conversation we had had with the lawyer. But when we finally got him home, Daddy only repeated the refrain that was by now familiar to us: "I got myself into this and I'll get myself out." He knew an attorney himself, he said. It was a friend of his, a man who lived in Espanola.

I did not come to the house the night that the attorney from Espanola and his wife came for dinner, but Mother gave me a full account the next day. She said the attorney was overweight and wore flip flops. What kind of attorney wears flip flops? she wanted to know. Mother was definitely not impressed. But Daddy wouldn't hear any opposition to his choice. "I'm fine," he said. "This will all work out. I can take care of it."

We believed him. After all, he was home with us, in a good mood, and he didn't seem any worse for whatever had or hadn't happened over the past few years. It was easy enough to simply be grateful for his presence. He said he would get off, and so that is what we all thought: Daddy will get off, and he will stay with us now, and we will be a family again. So confident was I that the trial would work in his favor that I didn't take off from work to attend. Instead I waited until my lunch hour and then hurried over to the courthouse to catch some part of it. As I walked in, something inside me froze. There were people in there who I knew from my political affiliations. It was embarrassing to see them under these circumstances. I glanced at the DA, at the handsome young Hispanic man sitting beside him.

The courtroom was quiet except for a recording that was being played on a tape recorder. It took me a few seconds to shift my mind from the embarrassment of seeing people I knew to actually listening to the recording, as everyone else in the room was raptly doing. The recording was of a conversation between a young Hispanic man, surely the one sitting next to the DA (surely an undercover agent) and my father. They were transacting, making a deal, a drug deal. There could be no doubt about what was happening.

In that moment I knew for the very first time that the man I respected and loved was also another man at other times, in other places. I felt as if I were sinking into the floor, into a hole in the earth. The recording was still playing and I was still hearing what I did not want to hear, what I never believed I would hear, with my own ears.

Later I would come to think that this was necessary, that if I hadn't walked in at that moment, I never would have believed it. I would have argued with other family members and argued with the law on his behalf. I would come to think that God guided me to walk in at that moment so that my understanding would be complete. But at the time, I could only think that I needed air, that I needed to get out.

Somehow I found my way to Mother and slipped in beside her. "Estoy desesperada," I whispered. *I feel hopeless.* Mother was hugging herself, rocking back and forth, looking straight ahead. The recording was still playing.

I had to return to work. I had said I would be back. I got up and left. It was easier to go back to the ethanol plant and, like a robot, dig in my bin to see what needed to be done before the end of the day. I was amazed to see how one part of me could carry on so efficiently while the other part remained pinned to the wall in the courtroom.

When I got off work I drove directly to Mother's house. Even though the sky was darkening, there were no lights on anywhere. I found her on the sofa, lying on her side, curled up against the cushions, crying her eyes out. She managed to tell me the results of the trial in between sobs: It had taken no time at all for the jury to make their decision. Daddy was guilty — guilty as charged. He had been sentenced to nine years. "Yo estaba sola allí adentro, sola cuando dieron el veredicto," my mother sobbed. *I was alone in there, all by myself when the verdict came down.* She was in hysterics. I could not quiet her down. And I was overcome with guilt. I had been so focused on my own emotions that I had done what seemed right for me. And in the process I had left her alone to take a blow like none she had every encountered — like none she had ever even anticipated.

Carol came, and the three of us cried together. We got Daddy's picture from the bedroom and brought it to the sofa and wept like babies. Our Daddy, nine years in prison. It might as well have been a life sentence. "How are we going to deal with this?" we wailed.

Oscar arrived. He tried to talk to Mother but she was completely hysterical by then. She might have been having a breakdown. Oscar was upset about Daddy too, but there was nothing he could do about that at the moment. In the meantime, here was Mother, nearly unable to breathe. He took her in his arms as easily as if she were a small child and carried her out to his truck. Then he and Carol drove her to the hospital, where the emergency room doctors gave her a shot to calm her down. I stayed at the house and waited.

I was still there at six in the morning when the phone rang. Mother was resting, finally, so I answered quickly. It was the Portales sheriff. "We're fixing to take your father over to the facility in Los Lunas," he said. "This isn't protocol, but I'm going to have him on the courthouse steps in a short time, and if you should happen to come by, you might get a chance to say goodbye to him."

I felt like someone had just removed a plastic bag from my head, allowing me to draw in a much needed long, deep breath. That the local sheriff would call and offer us such a gift was a testament to how much my parents were loved, how much of an aberration it was that my father had gone down this path. I woke up Mother and Carol and Oscar, and we were dressed and ready to go in mere minutes. I drove Mother and Carol in my car and

Oscar followed in his pickup.

And there was Daddy, standing outside the courthouse as promised, his face as ruggedly handsome as any Charlton Heston, dressed in his Levis and a yellow plaid western-style shirt, his hands behind him, cuffed. We headed first toward the sheriff, who was standing a few yards away, to offer him our profound thanks for his gift. But Daddy gestured with his head for me to come to him directly. I broke off from the others, and as soon as I was near him, he bent close to me and said that there was a piece of paper in his shirt pocket, that I should take it out and call the number, that the people on the other end would know what to do to get him out. I could see this was important to him. "Okay, Daddy," I said, and I reached into his pocket and pulled out the slip of paper. Daddy waited until I had transferred it into my own pocket. Then he straightened up and took a step back and greeted Mother and Carol and Oscar. The conversation that followed was mostly about how we would get another attorney, how we would find another way, how we would never give up and let him spend nine years in prison. And then the sheriff came forward and announced that the time had come for them to go. We tried not to cry as Daddy and the sheriff walked away from us. But once Mother and Carol and I got into the car, we all broke down, draping ourselves over the seats and the dashboard, crying for all we were worth. When I finally got the courage to straighten up and take the wheel, I glanced in the side view mirror and saw that Oscar's blue pickup was still parked behind me. At first I thought he hadn't gotten in yet, but then I saw movement. He had collapsed onto his steering wheel. His shoulders were heaving up and down, up and down.

Later that day we got a call from Daddy's lawyer, the man with the flip flops. Again I answered the phone. "If you can give me $500—" he began. I didn't let him finish. "What the hell did you do for my Daddy?" I screamed. "You did nothing for him. Don't you ever call here again. Ever!"

And he didn't. Nor did I ever call the number Daddy had given me. We had to get Daddy out, but getting more deeply involved with the criminal element that had gotten him in trouble in the first place surely was not the answer.

John was the first to go see him at the facility in Los Lunas. He and Ernestine had had a hunch for some time that Daddy was in trouble, but they respected him too much to question him about it. It was a long trip for them, from Juarez to Los Lunas, and it required getting special permissions to cross the border. But it was worth it to them; they loved him that much. A week later Mother and Leo and I went to see him. We left very early in the morning because it was a five-hour drive and we had been assigned a specific time for our visit. Leo and I brought Leah Dawn along. I'd never been to a prison before, and it had never occurred to me that there might be a dress code for visitors. I was wearing a dress with a halter top. The first guard we encountered said I could not go in like that. Luckily Mother had a sweater in the car. I went back to fetch it. "I never thought I would have to bring my children to a place like this," Mother lamented as we followed a succession of guards to the visiting area.

The large room was arranged like the lobby of a hotel (albeit a third-rate one), with chairs grouped together so that families could gather with some amount of comfort and privacy. We settled ourselves into one of the groupings. Daddy was brought out a few moments after our arrival. He was as straight and tall in his khaki pants and shiny work boots as he had ever been. For all that had happened, I felt a surge of pride.

All around us families were meeting with their prisoners, all young men, 18 or 19 years old. "You should be ashamed," Mother began as she took in the other inmates. "You, an old man, getting into this kind of trouble. I can't believe it. And here you were so hard on our kids." Daddy hung his head and nodded. When Mother got rolling, there was no point in arguing. And what was there he could say anyway? She was right. The minute she let up, Leo and I jumped in, asking Daddy questions about prison life, his daily routine, what he ate, when he slept, anything to lighten things up.

So this would be our future, I thought as we drove home that day, endless hours on the road, driving back and forth to Los Lunas so that we could spend a short time with Daddy. We had already committed ourselves to it. We were a family; we would do what had to be done. We would take turns, Oscar one week, Carol another, Mother and me, John and Ernestine, and this way Daddy would always have someone. We would never let him be alone again.

But the future I envisioned was not the one that actually came to pass. Not two months after his arrival in prison, Daddy was sent out for a routine medical examination. Daddy felt fine, so no one worried about the results. But when they came, the news was bad. It was, in fact, a death sentence: cancer.

Chapter Seven

A Second Chance

Back when we were all kids, Daddy flipped his truck once while trying to scare some coyotes away from cattle he was tending. Except for having to have a finger amputated, he wasn't hurt. But the finger was his left hand ring finger, and it upset Mother that that was the one he had to lose.

We didn't learn this story until we were older. I at least assumed for several years that all daddies were missing the best part of their ring finger. My Daddy was tall, well-built, strong, and handsome...so it stood to reason, in my young mind, that one four-fingered hand was part of the plan.

In some ways the cancer seemed to be part of the plan as well. I believed that with my political connections, there was a good chance that I could get a "sickly" Daddy out of prison. And since he had never been sick before, since he professed not to feel sick now, and since we lived in times when medical miracles happened daily (my mother herself was one), we would deal with the cancer once he was home. We would smother him with love and he would heal and we would be a family again.

At first the doctors who initially examined him told us only that he had cancer, but not what kind. Then we were told it had something to do with his lymph nodes. Finally someone gave it a name: Hodgkin's Disease. We read everything we could find about Hodgkin's and learned that it had a cure rate of 93 percent. We were more hopeful than we had been in a while.

The next step was for me to write a letter to Governor Anaya to ask for clemency for my father. This was no ordinary petition. I took the time to tell the governor my Daddy's life story, how he had come here as a boy to work in the Bracero Program, how well loved he was by all the ranchers he worked for, how, against all the odds, he rose to the position of being a rancher himself, how he had loved the cattle and the hogs he kept, how he had made a mistake, gotten involved with some bad men and lost his way.

In the meantime, Daddy was spending more time out of prison than in. He was sent to St. Joseph's Medical Center in Albuquerque for treatments, then returned to the facility in Los Lunas, then back to Albuquerque for more treatments. He even came back to Portales once during this time. Officials at the Portales courthouse needed his signature on some paperwork, so it was arranged that a correctional officer at Los Lunas would escort him.

During the five-hour trip from Los Lunas to Portales, the officer in charge of my father fell under his spell. Except for when he was drinking, which was now a thing of the past, Daddy had never had a shortage of charisma. So impressed with him was this officer that while my father was doing his paperwork in the courthouse, he called my mother to say that Daddy was in town (we hadn't known) and that he couldn't see how it would hurt to bring him by for a quick visit before they headed back to Los Lunas.

Mother called me at work to share the good news, and on the way home I made an emergency stop at Kentucky Fried Chicken so as to ensure that there would be enough food for Oscar and Carol and whoever else might come by.

The officer ate with us, at the kitchen table, and afterwards, stuffed full of chicken legs and buttery mashed potatoes, he went into the living room to rest "for a moment or two." An hour or so later, Mother remembered him and went in to check. "Oh, look at this," she whispered, and we all got up from the table and looked over her shoulder. The officer was sound asleep, his big hands resting on his belly, his head tipped back, his mouth open, snoring. We could have hit him over the head and let Daddy run out the back door, and his nine-year sentence would have been deferred permanently – and this guy, kind soul that he was, would have been out of a job. But instead we laughed. This was a gift, we knew, a blessing from God that Daddy's presence should have been required in the Portales courthouse in the first place, that this man should have been chosen to escort him. You don't really appreciate the joy of laughing with a loved one at the kitchen table until you've made a few visits to a distant prison visiting room.

And it was not the only gift. Shortly thereafter Toney Anaya got back to me. He agreed to grant my father clemency.

Our fear, when we calmed down from the excitement of knowing that Daddy was coming home, was that he might want to take revenge on the people who had let this happen to him in the first place. But that turned out to be the furthest thing from his mind. Now the only thing Daddy wanted was peace, and a chance to do a little ranching.

He had started reading the Bible, a Spanish version, in prison, and when he came back to us, Bible reading quickly became part of his daily routine. I think this was something he had always wanted to do, back since the time when he had first followed Oscar's example and gotten baptized in the Baptist church. But he had troubles in front of him, first with drinking and then with keeping bad company, and somehow he never got to it. Now that his vices were behind him, it was one of his greatest pleasures to slip on his glasses and pick up his Bible and begin reading right there at the breakfast table, with the bright blue New Mexican sky shimmering in the window and Mother moving about at the sink, and the knowledge that he was surrounded by people who loved him.

The other thing he wanted was to spend time with his mother and sisters, and Mother began to drive him down to Juarez on a regular basis. It broke my heart to imagine how much mother-love he must have missed, having left home at such an early age and having waited so long to contact his family thereafter to let them know he was alive and well. But he was making up for it now, basking in his freedom to spend as much time as he wanted with his family.

By this time Leo and I had already decided that our attempt to hide our separation from our kids was pure folly. Since he was there at the house with them, he used his position of control against me in ways I had never expected. It was, after all, their home. Many times I went to pick them up at a time we had agreed on, only to find the house empty, that Leo had taken them out somewhere and hadn't left as much as a note to let me know when they might return. This left me with no choice but to come at times when I wasn't expected, which sometimes meant taking longer lunch hours or leaving before the end of the work day to pick them up. My boss was not impressed with my disregard for the rules; nor was he impressed with my emotional state, and I was eventually fired.

I needed some air; I needed to get away.

Mother had an idea. Daddy was constantly needing to be in the hospital in Albuquerque for treatments, and sometimes he had to stay there several days consecutively. Since she was still working, still cleaning houses to pay the bills, Mother would often drive him to St Joseph's and then return home and pick him up again a few days later.

The traveling was taking its toll on her. Once, coming back alone from Albuquerque, she had a blowout in Santa Rosa. Luckily, she hadn't been going that fast and she managed to pull off the road. A minister and his wife happened to be driving by, and they stopped and helped her to change the tire. Another time she got caught in a sudden snow squall. She pulled off the highway onto the shoulder of a secondary road, where she thought she would have to wait out the blizzard in her car. But a rancher on his way home in his pickup saw her sitting there and brought her back to the house to stay with his family until the weather conditions improved.

If I found a job in Albuquerque, Mother reasoned, I would be going back and forth regularly to see my children, and sometimes I could take Daddy, or bring him home. And what's more, when he had to stay overnight at St Joseph's, I would be there, in the same town, in case anything went wrong. So I packed up some clothes and drove to Albuquerque to see if I could clear my head.

I found a job right away, in a bank. But the two days I had off each week quickly proved to be too little time to be with my kids, so I found another job, working nights in a law office, Monday through Thursday. This meant I could leave first thing Friday morning and spend Friday, Saturday and Sunday with my kids. I did not have to be back until late Monday to start working again. My split life was challenging, and typing alone in the quiet law office after hours was not very stimulating. But I had made up my mind that I would make the best of the situation.

Daddy set the example, for all of us. Though there were plenty of days when he didn't feel well at all, he refused to talk about death. If anything, he had fallen in love with life. His hair fell out, and as he didn't like the way he looked bald, he went out and bought himself a toupee. He bought a little bit of land as well, and a few cows. With Oscar's help, he began plowing, and caring for his cattle. He even took a vacation — with Carol.

Daddy's intent was to visit an Indian medicine man deep in the heart of Mexico. He had read something about this healer, and he believed strongly that he could help him in ways that western medical doctors could not. The trip was a dream for both my father and my sister. They went to the sea and spent long days listening to the surf pound the sand. In the evenings they ate fresh-caught fish at seaside restaurants. They talked.

Carol has always been the caretaker in the family; she has the healing touch. It's likely that her being with him was as beneficial as whatever the medicine man was able to do. Daddy returned refreshed, positive about every aspect of his life. And for some months, things went very well indeed. Then one day I got a call from Mother saying that Daddy was having a relapse and that he would be coming to St Joseph's by ambulance from the hospital in Roosevelt County.

We were certainly used to fluctuations in his health. Daddy would lose some weight and appear sickly, and then just as quickly he would regain the weight and be fine again. We had come to believe that he would continue this balance of sickness and health for many years to come. But just in case, I stayed in the hospital with my father all that night. I slept bent over in my chair with my head on the foot of his bed, my hand extended so that my fingertips just brushed his leg. That way, if he moved during the night, if he needed something, I would know right away. Mother came the next day. Then other family members. Daddy wanted his mother there, and so Carol helped to arrange for her and his sisters to come up from Juarez. His mother, who was in a wheelchair, was like an angel by his side, a beautiful, gentle woman with long silver hair that was further graced by the lacy mantilla she always wore on her head. She dressed always in long dark skirts and high-collared white blouses. She wore granny shoes, with one inch heels and laces up to her ankles. Daddy's niece came from Colorado too.

This time was more serious than other episodes had been. Daddy's doctor told me that the cancer was spreading. She said there wasn't much they could do, that we could take him back to Portales and make him as comfortable as possible. She said it would get worse as time went by, that at some point he would be unable to speak, and then unable to see. It was hopeless.

Despite the cure rate that the statistics promised, despite the treatments, despite the medicine man, Daddy would not get well. I couldn't believe this news. I refused to believe it. But I told Mother what the doctor had said because I felt responsible to do so. She didn't believe it either.

Carol and Oscar and Mother and Grandmother and the aunts all left to return to Portales, to get the house ready for Daddy's return. I was still there when they put him in the ambulance that would take him back to the hospital in Roosevelt County. "I'll see you in Portales," I called out to him through the open doors in the back of the vehicle. He sat up in his stretcher to wave goodbye, a big smile on his brown face. "Adiós, Flaca!" he said. *Goodbye, Skinny*. The attendants shut the back doors, but I could see that he was still repeating the words — "Goodbye, Flaca" — and waving heartily with his four-fingered hand. We waved until we couldn't see each other anymore.

The Roosevelt County hospital kept Daddy for a day and then released him to us. We got him a hospital bed so that we could make him comfortable at home. Mother's small house was full of people. Daddy's mother and his sisters stayed on, not wanting to leave now that Daddy had come back into their lives. Even though he was terribly weak, Daddy showered the next day and put on fresh pajamas. He was proud and he wanted to be clean. Daddy called me over to him. "You should go back to Albuquerque, Flaca," he said. "You have no one to take care of you now. You need to work." He was right, of course. I wanted to say to him, Daddy, please don't die while I'm away. But naturally I could not say that. So I simply said goodbye.

I was just about to finish my shift at the law office a few nights later when I got the call. Since it was almost two in the morning, I knew right away that the news could not be good. It was Oscar. "Daddy's not doing well," he said. "He's back in the hospital. If you leave right away, I can meet you in Santa Rosa so you don't have to drive all the way here alone. I'll arrange for someone to pick up your car."

I rushed home to my apartment and packed. I made sure to pack something black. I knew in my heart that I would need it. Then I drove as fast as I could, praying straight through from Albuquerque to Santa Rosa. "Please, Lord," I prayed aloud.

"Please don't let him die. Let me at least say goodbye."

I pulled into the designated parking area and got out of my car, leaving my keys under the mat for the person Oscar had made the arrangement with. Oscar was already there waiting for me. During the drive back to Portales, Oscar was silent. For weeks he had been pleading with Kathy to let him pick up his little girls and bring them to Portales so that they could spend a few moments with their grandfather before he died, so that he could give them his blessing. This meant everything to him. But Kathy had said no. Nor would she agree to bring the girls herself. Her unwillingness to bend was devastating to Oscar. I tried to be strong and silent like him, to hold it all in, but I couldn't control my tears. I cried all the way to Portales. We arrived about five, just as the sun was coming up, and went directly to the hospital.

My prayers were answered. Daddy was still alive. I must have looked a sight because Daddy said, "Don't cry, Flaca. It will make me weak to see you cry." I forced as big a smile as I could muster onto my face. "These are tears of joy," I exclaimed. "I'm just so happy to see you."

Daddy stayed in the hospital for a few days. In fact, we all did. We prayed in the hospital chapel, and much of the time we slept there too. When we went home, it was only to shower, to sleep a few hours more in an actual bed, and then we rushed back again. Daddy's mother sat at his side, sage and elegant in her wheelchair. Every day the preacher came and together he and Daddy read from the Bible. The cousin from Colorado brought a tape and a player and placed the earphones on Daddy's head — music that would help him to heal, she said. One of the songs on the tape was "Amazing Grace," Daddy's favorite. He listened to it raptly, as if it was his life story being sung back to him.

And there must have been a bit of amazing grace going on, because Daddy got a little better, and after three days, we were told we could bring him home again. We were thrilled to know that we would have more time with him, and we tried not to let our thoughts wander away from the present moment. On the Sunday following his return to the house, Daddy called Carol and me to his side and said that he wanted us to take him out to see his cows. Over the months — almost a year — since his release from prison, he had managed to obtain about 20 cows. Daddy was very weak, and at first Carol and I argued that he didn't need to be thinking about cows; Oscar was taking good care of them. But he insisted, and we quickly came to understand that he wanted to see his cows for the simple reason that he loved them, that they were his source of pride, his own cattle, the thing he had cherished before he had gotten waylaid on his path to becoming an independent rancher.

When we told the rest of the household where we were going, Daddy's sisters got upset. "You can't drag him out," they exclaimed. "Leave him here. How can you do this?" "We're taking him," Carol said resolutely.

I had never been out to see Daddy's cows before. His land was not too far outside of Portales; I could have gone many times, but I had never had the desire.

As the doctor in Albuquerque had warned, Daddy's eyesight was failing. He was frail and he could barely see. But when we got out of the car and started across the land, you could hardly miss the beauty of our timing. The sun was just going down, and the sky to the west was golden. So was the milo that Daddy had planted. It was surreal to be standing there in the setting sun, Carol and me and our Daddy between us, surrounded — enveloped — in gold light. I thought back to one day a month or so earlier when Daddy had come in from a day's work on the tractor and I had said, "Daddy, you know you don't need to work so hard. You don't have to be out in the sun." "Yes I do," he'd said. His answer had been quick and decisive. Now he whispered in Spanish, "La tierra puede ser tan bonita." *The land can be so pretty*. And he was right.

We reached the cattle. They were fat and black, as healthy as any I'd ever seen. Why had I not come out to see them before? Daddy said, "See that pail over there. You girls go and get it and fill it with water from that barrel." We did what he said but the water bubbling out of the faucet looked like mud. Carol and I looked at each other. This was a sign, we were both thinking, a sign that our Daddy's mind was slipping. Daddy started to get angry. "I said, fill the pail with water and bring it over," he insisted. "Give it to my cattle. I can't believe all these years and I didn't teach you a thing." Then one of us, Carol probably, figured out that what we were filling the bucket with wasn't supposed to be water, though Daddy kept calling it that. It was waste from the ethanol plant. We filled the trough and went back for more. The cattle couldn't get enough of it.

When we finished, I noticed that Daddy had one eye opened and the other closed, like a permanent wink. And with that one eye he looked at the sky, which still held a golden glow, and he looked at his milo and he looked at his cows and he looked at us, his daughters, and I could see that he was satisfied.

That night he got very sick and the ambulance came and took him back to the hospital again. Over the next few days, he lost his voice. Previously when the preacher rested between the reading of Bible passages, Daddy would exclaim, "Praise God," or "Praise Jesus." Now he clapped his hands instead. Sometimes the preacher would say, "John, you know the Lord loves you," and Daddy would clap his hands at that too.

I heard wailing a few days later as I was approaching Daddy's room. I took a deep breath and entered. Carol was holding Daddy in her arms, rocking him, crying, "My Daddy died. My Daddy died." Daddy's mother and two of his sisters were there. John and Ernestine were there. Nurses came in and tried to coax Carol to take something that would calm her down. I poured some water from the bedside pitcher into a glass and went out in the hall. Mother had taken one of Daddy's sisters to dinner. Now they were on the way back, coming toward me. As soon as

Mother saw my face she cried out, asking me what was wrong. I went up to her and kissed her cheek and said in Spanish that Daddy was with Jesus now, that finally he would be at rest. She collapsed on the floor immediately crying, "¿Oh, por qué lo dejé, por qué lo dejé?" *Oh, why did I leave him?* I held her and rocked her and whispered that God didn't want her to be there, that it would have been too much for her.

We went back into the room together, all of us crying in one another's arms. I lay my hand on Daddy's forehead, which was still warm. I kept it there, unwilling to break the connection while any warmth remained. After a time he grew cold. Still, none of us wanted to leave him. More time passed, all of it contained in a cloud of grief too dense to describe. Then a doctor came in to say Daddy had to be taken to the morgue. As requested, we went out in the hall while they prepared him. Once he was gone, we went back in to collect his things. We gathered his clothes, a few personal items. There were pill bottles on the bedside table. I began to collect them, some grief-shattered part of my mind thinking we would need them at home. We had always transported his pills back and forth. Then the rational part of my mind kicked in, with a stab of pain that was sharper than anything I had ever experienced before, reminding me that this time was different. I swept the bottles into the trash. My Daddy was gone.

Still, who can deny God's mercy? Daddy might easily have died in the street, or he might have pined away in prison. Instead he died with his loved ones all around him. And he died satisfied. He had made something good of his life after all.

Chapter Eight

When The Fat Lady Sings

We cried all night, and in the morning we were zombies. Still, there were things that had to be done, a casket to buy, arrangements to be made. Carol and Oscar and I were too worried about Mother's condition to allow her to be involved. We wanted to take care of everything.

I drove to the plaza at the heart of Portales and parked in front of a store called Anthony's. I found the aisle where men's socks and underwear were displayed and grabbed a package of each. A friend of my mother's was there, and like all the women who knew Mother, she loved her very much. When I told her that my Daddy had died, she folded me in her arms. Then she insisted on giving me money to pay for the shirt he would wear in his grave.

I wandered from one aisle to another, aware of my surroundings and my purpose only some of the time. A clerk saw me standing senselessly in front of the shirt rack and approached to ask if I needed help in finding a size. I did. I told him Daddy's size and he helped me pick out a white shirt. We went to the register together. "Would you like me to wrap it?" he asked. "No," I said. "It's for my Daddy, but it doesn't need to be wrapped because he's dead."

I left my packages at the register and went into the aisles again, this time to the ladies' section. Tradition required Mother to dress completely in black for a full year. As for Carol and me, we would wear veils or mantillas, a sign of respect for the dead according to Mexican beliefs. I bought three, one each for Carol and me and one for Mother. Daddy had wanted to be buried in Mexico, but we were not about to have him so far away from us. Still, we intended to honor all the traditions that go along with a

Mexican funeral.

When I returned to the house Mother was already getting Daddy's suit ready. It was the same blue suit that he had worn to walk me down the aisle when I got married. How it had broken his heart that my marriage had come to an end, and Oscar's too.

Mother and I made a list of people we could call to be pallbearers. Some of the names were local ranchers, people who Daddy had lifted up financially, by tending their land, by raising their cattle. Now they would have the chance to lift him up, onto their shoulders, their Mexican ranch hand, the hardest worker, surely, they had ever had.

We went to the mortuary, and since Daddy's favorite color was blue, we chose a blue casket. We told the director that we might decide to keep the lid closed. Daddy had been so frail and sickly looking in his last days, and we didn't think he would want to be seen like that. People would not recognize him as the same handsome rancher they had known. We requested only a one-day viewing. We were worried about Mother, and also about Grandmother. We didn't know if they could hold up any longer than that. We didn't know if we could.

The mortuary called us the following day to say that Daddy was ready to be seen. We drove over and entered the viewing area apprehensively. Oscar and I held Mother between us; she felt as limp as a rag doll. But as we approached the casket, she seemed to gain some strength. Daddy looked great; he looked the way he had before he'd gotten sick. In fact, he looked angelic. They had filled out his face nicely. Mother said, "Sí, tendremos el ataúd abierto." *We will have the open casket.*

Mother and I held each other and cried like babies. Oscar stood with his teeth clenched. His eyes were wet, but he wouldn't allow himself to lose control. A week or so earlier, he had taken Daddy's watch to be repaired. I had forgotten all about it. But as Mother and I clung to each other, I saw out of the corner of my eye Oscar slipping the watch onto Daddy's wrist. I was touched that in all the chaos of the last several days, he had thought to pick it up from jewelry repair. I was touched that he would send Daddy off with a working watch — nothing less.

We took turns embracing Daddy in the casket. Even while hugging him, Oscar kept his teeth clenched. He was the head of household now; he was handling the situation just the way Daddy would have. Later, when people started arriving, Oscar stood back; he stood erect and tall and let them come through to say their last farewells. There were ranchers there from Elida; ranchers from Portales. There were neighbors and friends and relatives from all over Mexico and New Mexico and Colorado. Everyone spoke of Daddy with great respect, as if his transgression in recent years was nothing more than a short chapter in the longer book that was his life. I had to wonder if it would have gone like that if Daddy had died in prison, or worse, in an arroyo somewhere, shot to pieces. Again, I was full of gratitude. Mother bent low before we left and whispered to Daddy, "Recuérdanos. Recuerda a tu esposa y a tus niños." *Remember us, remember your wife and your children.*

Once we were home, Oscar disappeared. We were so beside ourselves with grief, falling to pieces left and right, that no one saw him go. But when we realized, we all felt certain that he had gone out to Daddy's land, a place where he could be alone to shed the tears that he had been holding back all day.

The funeral service the next day was in the chapel of the mortuary. Again, it was well attended. There was an a capella choir there and they sang with the voices of angels many of the songs that Daddy loved best, including "Standing On Higher Ground," "Lighthouse," and, of course, "Amazing Grace."

Daddy was buried in Portales. We stood close and cried, Grandmother and Mother and Daddy's sisters and Carol and me, and Oscar. He held on to Mother, and surrounded by women, he clenched his teeth ever more fiercely, so that the effort made his jaw tremble.

We kissed the casket and left; we did not stay to watch Daddy being lowered into the ground. It was not an option for us. In our grief, we would have followed him. We started the Novena, nine days of praying the Rosary, the next morning. I stayed at my mother's house the entire time, along with my children. Daddy's mother and sisters were there too, of course. And Oscar. We were used to having many people at our home, and with all the food that friends kept bringing us, we had plenty to eat and did not have to use any of our valuable prayer time for shopping and food preparation. But when the nine days of Novena came to an end, Oscar said gently to our house guests, "You were so kind to come to be with Daddy in his last weeks, and to stay to pray with Mother in these hard times, but now the Novena is over and I'm ready to drive you back to Mexico." And Daddy's sisters and mother all retired to the bedrooms and began to pack.

My return trip to Albuquerque was the most difficult one I'd ever made. Not only did I have to say goodbye to my children and my mother yet again, but I felt that I was burying Daddy all over. I cried all the way back, for four hours, and arrived at my job just in time for my evening typing shift. All the women from the day shift, who were just getting ready to leave, lingered to talk to me. They embraced me and did their best to console me, but anyone could see that I would be carrying my grief for a very long time.

Oscar, meanwhile, returned from Mexico and took over as head of the house, caring for Mother, caring for Daddy's cattle and his land. His grief might have been less conspicuous than mine or Mother's or Carol's, but it was no less bitter. He had lost everything, his father, his wife, his children, his career. He was there and not there, Mother said when I spoke to her. He was far away much of the time, silent, always thinking. I was worried about him. But then one day, maybe six weeks after Daddy's funeral, Oscar showed up at my doorstep in Albuquerque and announced that we were going to be roommates. We would get an apartment together, he said, a bigger one than what I had, and we would start a new chapter in our lives.

I was ready for this kind of change. I jumped into Oscar's pickup and we drove around looking for a new place. In the town of Corrales, which is just northwest of Albuquerque, we found one. With its roosters and cows and horses and sheep, Corrales was rural enough for Oscar. And with its desert scrub and view of the Sandia peaks, it was stunning enough to take me outside of myself from time to time.

Oscar landed a job that would keep him busy from dawn to dusk, just the way he liked it, working for a monastery, building fences, welding, whatever was necessary to keep the grounds in good repair. You would think that he would be exhausted at the end of the day, but he was just getting started. He would come back to our apartment just long enough to shower and change and then he was gone again, dancing his evenings away at clubs like Caravan East and Denim and Diamonds. He had always loved dancing, and he had always been a great dancer, as smooth and surefooted and unpredictable as he had once been out on the pitcher's mound, winding up to launch a fastball, but now it was an obsession, something he had to do. He danced every night of the week and on the weekends as well. He loved George Strait and Hank Williams Junior. He loved dancing to songs like "Born to Boogie," and "All My Rowdy Friends Are Coming Over Tonight." I was still typing from four o'clock in the afternoon into the wee hours. Consequently, I didn't see him all that often. Women called the house all the time. They left messages. Was he going to this place or that place and on what night? They were all different voices, all different names. One week I counted 13 of them. I didn't know whether to be happy or alarmed. "What about baseball, Oscar?" I asked him once. "Do you think you'll ever go back?" "I don't want anything to do with baseball anymore," he responded.

I had a couple of opportunities to go out myself during this time, but nothing much came of them. I met Bobby Unser Junior, the son of the famous auto racer, at a political function and accepted his invitation to have dinner with him at his mother's house and then watch a video of him climbing Pike's Peak. Oscar happened to be home while I was getting ready for Bobby to pick me up and I could tell he wasn't happy that I had a date. And I had to wonder whether he said something to Bobby on his way out to his own Saturday night event, because Bobby seemed a bit more reticent than when I'd first met him. But we had a nice evening together, eating lobster that he said he had prepared especially for me, and then sitting down to watch the video with his mom.

Another man asked me out, Tony G, a young lawyer on the verge of breaking into the political arena. At the time, Garry Carruthers was just about to take the reins from Toney Anaya and become the governor of our state. Tony G invited me to attend Carruthers' inaugural ball. But it seemed that his position in politics required him to meet me there rather than pick me up, because he had to "baby-sit Carruthers," as he put it. Oscar didn't like this at all. "Either you're with him openly or you're not," he lectured. And he stomped out of our apartment frustrated that he couldn't prevent me from going.

I went out with Tony a few more times, but my heart wasn't in it and it soon came to an end. The new governor, however, would unwittingly become the catalyst for the real romance that was coming my way.

Carruthers, people were saying from the get-go, lacked an open-door policy. He wasn't letting other Republicans in to talk to him. This was bad for the party and a lot of people were complaining about it. Who was this guy? And how did he plan to run his office? I really wanted to know. The word was that the only people who could get in to see him easily were reporters. He loved the media.

While my weekends remained crazy with the long drives

back and forth to Portales to see Mother and my kids, I had too much time to myself during the day — too much time for thinking — while I waited for my evening typing shift to begin. So one day I called and made an appointment to speak to the publisher of our local Spanish language newspaper, *El Hispano*.

"Look," I said when we sat down to talk a few days later, "I don't really know how to write that well in Spanish, but I do understand politics. I know the issues. I want to interview the governor. I want to work for you. I'll write down all the questions and record his answers, and then maybe you can get someone here to translate and write up the article." Not only did the publisher think it was a great idea, but he promised to make my political stories front page news.

I called the governor's office immediately and introduced myself to his secretary as a reporter for *El Hispano* and requested an interview with Governor Carruthers. We set a time right then and there. In the meantime, I met my friend Mickey Barnett, a former state senator from Portales and now a lawyer in Albuquerque, at a restaurant with a few other people, and together we generated the list of questions I would ask Carruthers. One thing Mickey suggested was that I ask him about his budget, why he wasn't more of a fiscal conservative. A few days later I marched into the governor's office with a photographer from the paper and my new tape recorder. My tape recorder was not the only one there. He had one of his people there with a recorder as well. Interesting. I asked some pointed questions — including why he had shut the door on the very people who had put him into office — and while he danced around a bit, in the end I got some good answers. The photographer snapped a few photos of us together, and my part-time career as a newspaper reporter was launched.

This was the first activity following my father's death that really knocked me outside of myself. Meeting with other people from the paper, figuring out the angles, writing up the questions, and doing the interviews required my full attention and didn't leave any space to tune in to the part of my heart that had been scraped raw. I interviewed Senator Jeff Bingaman and Councilor Steve Gallegos. One day at the Round House in Santa Fe, I found myself standing beside Mickey Barnett looking down at the senate floor. The speaker at the moment was Raymond Sanchez, a former political rival of Mickey's who was currently the state speaker of the house. "Take a good look at him," Mickey said. I did, and what I saw was a handsome, articulate, passionate Hispanic politician, someone with the kind of power that was needed to bring attention to the Hispanic political voice. In a way, Sanchez reminded me of my older brother, John. I promised myself that I would interview him before the month was out, and I did. Like all the others, our picture appeared in the paper together, on the front page.

Before long I had a team of people at the paper to work with me. We would meet once a week at a restaurant called Tenth and Central, a lounge that was frequented by judges, politicians, and other people who worked downtown, and bounce ideas off one another. I would know some of the issues, but they would know others, and together we could ensure that my stories really dug in deep. I was spending a lot of time in Santa Fe, where most of the interviews were conducted. It was an exciting time for me. It offered me what the non-stop dancing offered Oscar.

One day I interviewed State Attorney General Hal Stratton. After we got through the questions, we had a conversation — about me. Hal, it seems, was aware of my activism. He had an opening for an administrator in Consumer Protection. He asked if I would consider coming to work for him. "In a New York minute," I answered.

I told Oscar later that day. He was very proud of me. We both agreed that this could be a stepping stone to a career where I would really be in a position to make a difference in people's lives. I gave a week's notice at the law office. I would have to quit the paper too, though I still had one interview to complete, with the woman who owned the local Spanish TV station.

Oscar and I agreed that it would make sense for me to find a small apartment in Santa Fe, close to the Round House. This would eliminate the traffic problem getting in and out of the village each day. I started looking immediately, and while I knew I would miss sharing a home with my brother, he had told me many times, and told others as well, that living with me was the least stressful living arrangement he had ever had. These words were a gift to me, and I knew I would cherish them until my dying day.

Oscar took a day off from work during my last week in the apartment. I heard him leave early in the morning and I did not see him until very late that night, when I got home from my typing shift. He was waiting up for me when I walked in. He made me a drink and we sat down together in our small kitchen. "Do you know where I was today?" he asked me.

"Portales?" I guessed.

"I did go to Portales, but just long enough to pick up Naomi. Then Naomi and I drove to Lubbock and sat in front of the school."

By "school" I knew he meant the school that his little girls, Melissa and Amanda, attended. It was a four-hour ride to Portales and another two hours to Lubbock. Six hours is a long way to go to sit in front of a school. I reached across the table to touch his hand.

"I parked across the street and Naomi and I waited until the kids came out on the playground. Melissa and Amanda came out holding hands. We watched them play. We watched them on the swings, Amanda with her dark hair flying out behind her, Melissa with her gold hair. They never saw us there. I just wanted to see them. My girls." He closed his eyes and pressed his lips together.

The night before I was due to move to my new place in Santa

Fe, I pulled up in front of Tenth and Central to meet with my newspaper team to prepare for what would be my last interview. As I parked, I couldn't help but notice the white Rolls Royce limo out on the street. I climbed out of my car and went in, but before I could get to the table where my team and I usually met, a man by the name of Ernie jumped in front of me and pulled me in the other direction. "Yolanda!" he cried. "How great to see you! You've got to join our party! You've got to come meet my friends."

Before we both became so busy with our extracurricular activities, Oscar and I had considered buying a house together. Even if we didn't wind up roommates forever, it would be a good investment. To this purpose, he had taken me once to meet Ernie, who was a realtor. Ernie was also a roper, and he and Oscar had roped together at the arena at the county fair grounds in Albuquerque. The house idea had fallen through the cracks, but Ernie, apparently, still remembered me. I freed my arm from his grasp and explained that I had my own party to meet with.

But Ernie was insistent. He was also drunk. If the level of noise from his party was any indication, so were all his friends. There were quite a few of them. I tried to explain about the paper, about how I had to do a last interview, but he wouldn't give up on me. "At least come in and meet some people first," he said. "It will only take a minute."

Reluctantly, I took a step or two in the direction of their table and I said a quick, collective hello. Everyone seemed to respond at once. I gleaned that it was the birthday of one of the men, Anthony T. "You have to stay," Ernie insisted. "Don't you want to talk to everyone?"

"The only person I want to talk to," I joked, "is the owner of that Rolls outside."

"That's Ralph!" Ernie cried, and he pointed to one of the men sitting at the table.

"Oh, God!" I exclaimed. "I was just kidding. I didn't think...."

Tenth and Central was a busy place, bustling with private parties as well as more intimate gatherings. It hadn't occurred to me that the Rolls might belong to one of the men in Ernie's group. Since the only thing I knew about Ernie was that he was a realtor and roper, I had made the assumption that these people were either realtors or ropers too, and everyone knows ropers don't make much money, and realtors in Albuquerque in 1988 were not making big bucks either. Ralph lifted from his seat. "Let me take you for a ride in it," he said.

I looked from him to the woman sitting beside him. She was leaning against him and was obviously his date. "Judy from New York," is how Ernie had introduced her. "Oh, no, no, no. I was just kidding," I said, laughing at myself.

"No, come on," Ralph insisted. "Let me give you just a short ride." He turned to Judy from New York. "We'll be right back," he said as he pushed back his chair. She only shrugged, as if she didn't care one way or the other. He looked back at me again, questioningly, as if to ask if I would really go with him.

Sometimes you look into somebody's eyes and what you see is that there is a bond. Never mind that you may be strangers. I was going for a ride with him, just around the block, just a long enough time in his company so that I could explore this feeling of connection a little further. But I didn't want Judy from New York to be upset. I had an idea. I knew the bartender well. I went to him and told him that I was going for a short ride and would he stick my purse behind the bar. He took it from me. I turned back to the table to make sure that Judy had been watching. I wanted her to know that I fully planned to get her boyfriend right back to her.

"I'm so sorry to have forced you into this," I said to Ralph as we settled into the lush leather seats of the limo a few moments later. "I didn't know it was your car or I never—"

"Where would you like to go?" he asked.

I laughed. "Just around the block."

"No," he said, "let me at least take you somewhere."

"No, no, you really don't have to. I have my people waiting and you have yours...." I began, but in fact we'd already passed the turn that would take us around the block and were heading west.

We went to Epies, up on Coors Boulevard, and had a drink. The conversation flowed. I found myself telling him all about my father. Ralph told me that he had come from Mexico too, at the age of 11, in 1955, the year I was born. The facts of our lives seemed rife with coincidences. On the way back, Ralph said, "You know, I think I would have liked your father. I think we would have gotten along very well." And I had to admit that he seemed to be the kind of man my father enjoyed joking with. "I think your father wanted us to meet," he added. I had been thinking that too.

It didn't seem that we were gone all that long, but when we walked back into Tenth and Central, everyone was gone, from both our parties. I got my purse from the bar. Ralph said, "Well, everyone is gone. Why don't you let me take you to dinner."

We went to the Ranchers Club at the Hilton. And by the time we were onto dessert, we had already raced through the facts we needed to know to comprehend each other's lives to date and moved to a tacit agreement that we were about to begin a relationship. I told Ralph all about my new job at the attorney general's office in Santa Fe, that I was moving to a new apartment up there the next day. I wasn't planning to take much from the Corrales apartment, but there were a few heavy items, and I thought Ralph might want to help me move them. Really, I wanted to get Ralph and Oscar's meeting out of the way. I didn't know what Oscar would think of him and I was concerned. Ralph laughed. He said, "Leave your furniture with your brother. I'll buy you new furniture. I'll buy you whatever you want."

"I couldn't do that," I said. "And anyway, I have boxes of

personal items, clothes, shoes, things I need."

He saw my point and agreed to come the next day. Before we said goodnight, I looked at his hands, at the rings he wore on his fingers. I said, "Ralph, you need to be ready for my brother's handshake. My brother has huge hands. His grip can bring men down to their knees." I was used to ranchers, men with callused hands and broken nails. Ralph was a business man; he owned two redi-mix cement companies (one he owned outright and one he co-owned with a partner), but it was the hands of the people who worked for him that actually made contact with the cement. The handshake warning was my way of letting him know that Oscar wouldn't respect him if he didn't show some masculine pluck.

"I can shake hands as well as anyone," Ralph responded.

I needn't have worried. Ralph passed the handshake test the next morning with flying colors — and things went forward from there.

I moved to Santa Fe and started my new job. Ralph came every day to pick me up to take me out to dinner, usually in Albuquerque, and drive me back again. He didn't want me meeting him and driving myself home. In fact, what he really wanted was for me to move back to Albuquerque. Ralph had five children, the oldest of whom, a 17-year-old boy named Mark, was living with him. Three of the others were teens and the youngest, a little girl, was the same age as my Brandon. The younger children lived with his ex-wife. Ralph's argument was that he could easily buy me a house, and as I would have no expenses, I wouldn't need to work anymore. And if I didn't work, then I could go back to the court in Portales and get full custody of my children and bring them to Albuquerque to live with me. It was a tempting offer.

Looking back I realize that Ralph was domineering, possessive, and jealous. He was jealous that I had been married before; he was jealous of people I had merely dated. He was jealous of everything that had happened in my life to date and everything that happened each day when I was away from him. But at the time, I took his possessiveness for complete and utter devotion. I saw only that no one had ever loved me so much, and I returned his love with my heart and soul.

His friends, however, were another matter. Anthony T was a case in point. Anthony was Ralph's business partner, co-owner of one of the two redi-mix cement companies, the one in Rio Rancho. They couldn't have been more different. Ralph was kind and gentle and calm. He knew what he wanted out of life. Anthony was a loose cannon and it didn't take much to set him off. When I met Ralph, I would later learn, Anthony had just gotten out of the federal penitentiary where he'd done time for transporting cocaine. All during the time he was imprisoned, Ralph had had to run the company they co-owned on his own. Ralph split all the profits with him down the middle, even though Anthony hadn't been there to do the work. His sense of fairness was not unlike Oscar's in that way. Sometimes people, including some of Ralph's so-called friends, would pull me aside and warn me about Ralph and his partner. "How do you think he makes his money?" they would ask. Some people went further, saying that Ralph and Anthony T had both been involved in drugs and that Anthony took the fall for Ralph. I confronted Ralph of course. I looked him straight in the eye and said, "If what these people say about you is true, please get out of my life now."

Ralph smiled kindly and spread his arms and waited for me to fall into his embrace. "That is one thing I don't do," he said. He said people were jealous. He had done very well in business, and he had made a lot of money, and people just didn't want to believe that he could come by that kind of success without doing something illegal. Even the police, many of whom were his good friends, assumed he had something going on on the side. They would come to him and warn him when undercover agents applied for jobs driving his trucks. Ralph would laugh. He had nothing to hide.

As the months went by, I tried to keep at a distance from Ralph's friends. Besides Anthony, there was Chava, Ralph's nephew, who owned a trucking company, and Dennis C, a two-bit horse trainer. And there were others. All of them were blowhards, always boasting about the money they had. In Elida, the men I knew took their hats off to greet people; when they spoke, they looked you in the eye and you knew they meant what they were saying. "Sooner or later, these people will betray you, one by one," I told Ralph on a number of occasions. He only laughed.

One afternoon when he was out with his friends, Ralph called me and begged me to join them at Tenth and Central. Against my better judgment, I agreed to meet them for a drink. I hadn't seen any of them in some time by then, and I knew that Ralph was continuously making excuses for why I wasn't with him. Also, Ralph had recently turned down some of their invitations at my request. If I pushed too hard, I worried, I might push Ralph right out of my life. There had to be a middle ground.

I knew I had made a mistake as soon as I walked in and saw that Ralph and his friends were attempting to pitch dimes into a paper cup. There was a stack of hundred dollar bills on the bar, the booty for the winner. One of his friends sunk a dime, and while he reined in the bills, he called for more drinks for everyone. The others hooted excitedly and reached into their pockets to find more hundreds for the next round. Why had I come?

All the shouting and dime pitching made Ralph and his friends hungry. No sooner had I sat down than they wanted to climb into the limo and have Ralph drive them to the Ranchers Club at the Hilton to get something to eat. It was one thing to be in their company at Tenth and Central, which was, despite its mostly upscale clientele, a drinking establishment, but it would be something else entirely to be at the Hilton with men who acted like pigs. Reluctantly, I left my car at Tenth and Central and got into the limo with the rest of them. Sure enough, when we reached our destination, they walked in like they owned the place, shouting, "Get a table, a good table." The Albuquerque Hilton is a four-star hotel. The Ranchers Club is a fine restaurant, a quiet place where the waiters know what you want before you do. I had the feeling that Ralph's friends were being especially boisterous because I was there, because they knew their behavior was disgusting to me. No sooner had we sat down and ordered drinks than Dennis C took off his boot and announced that he was going to drink his beer out of it when it came. I tried to ignore the riotous laughter of the men and instead concentrated on the piped-in background music. If I let them see how upset I was, it would only get worse. But they kept it up, and finally I said to Ralph, "I can't handle this. I really can't." Chava, the nephew, overheard and turned to me and roared, "Who do you think you are? You think you're some high class woman, don't you? Well, you're nothing but a little bitch."

I struck back immediately. "You all think that because you have a couple of bucks in your pocket, you're something special," I said. "Well, let me tell you something. I've sat down with billionaires. Men like Bob Dole and Robert O. Anderson. And none of them acted like you. And I've sat down with ranch hands who did not have a penny in their pockets, but had more class than you'll ever have."

I got up and walked out. Ralph called after me, but he didn't *come* after me. My car was back at Tenth and Central; he probably didn't think I'd get very far. But I called Oscar, and minutes later I was in his truck, heading back to Tenth and Central to get my car.

It was late by then. Oscar insisted I stay the night at his apartment instead of driving back to Santa Fe. I would stay in his bed and he would sleep on the sofa. Before we said goodnight, he lectured me sternly. "I want the telephone receiver taken off," he said, "because I don't want Ralph calling you, because he didn't have the balls to respect you or defend you in front of his classless men. You don't need him, Yolanda. He needs you because you make him look good in public. Whenever you walk into a room, all heads turn to admire you. I've seen it time and time again. Mother didn't teach us to worship money nor did she teach us that money makes a person. Get away from that group, and don't look back. That group has no love for one another. Their god is money and envy is their curse."

I did as he said and took the receiver off the hook. Then I spent a miserable night missing Ralph, thinking I could get through to him and get him to see the light concerning his so-called friends, knowing in my heart that what we had going was too big to be crushed by a bunch of rowdy fools. I awoke at five and put the receiver back on the cradle, and immediately the phone rang. I picked it up quickly so it wouldn't awaken Oscar in the other room. "Yolie," Ralph cried, "I'm so sorry. I didn't sleep at all last night worrying about what I've done. I'm coming to see you. I must see you right away."

"No," I whispered. "Oscar is too upset. I'm going to work. We'll talk later."

"I'll drive you to work," he insisted.

In the end, he talked me into leaving my car in the parking lot of a hotel right off the interstate. He met me there and drove me to work, and at the end of the day, he picked me up and drove me back to my car again. Oscar only shook his head when I told him that Ralph and I had patched things up. And over time, the incident was forgotten.

I held out for about a year, and then I told Hal that I would be quitting and moving back to Albuquerque. He looked at me for a long moment, as if he were deciding something, and then said, "Yolanda, I was in a relationship with a very jealous woman once. They don't change. You think they will but they don't. You know

I wish you the best though." Mickey Barnett offered a polite warning as well. And so did Raymond Sanchez. These men were my friends as well as my colleagues, and we talked and joked whenever we saw one another...unless Ralph was with me. When Ralph was there, they treated me like a mere acquaintance, someone they hardly knew.

Not long after Ralph and I moved in together, his business began to fall off. The economy was on a downswing, and all businesses that supported new construction were doing poorly. Ralph was not really worried. He had the ability to focus on the bigger picture, and he sincerely (and correctly) believed that Albuquerque was on the verge of incredible growth, and as soon as the economy settled, it would begin to happen. In the meantime, I had some ideas for ensuring that the people who did need concrete would come to him and not a competitor.

One of the benefits of being in a relationship in which you are regarded with blind adoration is an automatic boost in confidence. You begin to feel that you can do anything, even if it is outside the realm of your experience. Ralph and I watched the Univision channel in the mornings, and during one show I said to him, "We can do that. We can have our own show and your company can sponsor it, and it will generate business." Ralph loved the idea, and in the next few weeks we met with the right people and put it all together and before long we were the Spanish-speaking co-hosts of the "La Hora del Coyote" show, which essentially had a talk show format. We interviewed people from the community — politicians, business people, artists, authors. We showed videos. We put together raffles. And soon other companies came along and wanted to sponsor the show as well. It was a fun time for me, but it was not enough to complete my life. I seemed always to find myself standing at the window, looking east, thinking of my children, thinking of Mother. I was still driving back and forth on weekends, sometimes with Ralph and sometimes alone. Either way, I always cried on the way home.

Sometimes Oscar and Ralph, who had become friendly again, went out without me, for a drink and a bit of male conversation. Once they went to the same bar where Tony G, the man who had me meet him at the governor's inaugural ball, was having a bite to eat. Tony recognized Oscar from his baseball days and asked the waitress to bring him and Ralph a drink. Oscar, of course, was still upset that Tony hadn't come to the apartment to pick me up for such a major event, and when Ralph heard the story, he was upset because poor Tony was someone I had once known. Oscar got up with the two drinks that Tony had paid for and walked across the room and swished the liquid like he was going to throw it and set the glasses down hard on the table. "We don't need any drinks from you," he said, and he walked back.

Living with Ralph was challenging. Though I never doubted for a moment that he loved me, he had a tendency to put off telling me important things until he absolutely had to. One day, for instance, the phone rang, and when I answered it, the woman on the other end introduced herself as Sister Josephine. Ralph had told me about her. She was his sister, and she was a Carmelite nun living in Houston. But I'd never had occasion to speak to her before. I was in the process of telling her how happy I was to talk to her when she interrupted to say, "Yolanda, what are you doing with my brother?" I laughed. What kind of a question was that? Before I could muster a response, she went on to explain that Ralph was still married. "No," I said. "When I met him he was with a woman named Judy. It was just a date. His marriage was a long time ago." "No, no," she insisted. "He's still married to Teresa. Teresa is his wife." Ralph walked in just then, and seeing the bewilderment on my face, he asked me who I was talking to. I mouthed "Sister Josephine" and he immediately took the phone out of my hand and hung it up.

When I asked for an explanation, he said, "She lives in a convent; she doesn't know anything about real life." But later he conceded that it was true that he and Teresa had never gotten their divorce. It made my head swim to think he had deceived me about this. But he promised to begin the divorce proceedings the very next day, and he did.

While I knew very little about Teresa, she seemed to think she knew a lot about me. One day Ralph came home from a visit to his mother's and said that Teresa had told his mom that she would rather see him dead than with me. When I told my mother, she got very upset. She said that a wife who has been married with the sacraments should never curse or damn her husband, no matter how bad things are between them, because the Bible confirms that when life and death are on the tongue, there is much power in what one says.

My mother liked Ralph, and he adored her. He thought, and rightly so, that she was a woman with a backbone, and also a great conversationalist. He loved her kitchen, the gathering place for all our family. There was always something going on in Mother's kitchen, certainly food, but often much more that that. At times there was prayer, other times music and dancing, and almost always, laughter.

Mostly we traveled down to Portales, but sometimes Mother came to visit us in Albuquerque too. These days she was doing a lot of traveling, and she was enjoying it. She had even gone to watch John wrestle in Juarez. John, who had been wrestling for years, made his money in "entertainment wrestling," which is a non-competitive performance event in which the participants deliver blows and apply holds with no real intent to hurt their opponents. The participants have to be especially skilled in order to succeed in this dramatization, as they must make it look like they're killing each other but without anyone really getting injured. John had done very well for himself with this work. He was able to present each of his daughters with a house in Juarez, and on the two square blocks he owned, he built a gym for his son, Beto, who would succeed him one day in the ring. He wanted to ensure that his children would stay close to him, because his children were his life.

Ernestine and all of John's family were there at ringside the night Mother attended. These events draw about five thousand people on any given night. Mother was trying to have a conversation with Ernestine over the din when the announcer yelled out, "Aquí viene 'El Demonio Negro'!" El Demonio Negro was John's performance name. Mother knew that, but it didn't prepare her for the sight of my brother — wearing a dark mask as villainous as the moniker — jumping into the ring out of nowhere and rubbing his opponent's eyes with chili. Poor Mother was aghast, and even more so when the crowd started yelling at her first born, calling him names and cursing at him. To her surprise, Ernestine and the rest of the family yelled and cursed just as earnestly at his opponent.

When Mother came to Albuquerque, we tried to provide just as much entertainment, but without the fright factor. Once Ralph, Oscar, Mother and I went to the Caravan to dance. "Oh, how precious, how beautiful you look out there," she said each time we came back from the dance floor. She was so certain that we were the most beautiful people on the face of the earth that she insisted we have our pictures taken by the house photographer. He took "saloon" shots that we had to dress for: Mother dressed as a pioneer woman and Oscar and Ralph dressed as cowboys. I was a saloon girl.

At the beginning of the summer of 1988, Oscar picked up Noel, Carol's son, and brought him back to Albuquerque to work with him. Carol's husband had left her, with four kids, and Oscar knew it would help her greatly if Noel had some kind of a male role model. "I'm going to teach him to be a man," Oscar said. Noel was 12 at the time, and he was a willing student. He adored his uncle and did everything to ensure that he wouldn't disappoint him. "You're going to be a man," Oscar told him. "You're going to work and you're going to learn the difference between doing things right and doing things wrong." Each day that summer they got up early in the morning, little Noel in his work boots and cowboy hat, looking as much like his uncle as a 12-year-old could, and off they went to work at the monastery. And at the end of the day they came home and cleaned and cooked together, or stopped for takeout. They were inseparable during the day, and my guess would be that Noel didn't mind much when Oscar went out at night because he had to be exhausted. Oscar was relentless. But Noel kept up and Oscar paid him fairly, and as a result, when the summer came to an end, Noel had all the money he needed for his school clothes, which was a big help to Carol.

That same year, Oscar and Ralph and I watched the baseball playoffs together and then the World Series. We grilled steaks or chicken every night during the games, and we washed them down with cold beers. Orel Hershiser was close to unstoppable in 1988, and I was glad to see that Oscar regarded him — and the games generally — without any bitterness, the way any other fan could enjoy the games, maybe even more so. One thing Oscar admired about Hershiser was that he wore his religious convictions on his sleeve. He gave a lot of money away to charities, especially the Cystic Fibrosis Foundation. Oscar was fond of repeating his famous quote: "You don't have to be a wimp to be a Christian." Oscar said Hershiser would calm himself down out on the mound by singing hymns. I got to see a display of his devotion for myself when, after pitching a scoreless inning in one game, he dropped to his knees and took off his hat and lifted his head and said a prayer of thanksgiving.

I liked watching him and I like the Dodgers' manager, Tommy Lasorda, too. He seemed like a child to me, someone who knew how to have fun. The Dodgers played Oakland that year for the series, and they won. But it was the first game of the series that no real baseball fan will ever forget. Kirk Gibson, the Dodgers' star hitter, had been injured the night before; he'd torn his left hamstring and stretched his right knee ligament. He watched most of that first series game from the training room, with his legs in ice. By the ninth inning, the A's had four and the Dodgers had three, thanks to José Canseco's second inning grand slam home run.

I remember Oscar standing up and announcing, "Man, we need to get Gibson out there now, before the fat lady sings." Determining when the fat lady would sing was a big thing with Oscar and Ralph. Each night during the playoffs, one of them would say, "That's it, it's all over," and the other one would say, "I don't think so. I didn't hear the fat lady sing yet." And they would laugh. Or one would say, "Ohhh, I see the fat lady coming down from the stands. She's all but ready."

Kirk Gibson must have been the kind of man who believed that if you were mentally prepared, you could win against the odds, even when the fat lady was standing right next to you, warming up her lungs with breathing exercises. It looked like the game was over, and you could see people moving around in the stands, probably hoping to get to their cars and beat some of the post-game traffic. Dennis Eckersley, the A's all-star closer, was pitching the final frame. He had had a good season and he looked pretty confident out there on the mound. Dodgers fans who had opted to stay were kind of quiet now, holding their breath, probably praying for a miracle.

Eckersley struck out the first two batters, and walked the third one, Mike Davis. So the Dodgers were still alive, but barely. "The fat lady is winding up," Oscar said. Though part of the joke required the two of them to feign opposing views about the fat lady's plans, this time Ralph broke rank and agreed with him. "Yeah, I see her standing right there, behind Anderson." Anderson was Dave Anderson, who was having a bad year and didn't stand a chance. He was just coming out to give it his best shot when Lasorda called him back to the dugout. Maybe he had been a decoy from the get-go — because a few seconds later, here comes Kirk Gibson out onto the field. He is limping, and he is carrying a bat.

The crowd went wild when they saw him. We went wild. Gibson got ready at the plate and Eckersley went into his windup, kicking his leg high in the air like Oscar used to. Fast ball. Foul ball. Davis stole second. Before we knew it there was a full count. And then Gibson hit a backdoor slider into the right field bleachers. It was the miracle the crowd had been waiting for. Gibson hobbled from base to base, in what was very evidently excruciating pain, his legs looking like they would collapse beneath him at any moment but his fist clenched tight and his arm pumping overhead. Oscar and Ralph, who'd been on their feet throughout the ordeal, did the same thing, limping, pumping their fists, howling excitedly. Their little dance looked so funny you couldn't help but want to imitate it. Ralph really got it down, and he would use it often over the next ten years of our relationship, whenever anything really good happened.

Maybe it was Kirk Gibson who got Oscar thinking. Or, more likely, he had been thinking all along. The fat lady, he must have known, had been nipping at his heels for a while.

Oscar was very particular about his clothes, even his work clothes. He liked his shirts and pants starched. Since he worked so many hours, I would generally pick up his stuff for the cleaners and bring it in when I was bringing mine. Then I would bring it back again a few days later and see if he'd left anything else for me to pick up. To this purpose, I let myself in one afternoon and was startled to see him sitting there in the kitchen, smiling like a Cheshire cat. "Guess what," he said calmly. "I called Doug Gassaway. You remember him; he drafted me for the Phillies. Anyway, I'm the new pitching coach for the Texas Rangers minor league, the Butte Copper Kings."

"Praise God," I exclaimed, dropping the laundry onto the table so that I could throw my arms around him. I couldn't have been happier.

"I'm going to start at the bottom, but I'm back in baseball," he said. "That's where my heart is."

Shortly after that, Oscar left for his new job. And not long after that, Mother got a call from him saying that he and Kathy had gotten remarried. When I saw him again in Portales, I said, "What made the change? She was so adamant about not wanting to be with you anymore."

"It's because I'm back in baseball," he replied.

Whatever the reason, it was okay with him. He had his girls back. "God is giving me this second chance," he confided. "I am going to do everything in my power to be a good father to those little girls, and no one is ever going to take them away from me again."

And not long after that, Mother got another call and promptly called me to pass on the good news. Oscar was going to be a father again.

Chapter Nine

A Season of Hope

Ryan Douglas Acosta, Oscar and Kathy's baby son, was the embodiment of our family's desire to pick up the pieces and give ourselves a second chance. His very name was emblematic of our raw hope: Ryan after Ryne Sandberg, Oscar's dear friend and teammate from back when he had played for the Phillies, and Douglas, after Doug Gassaway, who, of course, had given Oscar the opportunity to get back into the game.

Now that they were a family again, Oscar and Kathy and the children resumed their visits to Portales when they could, and we welcomed them with opened arms. Mother, especially, couldn't do enough for them. What did they want for breakfast? For dinner? What could she give them to make them more comfortable?

There were so many photos from that time: Kathy and Oscar beaming at the camera, their sweet daughters bending over to kiss their new baby brother's brow.... Baby Ryan being passed from one ecstatically-grinning family member to the next.... "This is the door that God has opened for me," Oscar told me sitting in Mother's kitchen, bouncing his son on his knee. "And I'm going to walk through it as best I know how. God and family and job."

Oscar began to attend services at the Baptist church again. His daughters were both baptized there. It was important to both Oscar and Kathy that their children know that Christ died for their sins and was their salvation. But even giving thanks regularly in church and at home felt like too insufficient a gesture when Oscar measured it against the second chance he'd been given. He actively began to seek other opportunities to express his gratitude. During the holiday season especially, he made a point of finding out — through Mother, who knew everyone — who in the Portales community was hurting, and then he would work with Mother to get gifts for that person and their family, a turkey and trimmings, some cash…whatever would help them most. It wasn't like he had a surplus of funds. Kathy and Oscar were just getting on their feet. And coaching for the minors was certainly not the same as coaching for the majors. He gave from his need, not his excess.

The rest of us only learned of his good deeds through Mother; Oscar never said a word about them. He gave back in other ways as well. With the help of his good friend Tom House he started organizing free baseball camps in Portales for any area kids who wanted to attend. When he could, Oscar got coaches from the Rangers to participate in these one-day events. What a time the kids had, being instructed by big name Rangers whom they had never thought to get any closer to than their baseball card pictures. The kids learned how to run, hit, pitch and field balls. "Baseball does not build character," Oscar told them. "It reveals it." The kids adored Oscar because he was tough, because he made them experience their own toughness.

In fact, he behaved like a kid himself much of the time. He laughed at almost anything. If he was at Mother's when Naomi came in, he would jump on Mother's lap, and when Naomi cried, "Uncle, what do you think you're doing?" Oscar would reply, "I'm the baby here!" Naomi, who had been partially raised at Mother's, would cry, "No you're not, I am." It was an occasion for a lot of laughter and silliness between Oscar and Naomi. As for Mother, she would relish the chance to have her towering son on her lap again, even if only for a few moments. She would wrap her arms around his waist and coo, "Oh, mi bebé, mi bebé."

One day Oscar said to me, "You know what, Sis? Eastern New Mexico University doesn't have a baseball program. Who do I need to talk to get them one?" I told him to see the senate majority leader, Manny Aragon. Ralph volunteered to go with him. The representative for Roosevelt County was Gary Robbins. Oscar and Ralph talked to him too. And sure enough, they made it happen. They got the funding and Robbins passed the bill. And Oscar's inclination to ensure that others had access to the same opportunities he'd had was made manifest yet again.

It gave me great pleasure during this time to see that Oscar and Ralph had so much respect for each other — and even greater pleasure to see how much Ralph cared about my mother and my kids. "Love me, love my family" was my maxim. The rest of it, Ralph's so-called friends, and his reluctance to tell me *all* of the truth *all* of the time, were small flaws in our relationship by comparison; I could put up with them.

A rupture occurred between Ralph and one of his friends, without any help from me whatsoever. Anthony T, the man who had partnered with Ralph on one of his redi-mix companies (and the man Ralph had shared profits with for the tax year that Anthony had been in prison), somehow failed to pay the IRS some money that was owed. When the IRS started questioning him, he worked with his lawyers to turn them on Ralph. Ralph was furious. He said he'd rather file for bankruptcy for his part of the business than find the money to pay for something that Anthony had professed to have paid. Anthony was in trouble again, and this time Ralph did not intend to bail him out.

He followed through and started bankruptcy proceedings. He planned to concentrate on Coyote Concrete, the company that was solely his, and let Anthony figure out how to climb out of the trouble he had got himself into with the other company. He didn't want any part of it anymore. But things got worse. One day Ralph came home in a state as close to tears as I had ever seen him. His oldest daughter, who had worked for him at Coyote Concrete, had argued with him in the office days before and walked out. Now Ralph learned that she was working for Anthony. There was also some indication that she was dating him. Ralph had never felt so betrayed in his life.

This was a setback that Ralph could do nothing about. He suffered over it, but he did his best to stay focused on things he could have an influence on. Our TV show was still doing great and it was bringing more and more customers to Ralph's business. It was also bringing in sponsors, people who wanted to help underwrite our show. One of them was a truck driving school. It made me think. I said to Ralph, "You know, you could start a driving school. You could get grants from the Department of Labor to fund each student and then you could hire the students to drive for you. Or they could get their education and training and move on." Ralph liked the idea. He had so much energy and passion for life. Once he decided he wanted something, he got up and went after it. If it failed, it failed, but he was never afraid to try. In this case, it was a success; in no time Freeway Truck Driving School was launched.

At about the same time that Ralph was getting his driving school up and running, we learned that the popular Telemundo network was about to launch a show in Albuquerque. We went immediately to talk to the people involved. Now that I had broken into TV, I could well imagine having a variety show on the Telemundo station. And I could imagine co-hosting such a show with Roberto Mondragon, who had been the lieutenant governor some years earlier. He knew so much about New Mexican culture. And he was a wonderful talent, a man who could mesmerize audiences not only with his singing but also with his dramatic recitations of beautiful poetry. So we talked to him as well, and he agreed to co-host with me.

While the early morning show was live daily, the Telemundo show, though it broadcast only once a week, had to be taped and edited. It took a lot more time. Our interviews took place in the studio. We were assigned producers and editors to work with us. Our guests were dancers, singers, historians, politicians. Ralph remained involved with both shows. He knew a lot of people and he had access to plenty of talent.

The economy at large, however, was still in a bad place. Without the driving school and the TV exposure, it would have been very difficult to keep Ralph's redi-mix company alive. There was a wage war going on at the time, among the redi-mix companies. Various owners would get together and set prices in such a way that anyone excluded got priced out. "You can't be fixing prices like that," I scolded Ralph when I found out. "It's totally illegal." Ralph promised to stop.

With all the work that we were doing, I was able to give my children everything they wanted. Leo was a great father and a great provider, but their time with me, on weekends, was fantasyland. I bought them clothes. I took them on trips. My kids were happy around me, and that was the way I wanted it. And I was glad to see that Ralph was the same way with his children. Except for the daughter who had walked out on him, and of course the youngest, his kids worked at his redi-mix company, and though they wanted nothing to do with me, he got to see them almost daily. Together, Ralph and I tried to extend the fantasyland we had created to include everyone, especially my mother. We treated her like a queen. We took her places she had never dreamed to see in her lifetime, places I had never dreamed to see. We went to California. We took cruises in the Caribbean.

Oscar, meanwhile, stayed in Texas for a few years, and then he moved up to a new position, as manager for the Oklahoma City 89ers, a triple A team also owned by the Rangers. Accordingly, he and his family moved to Oklahoma. He and Kathy also bought a home in Portales, which would be their base during the off season. Oscar loved the part of New Mexico that included Elida and Portales. He had had his sense of discipline — kindled, of course, at home — fortified in Elida's schools, just as his respect for the land had been fortified by Elida's fellow ranchers. And of course he had found God in Elida's churches. He was determined that his kids would be exposed to all the same influences. He felt that the fortitude they would gain in the southeast corner of the state would compensate for the fact that they would have to change schools part of each year when baseball season started up again. He wanted his family with him, and they wanted to be with him.

His old friend Jerry Stroud, the one with the huge gash on his cheek, died around this time, of cancer. Oscar had gone to see him on his deathbed. He was amazed when another visitor arrived, none other than Jerry's lifelong enemy Kenny Smith, who had given Jerry the gash. Kenny made amends that day, and Jerry and Kenny got to talking about how they had managed to change each other's lives with their hatred. Now that they had reconciled, they would change each other's lives again (though Jerry's life was only days away from its end). Before Oscar left, Jerry said to him, "I've lived life the way I wanted and have no regrets. But I want to pass on to you that there's a better way of life. You have to find that for yourself and your family." And that's what Oscar determined to do.

Oscar would visit the apartments and dorms of all the young Latin players on the team at the beginning of each season. He would talk to them about baseball but also about life in America. He would show them simple things that other people didn't think twice about — how to take out the trash, how to use the amenities, how to care for their lodgings. He would even take them shopping for food. And he would instruct them about social do's and don'ts that might otherwise have taken them years to pick up on. He was a natural as a mentor. Whether he knew it or not, he really made a difference in their lives.

During the off season he ranched, just as he always had. He still loved to care for cattle, and it didn't matter to him that the cattle were not his own. As little Ryan got older, he would take him with him and teach him how to feed the cattle, how to brand them, herd them. He was a strict father, with all three of his kids. Kathy had a gentle hand. "Now don't do that again, Hon," she would say when one of the kids stepped out of line. And if they didn't listen the first time, she'd merely repeat herself, just as tenderly as before. Oscar's approach was just the opposite. "Sit down and knock it off," he would holler in a booming voice. And between the timbre of his voice and the look in his eye, the offending child would desist immediately.

In addition to ranching, when Oscar was at home he visited his old friends and made some new ones. Tom Drake, one of the latter group, even looked like Oscar. Tom lived in Clovis, and besides sharing a love of baseball (they first met when Tom volunteered to help at one of Oscar's baseball camps) and a love of the cowboy life, they found they also both loved the same music—and that sealed it. (Ray Price was their favorite.) Taking along both Ryan and Tom's son, who was more or less the same age, they would hunt together, or play a game of golf. Sometimes they would go to visit Tom's family, who lived in Fort Sumner on the Pecos River. It was there that Oscar met Tom's grandfather, Chano, a man who, like Oscar, didn't really like Christmas. Of course Oscar (and the grandfather) loved Christ and believed it was good and right to celebrate His birthday, but what they did not love was the commercial aspect, and they could talk about that for hours on end. "Hey, partner," Oscar would cry when he greeted the old man, and he would take off his hat and extend his hand and offer him that hearty shake of his. Oscar called everyone "partner." I would hear him on the phone, exclaiming "Hey, partner," with the Texas accent he had developed over the years.

Before returning to Oklahoma for spring training each year, Oscar and his family would stop in Portales to say goodbye to Mother. During these intense farewells, Mother and Oscar would retreat to her bedroom where Oscar would kneel to receive her blessing. No matter how hard they tried to control their emotions, they would both reappear with wet eyes. Mother would then walk everyone outside and stand and watch –

through her rivers of tears — as Oscar and his family drove away. In one final effort to shower the disappearing vehicle with blessings, she would make the Sign of the Cross. No matter what the weather, she would remain at her post until the car was well out of sight.

Oscar's birthday was March 21, the first day of spring. When we were kids, Mother would always bake cakes for each of our birthdays, and then she would take photos of us holding them. When it was Oscar's birthday, Carol, Mother and I would all contribute to the elaborate decoration of his cake. He was the baby and our job was to spoil him, so no amount of creative time and energy spent was ever too much. During the years he was away for spring training, I, as the older sister, would offer him God's blessing on his birthday, over the phone. I would leave my message on his answering machine, a simple prayer that I hoped would contribute to his well being: "Oscar, Happy birthday," I'd begin. "I just want to offer you an older sister's blessing, that our Lord will keep you safe and healthy and that He may grant you the desires of your heart, in the name of Jesus. I love you, Oscar." Then I would call Mother and thank her for bringing my little brother into the world. This is a tradition in our family. Just as I called to bless Oscar, Carol called to bless me. This, our family has learned, is how blessings proliferate.

Once he was back in baseball, Oscar could never be there for Mother's birthday because it fell right in the middle of the season. But he would never forget her either, no matter how busy he got. One day, when Ralph and I were sitting in her kitchen visiting, she left in her car to get her mail from the cluster box at the end of the street. A few moments later she came flying through the door with a box in hand crying, "Mi bebé, mi bebé me ha enviado un regalo!" *My baby, my baby has sent me a gift!* She tore open the box and held its contents, a beautiful sweater, up to her chest and continued exclaiming while tears of joy flowed down her face. Then all at once she remembered that in her excitement, she had left the car running, down the block by the mailboxes, and she had to run back out to retrieve it.

We had always tried to shelter Oscar from any problems, any issues at home. Even if Mother had a mere cold, we kept it from him, because their bond was that strong and we knew it would affect him — sadden him, maybe even result in him making some sort of mistake out on the baseball field, and we didn't feel we could take that chance. He was the baby, yes, and he was also the head of our family, the one whose success in life was most important to us. We respected him as one respects someone born to lead. He was our Joseph, younger that Carol and me, but already distinguished, just as Joseph had been distinguished by his many-colored coat. He was our David, innocently tending sheep until such time as he should be called upon to ready his slingshot.

Once, in an effort to protect Oscar from unnecessary concern, Mother failed to tell him that she had been to the doctor to address a problem she was having with her feet. The doctor had given her shots which in the long term would heal her but the immediate effect was that she was completely swollen from her ankles to her toes and unable to walk. This was during the off season and Oscar was in Portales, but as she was not expecting him in the next few days, she decided not to tell him what had happened to her. As luck would have it, Oscar popped in one afternoon unannounced. Mother had been perched on one of the stools in the kitchen, so the island concealed her swollen feet, which, now wrapped in bandages, looked like two shabby zeppelins. Oscar pulled up a stool on the opposite side of the island, and for a long time the two of them chatted. At some point the conversation turned to a certain type of bread that Mother had made several times when we were kids, a kind of Mexican challah that we had all loved. All Mother needed to know was that something that Oscar had once loved was now being denied him. She insisted on making it for him right then and there. But of course she could not easily climb off the stool and begin without revealing her swollen, bandaged feet. So she told him she was out of yeast and asked him to run to the store and get it. "No, no," Oscar replied. "I was only recalling how good it was. I didn't mean for you to have to make it." But Mother would not relent. "Go, go," she commanded. "Go to the store and get me what I need."

As soon as Oscar was out the door, she let herself down from her stool gingerly and made her way, on her knees, from one cabinet to the next, only standing when it was necessary to get something from one of the upper cabinets. In this way she gathered the bowls, the salt, the oil, the flour — everything she needed. The pain was so great it brought tears to her eyes, but as always, a little (or even a lot) of pain was nothing compared to her fierce determination to make Oscar happy. By the time Oscar came through the door carrying a grocery bag — he had picked up not only the yeast but other items that had caught his eye — she had everything out on the island counter and ready to go. But when Oscar went around the island to set down the bag, he noticed her feet (really, no one could miss them), and his eyes filled with tears immediately. He hugged her and held her, our mother who would drag herself across the desert if she had to — for any of us, but especially for Oscar.

Our favorite holiday, during the years that Oscar managed the 89ers, was always Thanksgiving, because that was the holiday that Oscar would always be around for. Each year we gathered in Mother's kitchen, our family's lifelong sanctuary in whatever house she lived in—and held hands and offered thanks. As much of a believer as Oscar was, he did not care to pray aloud or lead the prayers. If Mother did not lead, he would say, "Kathy! Pray!" and Kathy would do it. On a few occasions, until he got too big to enjoy it, little Ryan would dress up as a pilgrim, replete with a buckled hat and a white collar. He was so cute we could hardly tear our eyes from him as we laughed and talked and passed platters from one end of the table to the other.

Mother and Ralph and I went to Oklahoma once to see the 89ers play. After we settled in our hotel, we hurried out to the ballpark to meet Oscar, who had promised us a tour. Even before we spotted him, at the end of the field working with his players, we spotted little Ryan riding around the periphery of the field in a cart that looked like a giant baseball cap. Around and around he went, as comfortable on the field as any other child would be in his own backyard. That evening, we sat in the stands along with Kathy and the kids, cheering, eating hotdogs and popcorn, and generally enjoying the thrill of knowing that we were about to see Oscar and his team in action. The weather was perfect; the sky was a brilliant blue, and the field was a vivid green — though I couldn't say whether the green was grass or Astroturf. The spirit of the game of baseball was in the process of overtaking us — as it has overtaken so many Americans over the years. The floodlights all around the field came on. The fans stood up and cheered louder. The announcer's voice welcomed the 89ers and their opponents onto the field — and out they marched: happy, fit, determined men who would represent us, who would uphold our best instincts, for the next few hours. And there was my brother, the manager, Oscar Acosta. We were overwhelmed with pride.

Mother and I had been praying for years for Oscar's career. We prayed for him when he was a player, and we prayed for him when he began to coach, and we prayed all during the time when he was insisting that he was done with baseball forever. And now that he was back, we prayed that he would succeed in his dream of working with the majors. But we had prayed not because we thought baseball was the best direction for Oscar but because — no matter what he said — we knew that he believed it was, and whatever made Oscar happy was worth our prayers. But now a shift was occurring; perhaps it started when Oscar had presented his baseball camps, for which Mother and Ralph and Kathy and

I, having prepared all the food for the kids and the volunteer coaches, were on hand to see. But this game sealed it; we were officially passionate about baseball. We understood that it was in fact the best path for Oscar after all, for anyone who got the chance to be a part of such an exciting, uplifting experience.

Oscar was low key about his own feelings regarding the sport. I would ask him over the phone how a particular game had gone and he would say, "We won," or "It sucked," comments that reflected only the final score. But Kathy would talk at length about the games. "Those guys love Oscar," she would say enthusiastically, referring to the players. And he loved them, she would confirm. He cared about their health and questioned them about what they were eating, how many hours they were sleeping.... He taught them the mechanics of the game, but also to honor the game and to honor the crowds who attended. If he saw someone with a cap turned around or shirt not tucked in, he would confront them sharply. He was a true leader, able to turn his teams around even when it seemed an impossibility, to take them to the playoffs time after time. The only problem, Kathy would ultimately lament, was that Oscar simply would not work with the media. If the media berated his players with duplicitous questions, he would kick them out of clubhouse. He didn't want any reporter making his or her career by running down his team. Kathy feared that Oscar's disdain for PR spin would ultimately keep him from going further up the ranks. But politics was one game Oscar wouldn't play. He didn't see it as his responsibility. He didn't like to do interviews, even when his team had done really well. "Where the hell were you when they weren't doing well?" he yelled at one reporter, at the end of a season in which he had totally turned his team around. "You didn't give my players anything. If you can't be loyal to them, then we don't need you." It was moments like this that got some people in the business — including some of the other Rangers managers — thinking that Oscar had an attitude problem.

Although Kathy talked to Mother and me about Oscar's unwillingness to kowtow to the press, she said nothing to Oscar. And as for Oscar, he saw his bosses' reluctance to move him along from an entirely different perspective.

One time when we were all gathered at Mother's house in Portales, Oscar said to me, "Yolanda, there are no Hispanics or blacks who are managers in the majors. Blacks and Hispanics play, but they don't manage. I won't ever be promoted. No matter how good I am, it won't happen — unless I do something about it. Who can I talk to?"

"There has to be equal opportunity for everyone," I responded. "They can't shut you out because of race. That's not how it's supposed to work here in America. Let's call Toney Anaya."

And so, for the second time in my life, I found myself calling the now former governor of my state, a man who wasn't even a member of my party and for whom I had never voted. Toney Anaya was an attorney now, and it was known that he served on various boards and with non-profit organizations that primarily focused on Hispanic issues. Moreover he had served as a member of Jesse Jackson's Credentials Committee when Jackson ran in the Democratic Primary in 1988. And he had been an executive board member of Jackson's Rainbow Coalition. I thought that if he took up this exclusion issue, he might be able to bring Jackson into it as well.

I got Anaya on the phone, and as he already knew quite a lot about our family from back when I'd contacted him on behalf of Daddy, we were able to dismiss with the preliminaries pretty quickly. I explained that I was calling because my brother was concerned that minorities were not making it to the top positions in the sports world. Then I put Oscar on. One minority who should have made it to the majors, Oscar strongly felt, was Larry Rojas, the first black Cuban to make it to a position of any power in baseball. But he hadn't made it to the majors. He had impact,

Oscar felt. He had instructed Ryne Sandberg, Julio Francos, George Bell, Keith Moreland and others. They talked for a while; Anaya said he truly understood my brother's frustration. But he didn't have any pat answers for him and it seemed unlikely he would get directly involved. In the meantime, Mother and I went back to our tried and true method of getting things done: prayer. And this time we recruited Ralph too.

In New Mexico any respectable believer in the power of prayer ultimately finds his or her way to Chimayo, which is considered by some to be the Lourdes of America. Chimayo is about 40 miles south of Taos, tucked into the Sangre de Cristo mountains and surrounded by gorgeous vistas such as were dearly loved by Georgia O'Keeffe. The chapel there, which is Catholic, is called El Santuario. It draws some 300,000 pilgrims each year—particularly during Holy Week, when special police patrols have to be organized to keep the steady stream of pilgrims, most of whom have to park their cars miles away and go on foot to the chapel, from being run over.

Ralph and Mother and I drove up to Chimayo one Sunday, but it was late in the day when we got there and we found the chapel closed. Undeterred after our long ride, we pushed one of Oscar's baseball cards through the crack at the bottom of the door and said our prayers outside. Make him a major leaguer, Lord, we prayed. Baseball is a good thing, good for the body and good for the soul. Let Oscar make it right to the top, coaching and managing in the majors. The story about Chimayo is that a friar back in 1810 was performing penances when he saw a bright light bursting from a hillside. He quickly ran to the site and began to dig. What he found was a crucifix. Thinking the circumstances of the event confirmed that the crucifix deserved a more prominent home, a local priest took it to Santa Cruz, but it disappeared and was later found back in its hole at Chimayo. Twice more people tried to remove it, and twice more it wound up back where the friar had first found it. So it was left there, and the chapel we visited was built on the site around it. And thereafter the miraculous healings began to occur. And they were so numerous that over time the chapel had to be expanded. Mother and Ralph and I made a commitment that day that we would go to a church in Mexico, the world famous El Santo Niño de Atocha, to give thanksgiving when our prayers for Oscar were answered. And we had no doubt that they would be.

Cousin Olga, Carol, Grandpa Jesus & Yolanda

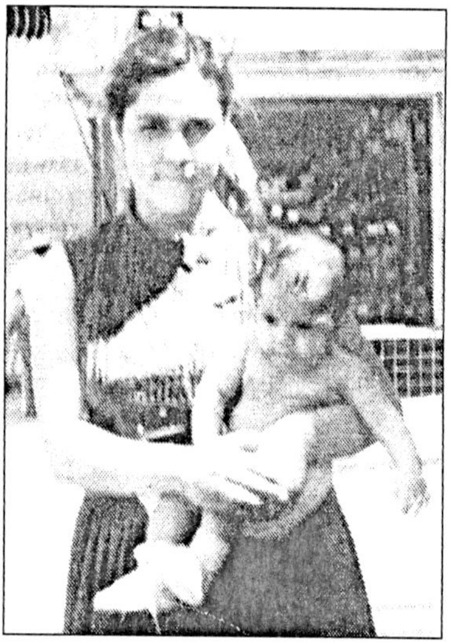

Concha & Yolanda

Teacher, Concha, Carol, Yolanda & Oscar

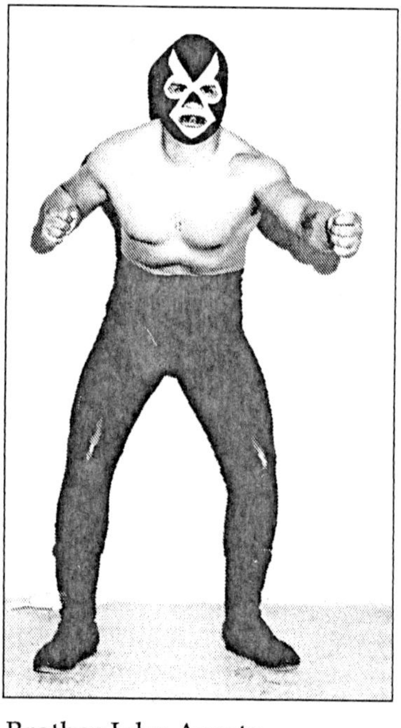

Brother John Acosta

Upper left: Yolanda with Jack Kemp; Upper right: Concha, Oscar, Yolanda & Ralph; Middle: Oscar, Concha, Carol, John & Yolanda; Bottom: Oscar

Former Elida star wins top honor

Oscar Acosta, 1975 graduate of Elida High School was named the most valuable pitcher after chalking up an 11-0 record in an independent amateur league in Dallas this summer.

Acosta threw four shutout and logged a 1.43 ERA in guiding the A's to the team title in the 20-team league. The A's, considered on a par to semi-pro teams have won the chance to play a AA team in Mexico.

Acosta, who played fall ball at Dallas Baptist and transfered to Lubbock Christian College, is hoping "to have one good year in a good program like they have at LCC."

His hopes are to be drafted into professional baseball, and for that he feels, he will need "just one super year."

While at Dallas Baptist, he compiled a 7-1 record; and when he enrolls at LCC this fall, he will still be a freshman.

His best pitch is his fast ball and a fork ball.

"I get some pretty good movement on my fastball and the fork ball keeps the batter off balance," he said.

He looks forward to playing for LCC because "they play a tough schedule and have a great winning tradition. They made it to the playoffs last year, and I think they will again this year."

Acosta, who racked up a 36-3 ledger while at Elida, has been offered one invitation to try out for a professional team, the California Angels.

He declined the offer because he would have had to pay for all expenses.

TROPHY WINNER — Oscar Acosta, a former Elida player, holds the trophy he won for being the outstanding pitcher in a summer baseball league in Dallas. (News-Tribune photo)

Upper left: Yolanda & Oscar; Upper right: Concha & Oscar; Middle: Oscar; Lower left: Oscar; Lower right; Yolanda & Ralph

Above: Oscar, Jason Bere & Kevin Tapani; Below: Yolanda, Oscar & Concha

Chapter Ten

The Calm Before the Storm

In spite of the fact that Toney Anaya was not in a position to level the playing field for Oscar and other minorities – and in spite of the fact that Oscar continued to aggravate (and be aggravated by) the press – he managed to negotiate a yet more attractive contract, this time leaving the Rangers to coach for a succession of triple A teams for the Chicago Cubs.

One of the young players he worked with was right-hander Terry Adams. He prodded him, saying that he would turn him into a reliever if he didn't shape up. Adams' problem, according to my brother, was that he could pitch one or two innings well enough, but he couldn't hold it together for more than that. Still, as Oscar worked with him, teaching him to perfect his pitch for however long he had it, he began to think that Adams really could be a great major league reliever.

Acting on Oscar's recommendation, the day came to pass when Adams made his debut at a doubleheader at Wrigley Field playing against the San Diego Padres. Adams pitched a scoreless two-thirds of an inning in relief of starting pitcher Frank Castillo. Then he returned to the mound in the second game of the double-header, pitching a scoreless eighth inning in relief of starting pitcher Steve Trachsel.

Meanwhile, back in Daytona, where Oscar was working with the Cubs minor league pitchers, he was seeing a lot of fielding problems. One afternoon he took all his pitchers outside and lined them up as if they were going to be executed, and slammed balls at them one after the other at close range. A few bruises resulted, but nothing too serious, and everyone got the point after that.

"Either you loved or you hated him," Cubs trainer Steve Melendez said in an interview. Melendez confessed that Oscar made him a better trainer. Oscar sat him down one day and told him the facts of life about being an athletic trainer and how he should always be prepared and go about his business.

Oscar had no qualms about sharing his opinion, on the field or off. We heard through the grapevine during this time that he went into a lounge one evening with several other guys from the team, all of them Anglos. Oscar stood out, not only with his darker coloring but also because he was dressed in his Stetson hat and a starched white shirt and Wranglers. He noticed some men across the room looking at him and smirking. A few drinks later, they were still smirking. When the apparent leader got up to go to the men's room, Oscar followed him in and locked the door behind him. He grabbed the smirker by the shirt and lifted him off the floor and asked him what was so funny and if he could join in on the laughter. Later he would say that he was just giving the guy an "Attitude Adjustment," as in the song by Hank Williams, Jr.

While Oscar was making a name for himself, Ralph and I continued to poke our noses into everything and anything that looked like it might be fun. Ralph had always loved horse racing, and he had owned horses in the past. At one time he had had twelve of them. "Why don't you get a racing license?" he said to me one day after we'd gone to watch a particularly exciting race. "Why not become an owner?" Ralph had had a few DUIs, which eliminated the possibility of him becoming an owner himself, at least not without going through a lot of red tape. But I was certainly game.

Paul Garcia, a friend of Ralph's who owed a local mortuary, agreed to partner with me on the ownership of a horse. Papa Bravo, the stallion we bought, became the object of many jokes, because of the fact that one of his owners was a mortician. "Look alive, here comes the dead horse," some of our friends would say. But that kind of joking ended quickly, because the first time we raced him, Papa Bravo came in first place, winning a Senorita Futurity $30,000 purse. Papa Bravo's trainer was Ramon Gonzales, who was well on his way to becoming one of the top trainers in the state of New Mexico.

It seemed, at that time, that wherever we went, whatever we did, victory was inevitable.

Some weekends Ralph would say, "Pack a bag; we're going to Las Vegas." I didn't care for casino gambling myself, but I enjoyed our trips, especially when they included tickets to boxing tournaments, to watch the likes of Evander Holyfield. As for Ralph, he was a high roller. Whether he won or lost, it was fun for him; it was the kind of stimulation he most enjoyed. We took my mother and my children on some of our trips, taking advantage of the family-oriented entertainment that Vegas offered at that time. We stayed at MGM and went to amusement parks and dolphin shows, whatever the kids wanted to do.

I never doubted for a moment that Ralph loved me and my family, and as I loved him wholeheartedly, I was grateful to have the opportunity to live the kind of life that I found unfolding in front of me. But there were times when Ralph got out of hand, particularly when he had been drinking. A few times he pushed me around. Once he hit me, and I called Mother and she dropped everything and drove to Albuquerque and picked me up and brought me back to Portales. When Ralph showed up the next day looking for me, Mother told him to leave. She said we didn't need or want his money, that he wasn't taking her daughter back with him. He pleaded, on hands and knees; he begged her — us — to forgive him. His persistence and sincerity were irresistible. At some point, we gave in. "You give me your man's word that you will never hit my daughter again," Mother said finally, and he said, "Concha, you have my word," and he extended his hand to her.

There were other instances too, not where he hurt me physically but where he became unreasonable over one matter or another and I felt the need to escape to Portales before the situation got worse. My departure always shook him up. On plenty of occasions within hours of arriving in Portales, I would hear music outside and I would know that Ralph had hired yet another Mariachi band to serenade me. I would go to the window and see them, Mexican men dressed in silver-studded charro outfits with wide-brimmed hats, playing violins, trumpets, guitars, and *vihuelas* – and Ralph there among them, his face as open and imploring as a child's, his eyes pleading for forgiveness. The true purpose of Mariachi groups is to use their beautiful music to build a bridge to the heart of the person to whom they sing. They have been around for a long time, and they are almost always successful at achieving this goal. Ralph knew plenty of Mariachis from being in the entertainment business. They loved him. They would play all night long if he asked them to.

Even though our spats had happy endings, Mother and I didn't tell Oscar about any of them. Oscar was having the time of his life. He was finally getting the recognition he deserved, not only from the Cubs but from the league generally. Several highly-regarded coaches from American baseball teams had been asked that year to coach the Melborne Reds for one summer, in Australia. Oscar was one of them. This invitation was so great an honor that even the most ornery sports journalists were forced to speak kindly of Oscar for a change.

In the months to come, things improved between Ralph and me. We started talking seriously about marriage, and I had no doubt that once we tied the knot, things would get even better. But there was so much red tape to be gotten through before Ralph and Teresa could even finalize their divorce. For one thing, they owned quite a lot of properties together, and all the properties would have to be sold in order for the profits to be divided equably. But the economy was still dragging, and properties generally were just not selling at prices that made any sense — except in those instances where a realtor had a vested interest in a particular property. So Ralph suggested that I get my real estate license and become that realtor with the vested interest. "You're smart," he said. "You could easily handle these negotiations." And so I did just that. I took the requisite courses and got my broker's license, and all of a sudden the properties began to move. During this time I also got out of the TV work that I had been doing and took a full-time job working for the Department of Labor. While it might not have been as glamorous as being a host on variety shows, I felt it was important to have one aspect of my life that was my own, that had nothing to do with Ralph. My job with the Department of Labor guaranteed not only independence but also the chance to help the people who needed it most, the unemployed.

After spending so much time in each other's company, my new job away from Ralph gave me the chance to regain some perspective, and that seemed only to increase my love for him when I was with him. Wherever we went, there was music, and if the band was composed of Mariachis Ralph knew, he would ask me to get up and sing with them and I would. Then he would lift his glass and say, "Salud, mi Yolie," with such love in his eyes that anyone who saw him would turn to his sweetheart and smile in a like manner. Alan Jackson's "Living on Love" became our song, and whenever we heard it we would stop what we were doing and dance. Once we were filling up at a gas station when we heard it on someone else's radio, and we began to dance right there, beside the pumps, while gas flowed into Ralph's limo.

Ralph loved and needed nature as much as he loved and needed the excitement of horse racing and casinos. Often we bought steaks and drove up into the mountains of Jemez and grilled beside the river in the shadow of ancient cliffs that wore their history in bands of colors — orange and pink and gold. Sometimes we soaked in the hot springs up there, beneath the

Ponderosa Pines. When we couldn't get away, it was enough for him to climb the cliffs on the west mesa right in Albuquerque. There, he said, he could really listen to the wind. And in the wind, he swore he could feel God's presence like nowhere else. Often we stood at the top of the cliffs with our arms wide, leaning into the wind, relying on its constancy to keep us — two large joyful birds — aloft. Ralph loved trees too. He loved to see the colors change on the cottonwoods. He was the epitome of purposeful living, and no one could be with him and fail to love life just a little bit more herself.

Finally Ralph's divorce came through, and Ralph suggested we get married on October 12, Columbus Day. He said, "Just as Columbus discovered a new world on that day, I am going to take the plunge and discover a whole new life." We were in the process of building our home at the time, on a 17-acre ranch in the South Valley of Albuquerque. We knew it wouldn't be complete by October 12, but there would be enough amenities in place for us to have our wedding there. The ranch meant everything to Ralph. He had bought the property some years ago from the dairy farmers that his family had worked for when they had first come north, immigrants from Mexico. Ralph was only 11 years old at the time. His job was to help sell the milk. Now he owned the property.

Ralph was the family's bright and shining star in that way, just as Oscar was the star in our family. Starting with nothing had not deterred him from becoming the man he aimed to be. In fact, it may have given him the impetus. Ralph had always had an entrepreneurial spirit. Even before he came north, when he was still a boy in Juarez, he displayed a tremendous talent for innovation and business savvy. When he was only eight years old, he was shining shoes and using the money to buy his favorite foods, white bread and coke. One of his sisters-in-law, Anita, had been a seamstress back in Juarez, and when Ralph was a little older, he began to take the beautiful dresses she created out onto the street to sell. He also learned early on that if he gathered up all the hay that fell when the livestock train went hurtling by, he could sell that as well, to local farmers who kept sheep or cows. And he learned that thirsty baseball players out on the field in his hometown would be willing to pay a few pennies apiece for a cup of water hand-delivered during breaks in the game. In the U.S., when he was still a very young man, he bought his first business, a gas station. He built it up, sold it for a profit, and bought a paving business. Then someone came along and offered to sell him the redi-mix businesses. And then there was the driving school. Most recently, he had started a construction company. In honor of my mother, he called it Concha Construction. It was already prospering. Soon Ralph would need to hire more people to help him run it. "Yolie," he would say, "can you imagine that a shoeshine boy in Juarez now owns so many businesses? Only in America."

All brides and grooms hope for a perfect wedding day, and we had one. My dress was not new; Ralph had seen it in a store some eight years earlier, and although we were then nowhere close to marriage (because of the complicated divorce he needed to get through), he bought it for me then and we saved it for this day. Ralph thought it made me look like a mermaid. The dress was white with gold trim, and in keeping with the white/gold motif, we had dozens and dozens of white daisies and yellow roses (I was the "Yellow Rose of Texas," Ralph said, since yellow roses were my favorite and I had been born in Texas) delivered, and they were put in vases everywhere throughout the tents where the wedding would take place. I attached gold and white ceramic angels to every post and structure.

The day itself was glorious, a bright blue cloudless New Mexican sky with temperatures in the mid 70s. Mother and my son Brandon came up from Portales to walk me down the aisle. My friend Sandra came with her husband, Tony Mirabal. Sandra was my maid of honor. My sister and her children came as well.

Oscar would have been there if he could have, but he was surely there in spirit. One of Ralph's brothers owned a restaurant, and our food was catered through him. Judge Brennan married us. When it was my turn to recite my vows, I also recited a prayer that I had written for Ralph on one of the pages of my Daddy's Bible. The prayer said everything that needed to be said; it expressed my wish that Ralph and I would find together the real treasures in life, the ones that depend not only on devotion to each other but also devotion to God, the higher power that makes love possible.

While I was reciting the prayer and for the few moments afterwards when I spoke briefly about my father, a breeze came out of nowhere and it sent some of the gold leaves from the cottonwood trees overhead floating down on the people seated in folding chairs in the first several rows. Looking out at the sight of the wafers of gold sailing in the air above our loved ones, I could not help but remember all the times that Ralph had told me that he best heard God's voice in the wind. Later he would tell me that he had been thinking the same thing as he listened to my words and watched the leaves flutter down. Ralph was not a religious man, but he was definitely spiritual. Though he never went to church, he swore to me that he started every day thanking God for many things, especially for the fact that I was in his life.

Once we had taken our vows, the Mariachis started up, and for hours they played and everyone danced. A friend of Ralph's looked around at the people laughing and dancing and joked that ours could easily have been mistaken for the wedding of Don Corleone's daughter Connie in *The Godfather*. At the end of the day, when everyone had gone and it was quiet again, Ralph and I fell into folding chairs, exhausted, and as we looked around we realized that our guests had taken all our decorations home with them — all of the flowers and the ceramic angels too. This made sense, we realized; it was the kind of day that absolutely required a keepsake.

For three full days after our wedding, Ralph wore his tuxedo pants — his own variety of keepsake. He was happy not only because we had finally gotten married, but because so many members of his family, some of whom had not previously approved of our relationship, had come to our wedding, and through their presence they had tacitly forgiven him and welcomed me into the family. This was particularly true regarding his oldest brother, Augustine. If Augustine was there, Ralph knew, everything was all right. Ralph's oldest son Mark had also come, and we knew that it could not have been easy for him and greatly appreciated his presence. Besides his other children, who had not come, the only one who Ralph missed was Chava, his nephew. Chava and I had never learned to get along; he was one of the loud, rowdy, rude people who had had so much influence over Ralph in the beginning of our relationship, who had tried very hard to keep us apart. Chava would never approve of me — nor I of him. Yet I knew Ralph felt his absence in his heart.

We flew to Matzalan some days later, and a week passed in a whirl of swimming, eating, lounging, and dancing. On our last day, however, the timbre of our trip changed. We went out on a fishing boat that day. The waves were high and the sun was extraordinarily hot. I knew better than to even think of having a drink. In fact, the movement of the boat made me just a bit seasick, and I found a place in the shade to lie down and wait it out. In typical Ralph fashion, Ralph stayed out in the sun all day, fishing and drinking and laughing with other men he'd met. He had a great time and caught a few fish, but that night, back in our hotel room, he had some kind cf attack. I can't to this day say how serious it was, but at the time I felt sure he was having a heart attack. In a panic, I called the medics at our hotel. They called for emergency transportation to the hospital. In Matzalan they don't come with an ambulance. They come in a vehicle that resembles a golf cart.

Holding Ralph in my arms, we bounced our way to the hospital. I stayed all night in his room, praying that our short time as man and wife would not end this way. The next day Ralph was feeling somewhat better. The doctors released him and we flew home. I hoped this would be the end of it. The episode was, in fact, the beginning of the end, but I had no way of knowing it at the time.

A few days later Ralph and I went to Houston, and along with other members of his family, we celebrated the 25th Jubilee of his sister, Sister Josephine, the Carmelite nun. Sister Josephine threw her arms around me and welcomed me into the family, another sign, in my mind, that ours was a marriage that would endure. I was also welcomed by the Mother Superior at the convent, a woman so tiny that the top of her head did not quite reach my shoulder, but a woman of magnitude in other ways. When she saw that Ralph and I, two divorcees, were reluctant to go up with the others to receive Communion during the Jubilee Mass, she came to us and whispered, "Hijos, vengan y tomen la Comunión. Está bien." *Children, come and get Communion; it's okay*. And so we did.

Our troubles began in earnest about five weeks after our wedding, on a cold, snowy November night. We were supposed to go out that night. The young daughter of the general manager at Ralph's redi-mix company was having a birthday party. I was waiting for Ralph to get home when I heard a car horn honking outside. I threw on a jacket and ran out. The man in the car was from the water conservancy and he had come to talk to Ralph about some business matter. Since I expected Ralph any minute, and since it was cold and snowing, I invited the stranger to wait for Ralph in our warm kitchen. We had just gotten our wedding pictures back. Ralph hadn't even seen them yet. In my excitement at finally having the photos of that wonderful day, I offered them to the stranger. He flipped through them one at a time, but when he was done, he looked up at the clock and announced that he'd come back to talk to Ralph some other time. He couldn't wait any longer.

Ralph went into a rage when he finally returned. He simply could not believe that I had let a strange man into the house. Nor could he believe that I had shared our wedding photos with him. I argued that I had done nothing wrong. Ralph was the one who was late, the one who had apparently forgotten about the party. But he was not hearing it. He came after me. He got a hold of my hair and yanked me close to him and screamed in my face. I broke away and immediately ran to the phone. I had promised myself that I would never accept abuse again in my life, and I intended to keep that promise. I called the police. "This is not the kind of marriage I intend to have," I screamed after I'd hung up. By the time the police arrived, Ralph had already left again. There were no arrests. There was no more trouble that night. But the honeymoon was definitely over.

In retrospect, there were a number of things that might have contributed to Ralph's behavior — for one, after the episode in Matzalan Ralph was surely very worried about his health. He had since been to the doctor, and while his physician did not seem overly concerned about his heart, he discovered that Ralph had diabetes and some other physical problems. He would need to change his diet, an unwelcome wakeup call for a man who loved food as much as Ralph did. And because he wasn't feeling healthy, I believe that Ralph experienced a great deal of insecurity regarding his sexuality. Perhaps he felt reluctant to say all this to the woman he had just married, a woman who was 12 years younger than him. Perhaps it seemed easier to go out and act in ways which, in his mind, would negate his concerns about his health.

None of this, of course, excuses his behavior. And at the time I did not have the clarity of mind to even consider these factors. All I knew was that Ralph remained furious at me, for calling the police, and that he continued to come home late.

At a loss for a clue as to how we might move forward,

eventually I called Sr. Josephine. I called her because she was a Carmelite nun, someone who prayed from morning till night, and because she had been so warm to me. I imagined that we would pray together over the phone, and that our combined prayers would begin to work to restore my marriage to its former state. But Sr. Josephine spoke to her lay sisters, Ralph's sisters, on a regular basis, and she knew as much — or possibly more — about what was going on in anyone's life as any other member of the family. "Yolanda," she exclaimed when she heard my voice. "I'm so glad to hear from you. Ralph has been running around with this young woman…."

She went on to tell me all she had heard, that the young woman had come from Mexico and that her ex-boyfriend was a drug dealer in Oklahoma. In fact, she had heard that Ralph and Chava, the infamous nephew, had been seen with other women as well, prostitutes, and that they were getting involved with drugs. I heard everything she said, but it was as if I were hearing her voice from under water.

When Ralph came in that night I stood up to him. "What is going on?" I demanded to know. "You know how I feel about drugs."

"Why?" he countered. "Why would you even say something like that?"

"What about women? Is there someone else?"

Ralph denied everything.

We believe what we want to believe. Even Sr. Josephine had agreed that the news about Chava and the drugs and the prostitutes had come from an unreliable source and could just be a rumor. On the matter of the young girl, however, she was quite certain. But I convinced myself that she could be mistaken there too.

Still, I took to driving around looking for Ralph when he was late. Once I saw him on the freeway in his pickup truck, and I speeded up and followed him for several miles, tooting my horn each time I got close. The fact that he was trying to outrun me convinced me that he had someone with him, but when he finally pulled over, amused that I had given chase, I saw that he was all alone. We laughed a bit. We were like the Coyote and the Road Runner, we concluded. His redi-mix company was Coyote. And with my hand on the horn...*beep beep*....

Not every day was a bad one. There were enough good ones in between for me to think that whatever he was going through would play itself out and then we could begin to pick up the pieces. But in January I called Sr. Josephine again, and this time she told me that the young girl, the one I still didn't quite believe existed — Karla was her name — was pregnant.

There was no more pretending after that. I couldn't eat. The pounds began to melt away, and before I knew it I'd gone from 112 pounds to less than 100. My tightest clothes swam on me. I was on the phone with Mother constantly. We cried together; we prayed together. I was also on the phone with Ralph's sisters, gathering information laboriously, a bit here, a bit there, trying to create a full picture of what had happened to my life. When I learned that Ralph had hired Karla to work in his office at Concha Construction, I grabbed one of our wedding pictures and drove right over there. Karla was not there — she had gone to Mexico to visit her family — but her brother-in-law, who Ralph had also hired, was there. I wrote a letter to leave on Karla's desk along with the picture. "I am Ralph's wife and you are a piece of trash," it said, and more. I told the brother-in-law to make sure she saw it when she returned.

If nothing else, leaving the note and the wedding photo was a way to insure that Ralph — who was still denying having any other women in his life — knew that I knew. With the cat well out of the bag, and the other woman pregnant to boot, Ralph fell into full confession mode. He cried like a baby as he told me all the details he had suppressed for so long. He'd been drunk at the time. He'd been angry with me. He'd wanted to get back at me.

She'd given him signs. They'd done it in her office, on the desk there at the construction company that was named for my mother and for which I was in fact the licensee. "Please forgive me," he pleaded. I asked him again about drugs, but he insisted he'd never had anything to do with them, that he never would.

The brother-in-law, the one who'd been there the day I ran in with my wedding photo, my sources confirmed, was the one who was dealing drugs. If Ralph was involved too, then I wanted to know. I had already gone far beyond my pain threshold; a little more wouldn't matter one way or another. I called Albuquerque Narcotics Bureau and demanded to know anything they knew. Surprisingly, they knew quite a lot. They knew that Karla's brother-in-law was a drug dealer and that Karla's ex-boyfriend was one too. They were keeping an eye out, waiting to see what else they would learn before they made any arrests. What about Ralph? I wanted to know. What was his involvement?

They didn't have anything on Ralph, they said. But that didn't mean that he wasn't involved. They told me to start looking in his pockets. See if I found any small scraps of aluminum. Take note whether he was grinding his teeth.

I found nothing in his pockets. As for his teeth, sometimes I imagined he ground them, but other times I was sure it was only my imagination.

I kept in touch with the Narcotics Bureau. Whenever I suspected anything, I called and told them, and they told me to watch my back, just in case it was discovered that I was an informant. Once a woman called me, a stranger, and told me that she and some other women had been driving to Alamogordo when their car broke down. Now they were stuck in the mountains with no way to get back to Albuquerque. If I would drive up and rescue them, she said, they would return the favor by telling me everything I wanted to know about Karla and Ralph. This was tempting. No matter how much I found out, I always had a feeling that the whole truth, the bigger picture, was eluding me. But when I called one of Ralph's sisters to get advice, she said, "No, whatever you do, don't go pick them up. It could be a trap." And I began to wonder if my life might really be in danger.

I found myself a small apartment and moved out. I tried to focus on one day at a time: get up, drive to work, get through lunch, work some more, come home, try to eat something for dinner.... But almost every evening the doorbell would ring and I would be distracted from my determination by the sight of Ralph there on the stoop, begging me to forgive him, begging me to come home. I didn't want to go home anymore, but I did let him in, and we spent hours talking, talking, talking, and getting absolutely nowhere. The bottom line was that Karla was pregnant. In October she would have his baby. And I was not about to move back home and risk his leaving the house when the baby came to sit with her in some hospital and tell her to *push, push*...or *wait, don't push.* Nor did I want to be the one to stand in his way if that was in fact what he wanted to do. Princess Diana, who had been dead less than a year, had once said about her marriage, "There were three of us in the marriage, so it was a bit crowded." I said to Ralph, "There's three of us in this marriage now, and soon there will be four. That's more than a bit crowded."

Still, I gave in to Ralph's pleas to spend time with him and accompanied him to see Johnny Tapia box in Las Vegas. Johnny Tapia was a hometown hero, and lots of people I knew planned to attend the event. On the plane, when Ralph got out of his seat to use the bathroom, a mutual friend of ours approached me. He said, "Yolanda, Ralph came to me the other day with tears in his eyes. He said to me, 'I really screwed up. I'm going to do everything in my power to get Yolanda back.'"

If Ralph thought our short time in Las Vegas would make me want to come home, he was wrong. In fact, the trip had the opposite effect. When I got back I called my old friend and attorney Mickey Barnett. "I want to file for divorce," I said. But in the meantime, I continued to spend time with Ralph. I continued to listen to his pleas and apologies. I couldn't help myself.

In March that year, the movie *Selena* premiered in Albuquerque. My son got a ride from Portales to Santa Rosa, and I picked him up there so that he could see it with me. Leah Dawn would have come too, but she was playing basketball at Highlands University, proving herself to be a superior athlete. Mother didn't care to go, but when she heard that Ralph would be there, she said, "Please tell Ralph to take my name off his construction company. No soy la broma de nadie." *I'm not anybody's joke.*

Selena was more than a great singer to us. She was a cultural icon for many Latinos; we saw her as a woman who remained proud of her roots as she set about achieving her goals. My children and I had seen her perform in Clovis a few years earlier. At the time, Leah Dawn had said to me, "When I get married, I want Selena to perform at my wedding." Ralph and I had seen her in El Paso, the year before she was shot.

Jennifer Lopez, who of course played the adult Selena in the film, could not make it to the premiere, but many of the other actors, including Becky Lee Meza, who played the young Selena, and Lupe Ontiveros, who played Selena's killer, were there. When Ralph, who met us at the theater, first saw Brandon, he cried, "Brandon, how is my son doing?" And my son, who was 15 at the time but already showing himself to be a quick wit, replied, "Well, I'm pretty good Ralph. How about you? I hear instances of teenage pregnancy have gone up a notch in Albuquerque recently." I laughed out loud, startling myself. I hadn't laughed like that in months. It felt good.

Mickey Barnett drew up the papers and had them served. Ralph received them. I wanted nothing — nothing — but to know that time would heal my wounds and that I would be able to think clearly again one day in the future.

In the meantime, with the divorce about to unfold, there was no longer any way to keep the news from Oscar. He called me as soon as he heard. "Stay away from that sewer," he said. "It stinks to high heaven."

At work, I made friends with Ernesto Gomez, a Christian man who took the time to pray with me almost daily. Sometimes at lunch we read the Bible together. We particularly liked to read about Sodom and Gomorrah. "Stay away from him," Ernesto warned me. "You've been given a clear sign. Don't look back or, like Lot's wife, you'll turn to salt."

No matter how many people I spoke to, no matter how much love and support I had from family and friends, I could not escape the loneliness I felt. I prayed continuously that I would forget Ralph, that I would meet a man with no wife, no children, no strings at all, nothing more than a nice home where we could spend time doing nothing. I didn't want love anymore; I didn't even want passion. All I wanted was a little peace — and not to always be alone with my thoughts. So the night I met Robert, of course I made the assumption that God had sent him along in answer to my prayers.

I was in the Northeast Heights area of Albuquerque looking for a larger and more permanent apartment than the one I had. I hadn't had anything to eat or drink all day. After checking out several apartments, any one of which might have been right if my heart had been in it, I walked into a bar called the Horse and Angel and ordered a Bud Light. As I took a sip, my eye fell on the three men across the bar from me, one of whom was sipping his beer too and looking right at me. The first thing I noticed was that his hair was so blonde it was almost white.

I realized I was too despondent to finish the beer and got up and left. A moment later, I turned to find Robert hurrying to catch up to me. "I have been in Albuquerque for three years," he said, "and I really didn't think this city had any beautiful women. But you are beautiful. Would you let me buy you a beer?" And all I could think was that my husband was pregnant with another woman, and I was lonely, and so why not?

I followed him back in and we talked for a while about politics in New Mexico and we had a few laughs; and when I said it was time for me to get going, Robert said that his house was just up the street and he'd love for me to see it, and he had some good wine there that he'd bought while traveling recently. I could see no way that a few hours of distraction could be a bad thing for me, so I left my car at the Horse and Angel and drove with him to his house, which we entered through the garage. No sooner did we step into the living room than he hurried to the fireplace mantel and turned a framed photo face down. Then he proceeded to tell me his story, which was basically that his wife Bonnie had died of cancer not three months earlier. Previously he had worked at McAllen Air Force Base in California, but after the base closed, they had come, reluctantly, to New Mexico. He worked as a military aircraft crash investigator, investigating, mostly, the causes of crashes of F-16s. He was an ejection seat and explosives expert, a civilian working for the Department of Defense. Like Ralph, he was older than me. Originally from Tennessee, he had fought in Viet Nam. He and Bonnie had never had any children.

Robert, it turned out, was as lonely and miserable as I was.

He gave me a tour of his home, all of which his late wife had decorated. Everything was done in peach: light peach, dark peach, orange peach, yellow peach.... After the tour, he put on some music and we started to dance. It felt so good to be in someone's arms. When he kissed me, I said to myself, Ralph, I loved you with all my heart and soul and you let me slip away. But the fact that I was thinking of Ralph while kissing Robert probably confirms that it was too soon to regard of my love for Ralph in the past tense.

We began to date. Robert seemed to be fun loving and certainly he was attentive. I enjoyed being in his company — or at least I enjoyed it as much as I could enjoy anything in the depressed state I was in. He told me right off the bat that he was a man who didn't pray, but then he also told me that he had prostate cancer. He'd been back to California for a few treatments, but to date he was still suffering with the disease.

He didn't resist when I offered to take him to San Felipe De Neri Church, a beautiful old adobe structure in the heart of Old Town, Albuquerque's historic district. San Felipe had been my sanctuary since my life had begun to fall apart. I was there all the time, praying, taking comfort, sometimes just crying....

I called Mother before we went. I said, "This man I met.... He's sick. We need to pray very hard for him." She promised she would do her part. Later, in the church, Robert and I sat in a wooden pew and I prayed aloud for his health. When I finished, he squeezed my hand and whispered, "Thank you." A week or so later when he flew to California for his proton beam treatment, the doctors told him they had achieved success. He was cured.

Robert and I had been dating about a month when I learned that Ralph had brought Karla to stay at the ranch, offering her a nice place to live while she waited for their child to be born. It was merely an act of kindness, he insisted; he didn't love her, she wasn't his girlfriend. She was simply pregnant and needed a place to stay until she figured out what she was going to do. To balance things out, I decided to move some of my things into Robert's home and, as he had been hoping, spend more time with him. His house was huge, some 3500 square feet, and all the floors, except the kitchen and bathrooms, were covered in white peach wall-to-wall carpeting. That alone should have told me that we didn't stand a chance together, but I was still acting on the fact that I had met Robert — a man with no attachments — right after praying for a man with no attachments. And Robert had allowed me to pray for him, in the San Felipe De Neri

Church. He had had cancer and now he was cured. So what that he was a bit obsessive when it came to his house. He had bought it when prices were low. He was planning to sell it when they went high again, so he wanted it treated like a model home. He preferred that I didn't cook in his kitchen. Too much wear and tear occurred in kitchens, he said, and he didn't want to have to replace any appliances. Fine, I wouldn't cook; I still couldn't eat anyway, so it didn't make much difference.

A few months later, Robert asked me to marry him. As soon as I had a minute alone I called Ralph at his office at Concha Construction. He answered the phone, and I heard his voice catch when he realized it was me. "Yolie," he whispered. "Please hurry and sign the divorce papers," I said. "I'm going to get married." Robert and I were hoping to be married by May. Ralph would turn 55 before then. I had spent a lot of energy in the past thinking about the birthday party I would throw for him. I had planned to call it a "Double Nickel" party. People would wear clothes from the 50s and we would rent a jukebox and dance to music — the swing and the cha cha — from that time. Now I would give him a divorce instead.

Karla had a baby boy. She was still living at the ranch. To keep myself from falling apart completely, I tried to focus on the part of my life that was moving forward. My divorce had gone through, and Robert and I were making our wedding plans, though it was to be a low key affair and planning it didn't take much effort. And that was a good thing, because the knowledge that Karla had given birth to Ralph's baby fell between any two thoughts I could hold, like a leaden punctuation mark between sentences.

I needed to get away for a while, alone. My ability to think clearly was completely diminished. My circular thoughts were drowning me. I needed perspective to pull myself out. I needed to go someplace where other people were suffering even more than I was. There were plenty of places to choose from.

The Zapatista rebel uprising in Chiapas had been in the news for about four years by then, ever since the rebels had declared war on the Mexican state in 1994, on the day after the NAFTA agreement went into effect. Chiapas was one of the poorest states in Mexico. That, I decided, was where I wanted to go. And I would not go as a tourist.

I wanted to live among the Mayans, 45 of whom had been killed on Christmas Eve when state-trained forces surrounded a Catholic chapel in the pacifist Tsotsil Mayan community of Acteal, Chiapas, and with the apparent consent of local Mexican Army units stationed not far away, proceeded to shoot to death those inside as well as many of those who tried to escape. Those murdered included 15 children, 21 women (four of them pregnant) and nine men.

I contacted a group called Global Exchange to see if I could travel to Chaipas as part of their organization. After a brief telephone interview, they decided that I was too headstrong for them and they refused to grant my request. So I began to make plans to go alone. I called Sr. Josephine, who had the wisdom to see that such a trip would be more beneficial for me than a trip to some island resort. She gave me the name of Archbishop Ruiz in Chiapas, who was a friend of hers. He would help me, she said. I also called then Governor Johnson, to ask for a letter of introduction for the government there. Reports of human rights activists being raped or killed were frequent; the more paperwork I could collect, the safer I would be.

And so, for one week in the middle of my own personal crisis, I became a grain of sand in a much larger sandstorm, staying in a refugee camp with 10,000 Mayan Indians. I slept with them on the ground in their crowded plastic tents. I made friends with several Mayan chiefs; and I watched as Blackhawk helicopters flew overhead in the hope of intimidating those of us below. I wanted to meet with Marcos, the Zapatista leader, but I was told he was deep in the jungle at that time.

I considered myself to be on a fact-finding mission, and in my opinion, the facts showed that the Zapatista rebellion was a Marxist movement. Pro-Zapatista support groups were emerging everywhere outside of Mexico at the time, particularly in the U.S., Argentina, Spain, Italy, Germany, Austria, Switzerland, France and Britain. They visited the area regularly, to instigate. When I returned I knew I would write letters to various senators. I would show them pictures and warn them that the communist movement was riding on a powerful wave of money, that they needed to open their eyes and see where all this money was coming from.

Ralph heard the news that I was away, and certain that I would be killed, he called my Mother once again to beg for forgiveness. But she was worried about me too, and the last thing she needed was to have Ralph reminding her that her daughter had placed herself in harm's way, and all for the chance to gain a bit of perspective. As for me, the trip did me a world of good.

When I returned, Ralph called and begged me to give him a second chance. I replied that unless he accepted Jesus into his life (and all the rectitude such an acceptance implied), I was never going back to him. In the meantime, my plans to marry Robert marched forward, seemingly of their own accord. I didn't think that Ralph had taken my proviso seriously until one day Ernesto, my friend at work, told me that Ralph had stopped in when I wasn't there and had gotten down on his knees and prayed with him. "Praise God!" I cried, and later that day, Ralph returned to the office when I was there and told me the news himself. "I accepted your Christ," he said. His eyes filled with tears. "I know," I responded.

Every day after that, he showed up at my office. Robert and I, in the meantime, had set a date: our wedding would be on May 23. On May 5, Cinco de Mayo, Ralph and I spent the day together, discussing my upcoming marriage. He begged me not to go through with it, and I insisted that I had to, that it was the best thing for me, and I had to think about myself. On May 20, just three days before the big event was due to take place, Ralph asked me to have lunch with him. I agreed and he picked me up at work and we drove to the Japanese Kitchen. After we'd ordered our meal, he said, "Yolie, you're not going to marry him. You don't love him. You're my wife. You'll always be my wife."

He was right of course. He was always in my heart, no matter where I went or who I was with. He went on repeating things we both knew to be true, and by the time we were done eating, he had convinced me to fly with him that very afternoon to Las Vegas and remarry him. I was giddy with the prospect of such a change in fortunes — in the eleventh hour. He took me back to the Department of Labor so that I could tell my supervisor that I was taking a few days off, that I would be leaving my car in the lot and to please make sure to lock the gate. Then we were off.

On the plane we couldn't stop looking at each other; we couldn't stop smiling. "We're like Elizabeth Taylor and Richard Burton," I said. Ralph agreed that there were some attractions that were just too hard to resist.

We got our license, and then we went to Silver Bells Chapel to make an appointment for later in the day. We requested yellow roses and white daisies, but the chapel director informed us that that would be impossible on such short notice. We could have red and white roses; that was the best they could do. I had never liked red roses. They reminded me of funerals. But on this day I didn't mind. If possible, I was even happier than I had been the first time we'd married. Ralph said he felt the same way.

After the wedding, we went to the room we'd reserved at Bally's and Ralph handed me the phone. "Call him," he said, and I did. Robert cried when he heard the news. Then he got angry. We hung up quickly — really, there wasn't a lot to say — and Ralph made his call, to tell Karla. She was angry too. She wasn't even legal yet. He was her sole meal ticket. "One thing," I told him in no uncertain terms after he'd finished talking to her. "You will treat that child just like you do the others. You will write out that support check with a smile on your face and each time you will remember that that check is the price you are paying for five minutes of ecstasy on a desk in an office at Concha Construction." "I will, of course," Ralph agreed. I thought of another thing. "Chava is going to be really mad because you've remarried me. They all are, Chava and all the others." "I don't care," he whispered. "I don't tell them who to marry. I don't say anything about their wives. You're my wife. You'll always be."

We stayed a few days, and we would have stayed longer, but Ralph had to fly back by Friday to do payroll. The crazy thing was that Karla was still at the ranch, and since she had the baby, we couldn't very well kick her out until she had another place to go. And while I still had my little apartment, I had plenty of clothes and other personal items at Robert's house. So, "Elizabeth and Richard" were forced to say goodbye at the Department of Labor and go their very separate ways for the time being.

I stopped at Robert's on the way home, to get some clothes. He was still very angry and he told me there was no way I was taking anything out of the house until I returned the engagement ring he'd given me. I reached in my bag and handed it to him. Not a week earlier he had gotten upset with me because every time I brushed my hair, which was long and black, strands fell on his light-colored carpeting and he felt compelled to pick them up. Remembering his anger over my hair on his carpet helped me to feel less guilty about the fact that I had just remarried my ex-husband, only days before I was supposed to marry him. I went into the bedroom and gathered up as much clothing as I could carry.

A few days passed. Karla was still in Ralph's house. He swore he was doing his best to make other arrangements for her, but it hadn't happened yet. In the meantime, my daughter had come to stay with me. She needed some clothes for the summer semester;

we had shopping to do. This kept me busy; it kept me from thinking about the strangeness of my situation. In the middle of the week, Ralph had a golf tournament to attend at the Santa Ana Country Club, about 20 miles north of Albuquerque. He asked me to meet him there and I agreed. Ken W, his friend and attorney, was also there. As I followed them around on the greens, I heard them discussing a horse race, scheduled to take place at the ranch.

My stomach sank. Some time earlier Ralph had mentioned that Chava, who he'd been spending time with again during our separation, had spent a lot of money buying some horses and wanted to race one of them at the ranch. Ken W also had horses. The plan had been for Chava and Ken to jockey their own horses, which was laughable as they both looked more like Baby Huey than jockeys, and the winner would get both his opponent's horse and some cash — $30,000. Since Ralph hadn't mentioned it again, and with all the other stuff that was going on, I assumed the idea had been forgotten. I, at least, had forgotten it. It was a preposterous idea to begin with. There would be big betting, drinking, lots of people who were not in this country legally, people who made their money through drug sales.... It was a very bad idea.

I was furious. I wanted Ralph's association with such people to come to an end once and for all. A quick end. So when I got home that day I called the Bureau of Alcohol, Gaming and Immigration and told a man named Richard that there was going to be some illegal gambling going on Saturday, May 30, and that they'd need to go over and stop it. Then I called Border Patrol and let a man named Tony know that there would be several illegals at the ranch on the 30th, some of whom were drug dealers. And then I called an editor of the *Albuquerque Journal* and told him about the sting operation going down at the ranch and that he would need to have a reporter there to cover it.

Since I remained convinced that Ralph himself had never been involved with drugs, I felt certain that the most that would happen to him would be that he would have to pay a fine. In the meantime, his bad friends would disappear; and he would never know that I was the one who had set up the sting. A day or two after my first series of calls, Immigration called me. They said they had walked the perimeter of the property, which was entirely fenced in. They wanted to know if I had a key for the gate. In fact I didn't.

Ralph called me a day later, while Leah Dawn and I were having breakfast, and told me that Karla was still there and he didn't know what to do to get her to leave. He also let slip that my arch enemy Chava had put some ideas in her head. He was telling her that she should stay in the house, that she shouldn't make it easy for me to come in and change everything that she had going for her there. "So what are you going to do?" I asked him impatiently. The whole situation was bordering on the ridiculous. I certainly didn't want to see any woman with a baby out on the street, but she had to have other options. She had a big family, and since some of them were drug dealers, there had to be enough money to get her out. And Ralph could give her plenty of money too. Ralph said he was going to put her in the limo that very morning and drive her to Juarez. Then he suggested that I drive down to Juarez and meet him at a hotel and we would come back together in the limo. He would have someone there drive my car back for me. I reminded him that I had Leah Dawn with me, and he said I should bring her, that we would have a good time together.

Leah Dawn and I got ready to leave a few hours later, but since in all this time Ralph hadn't managed to get Karla motivated to leave the ranch, I had no reason to believe that he would be able to do so now. I thought I had better check and make sure they were on their way before I set out for the long ride to Mexico. I pulled off the interstate and headed to the South Valley. When I got to the ranch, I saw that the gate was open. I drove in and parked close to the house. The limo, of course, was still there. "Please, let's leave," Leah Dawn begged me. I told her to stay in the car and then I marched up to the door that opened into the dining room. I remembered how that door always stuck; since it was ajar now, I assumed that Ralph had never gotten around to taking it down and planing it. From my vantage point, I could actually see both Ralph and Karla in the living room, her on one side of the room and him on the other. They were watching TV. Ralph was drinking something. Since there was an opened bottle of vodka and a container of orange juice on the table beside his chair, my best guess would be Screwdrivers.

The humor in the situation ran headlong into my intense feeling of fury, and without thinking twice about it, I lifted a high-heeled foot and kicked open the door. At the same time I yelled, "Honey, I'm home," in a crazily-inflected imitation of Ricky Ricardo from the "I Love Lucy" show. The two of them could only stare at me in horror for a moment. Then Ralph got up slowly from his chair. Karla got up quickly and grabbed the baby and made off into the far corner of the room.

"Let's go outside and talk," Ralph said.

"No," I countered. "We're going to talk right now, right here."

I could see his face tightening with anger, but I didn't care. He tried to push me out the door, and when I dodged him, I saw the anger in his expression intensify a notch. He lifted one hand threateningly, and all I could think was that if he hit me in front of Karla, in front of the 20-year-old that he had gotten pregnant while we were married, I would die of humiliation. I picked up an empty glass that was sitting out on a cabinet behind me and screamed in Spanish, "¿Cuánto tiempo más va usted a seguir haciéndole daño a la gente?" *How long are you going to go on hurting people?*

He kept moving towards me. I didn't know what was going to happen. I looked at Karla, almost as young as my daughter. Holding her baby tightly to her chest, she regarded me through narrowed eyes, as if I were the one who had invaded a home, ruined a marriage. He took one more step in my direction and I released the glass I had been holding. I had meant to send it crashing to the floor, a loud, gleaming, dynamic warning that would keep him from coming any closer. But that's not where it landed. It hit him in the shoulder. And it broke there. We both stopped moving for a moment to regard the blood bubbling up from under his shirt. Then I ran behind the drapes, ugly drapes that made the room look like a mortuary, drapes that only Karla could have chosen. But I must have pulled on them, for a moment later they fell in front of me, like a third-rate stage curtain at the end of an act, and I was exposed again — and Ralph was still coming at me. And then Leah Dawn was there, standing between Ralph and me, screaming for me to leave with her. I took one look back. Karla had gone into another room, and I could hear her talking. She was calling the cops. "Let's go," I said to Leah Dawn, and she was only too happy to steer me out.

As we drove down the road I heard the sirens. The cops were already on their way. "Leah Dawn," I said, "they're coming for me. We have to turn around and go back." She pleaded with me, but I pulled into a driveway and made a U-turn and back we went to await the arrival of Albuquerque's finest.

Two cops arrived right behind me. We got out of our respective cars and talked. They wanted to charge me with breaking and entering, but when I told them that Ralph and I were husband and wife, they changed their minds. The only thing they could charge me with was domestic violence. "Well, Yolanda," said one of them, "I guess you're going to jail." I nodded. Jail was where I wanted to be. "Fine, take me now," I said. And off we went. Leah Dawn followed in my car. As soon as we got there I told her to go back to school. I did not want to be bailed out. This was where my husband wanted me and this was where I was going to stay. "I got myself into this and I can get myself out," I said to her. And I had to smile when I remembered where I'd heard those words before.

Chapter Eleven

The Storm

If it was true that I was the wife and therefore couldn't have broken into my own house, a sheriff named Rhonda wanted to know, then who was the other woman, the young woman with the baby? The hired help, I told her, the hired help and her illegitimate child. The story at this point was much too complicated and bizarre to explain easily, but the bottom line was that I was, in fact, Ralph's wife, and the house was as much mine as his. Later, after another officer talked to Ralph and Karla, an officer appeared to say that I was free to leave on my own recognizance. But I didn't want to leave. There were other women in the cell with me, and we were sharing stories of love gone bad. In the frame of mind I was in, these stories were all important and I was not about to miss out on the opportunity to bond with other broken hearts. Exasperated and confused, the officer retreated.

The night went on and eventually I got tired. My cellmates told me to get some sleep, that they would look after me and everything would be okay. But only a few hours later, a guard came to say that there was someone there to bail me out. I told the guard to tell whoever it was to go away, and apparently they did. Then about four in the morning there was a pounding on the wall and one of the guards told me I had a phone call. I accompanied the guard down the hall. Robert was on the line. My daughter, who I had hoped had gone back to the university, was with him. She'd gone to him to plead for help on my behalf. "She's very upset," Robert said. "You'd better let us bail you out because I don't know what to do with her." When Robert and Leah Dawn arrived a few hours later, I left my heavy-hearted sisters behind and returned to the real world.

Once I had reassured Leah Dawn that I was okay and that she could get back to school, I called Sister Josephine and told her everything that had happened. I told her that Chava was egging Karla on, encouraging her to feel that Ralph owed her something more than child support, that Ralph had planned to take her to Juarez but then hadn't. How can this be? I asked her. I knew Ralph loved me and I knew I loved him, so how was it possible that we were both living our lives according to rules that had nothing to do with our relationship?

"Ralph is confused," Sister Josephine said. "Sometimes people get confused for reasons we can't understand. We need to pray for him."

I didn't go to work that day or the one after. But on the second day I knew at least where Ralph was and what he was doing. He had promised two of his daughters that he would take them to Houston, to a huge auto auction, to help them buy a truck that would be suitable for the landscaping business they planned to start. He had been teaching them the entrepreneurial ropes for months, and he would not have backed out on his promise to them under any circumstances. I knew this because I knew Ralph. For all that he was impulsive and prone to making bad decisions, and, as Sister Josephine had confirmed, confused, there were some areas of his life where he was very consistent, and the desire to be a mentor to his children was one of them. To pass the time, I called the undercover agents to make sure that they were still set to go forward with the sting operation at Ralph's racing event. The more I thought about it, the more astonishing the whole thing was to me. Ken W was Ralph's attorney; by encouraging Ralph to host this illegal event, he was doing him a great personal and professional disservice.

On the day that Ralph was in Houston, he called the Department of Labor to speak to me, but I wasn't there. I got the message from one of my colleagues and decided not to call him back. At this point, there wasn't much to say. I knew that once they had purchased the truck, Ralph would have one of his daughters drive the limo home and he would catch a flight. That was another way in which Ralph was predictable: he couldn't stand to spend that many hours in a car. He would fly back Friday and get a good night's sleep before the big event, which was set to begin at ten on Saturday.

Saturday morning at about eight, I called the numbers for Tony at Border Patrol and Richard at the Bureau of Alcohol, Gaming and Immigration and neither of them answered their phones. They had given me pager numbers, and so I tried those too, and again I got no response. It was as if they had gotten together and concluded that the events I was warning them about were no more than the ramblings of a distraught and jealous wife.

Their lack of support threw me into a panic. My intuition told me that it was imperative that someone with some authority be there to prevent things from getting out of hand. My feeling of foreboding increased as the morning went on. I tried their numbers again and again with the same results. At about 9:30, I called the state police. There was illegal gambling going on, I told the man who answered the phone, and it had to be stopped. His interest level was nil. He would have to have proof in order to act, he said. What I was telling him was pure speculation. I tried to make him see that if he sent someone out, he would have his proof, but it was like talking to a door. I was just wasting time. I called the Bernalillo sheriff's office and had pretty much the same conversation with the dispatcher there. It was closing in on ten by then, and my feeling of impending disaster was increasing with every minute. Since it seemed that I would not be able to orchestrate the sting that would get all these people out of Ralph's life for once and for all, I decided to focus on getting Ralph out of there. With this in mind, I called the ranch, but there was no answer. Then I tried Ralph's cell.

Karla answered. She must have been standing right in the

middle of a crowd of people, because it was exceedingly noisy, mostly with the voices of men. I could hear the excitement in the air. When she realized it was me, she started laughing. "¿Qué quieres, perra?" she screamed into the phone. *What do you want, bitch?* I told her I needed to speak to my husband and she said he wasn't there. I tried to be more convincing, but she only laughed at me and then hung up. I immediately dialed the house number, but again, no one answered. Probably the ringing wasn't even audible over all the racket. I waited a few minutes and then I called the cell number again. This time she didn't even talk. She simply put the phone down on a surface somewhere and let me listen to the voices. There was a lot of laughter. I could hear Ralph saying that he was going to have to up his bet by another $750. Jokingly, he asked someone if he could put it on his credit card. Then the phone went dead; Karla had decided I'd heard enough.

I called Richard and Tony again. Still no answer. Exasperated, I called the Child Abuse Hotline. After all, there was a child there — Karla's. I left a message begging someone to go to the address and check things out. Illegal gambling was going on, I said. Did anyone understand what that meant? There could be drugs, guns, drunks.... No one got back to me.

Minutes turned into hours and somehow the hours passed. My feeling of doom was so great that I even considered driving out to the ranch myself, but each time I tried to envision trying to convince a most certainly drunk Ralph to leave with me, I got stuck on the reactions that Karla and Chava and Ken W were likely to have. They had turned the ranch, the ranch that Ralph and I had built and were supposed to live in for the rest of our lives, into a version of Sodom and Gomorrah. In their minds, I was the bad wife, always calling her husband home to a life that did not include such outrageous activities. They would be drunk. They would not treat me kindly.

With no other option, I called Ralph's cell again. Again, Karla answered and laughed when she heard my voice. She must have been holding her baby. She put the phone near the baby's mouth so that I could hear him gurgling. Then she laughed again. Ralph wasn't there, she said, and she hung up. I tried the house phone. Nothing. I took some Tylenols and tried to rest. About nine that night I tried the house phone and the cell phone one more time. Karla picked up the cell and let me listen to the party for a moment. I could hear clearly that everyone was very drunk. There was a lot of noise, a lot of shouting and slurring. Once again I asked to speak to Ralph. In an agitated tone that confirmed that she was at the end of her patience with me, Karla replied that Ralph was not available. But then she added that I should talk to Chava if I wanted to talk to someone, and before I could respond, she called to him and I heard him ask who it was. "Es Yolanda," she said.

I did not want to talk to Chava. He was the last person in the world I wanted to talk to. My stomach was doing flips. My intuition radar was all over the place. "Todos estamos pasando un buen tiempo," she said as she waited for Chava to come to the phone. *We're all having such a great time.* Then Chava was on the phone, his voice so loud that he drowned out all the noise of the drunks surrounding him. "You fucking whore," he said. "You know what you need? You need a hole in your head."

Trembling, I hung up. I was right to believe that I would have been harmed if I had gone over. That was clear to me now. I had heard in Chava's voice that they would have torn me limb from limb.

I sat on the edge of my bed and opened my Bible randomly. The psalm I found on the page before me was Psalm 35, King David crying out to the Lord that his persecution had gone on too long: *Contend, O Lord, with those who contend with me…* and later: *May all who gloat over my distress be put to shame and confusion; may all who exalt themselves over me be clothed with shame and disgrace.*

Later I turned to Psalm 25: *To you, O Lord, I lift up my soul; in you I trust, O my God. Do not let me be put to shame, nor let my enemies triumph over me. No one whose hope is in you will ever be put to shame, but they will be put to shame who are treacherous without excuse.*

I read these words over and over again, until the repetition eased my mind and I thought I could finally sleep.

I have said that there were some things about Ralph that were entirely predictable. Just as I had known that he would not disappoint his daughters, and that he would fly rather than drive back from Houston, I knew he would call me in the morning. If he was still angry, he would call to boast about how much money he had won. If he had come to his senses, he would call to say how sorry he was. So when he didn't call, I knew that something was very wrong.

I called the house once again, and there was no answer. Then I called the restaurant that his brother owned, thinking that his brother would have catered the food the day before. He was not there; the waiter who answered the phone said that he would not be in at all that day, because there had been some kind of an accident the previous night. I hung up the phone and tried to keep my heartbeat even. In my mind's eye I saw excited horses trampling someone. I could hardly breathe for fear that it was Ralph. I called Ralph's sister-in-law, Alicia; I knew she would not have been at the event, but surely she would know if something had happened to Ralph.

What she told me was worse than anything I could have imagined.

They'd had the race and Chava's horse had won. There was a lot of drinking and celebrating, and that was still in the late morning. Then everyone drove to Chava's place and got into a school bus that he owned and drove down to another illegal horse race in the town of Belen. More drinking and celebrating ensued. So by time they all got back to the ranch, people were on the downside of a party that had gone on far too long.

Right after I called the house the last time and spoke to Chava (or, to be accurate, listened to Chava curse at me), Ralph came in from outside and Chava said to him, "Why the fuck did you go ahead and remarry her?" And Ralph, who loved his friends and drinking buddies and never wanted to have any confrontations with them, who had so many times let his friends get away with saying mean things about me rather than defending me, decided on this occasion to become my advocate. "She's my wife," he'd said. "I don't tell you about your wife, so don't tell me about mine." And one of them threw a punch and the fighting began.

The onlookers broke it up quickly and ordered Ralph and Chava to go outside and get some air, but they only started up again outdoors. No one could break them up after that, probably because all the others were as drunk as they were.

Karla, who had already proven that she knew how to call the police by calling them once on me, opted this time to call Chava's brother Henry instead. Henry was the white sheep of the family, the one who didn't drink or gamble or get involved in things over his head. The fight was still going on when Henry arrived on the scene moments later.

Although they were very different, Henry loved Ralph like a father. Chava did too for that matter. And Ralph loved them both as if they were his own sons. And given their love for one another, it makes all that happened seem even more tragic. Henry got out of his car and yelled, "The party's over, everyone's going home," and the fighting desisted at once. But Chava was still full of drunken anger when he got into his truck. His horses, the one he'd come with and the one he'd won from Ken W, were already in the horse trailer and the trailer was hitched to his pickup. In front of the spectators — everyone had come out of the house by then and they were grouped together at the edge of the driveway — Chava roared into gear and made an insanely fast U-turn to get himself headed out of the driveway. As he straightened out of the turn, he hit Ralph, who had been at the front of the watching crowd, pinching him, momentarily, between the truck and the trailer.

Ralph was in the hospital with a crushed pelvis, Alicia said. Karla and other witnesses told the police that Chava had aimed for him, that he'd done it on purpose. That was all she would tell me. I could tell she knew more, both about Ralph's condition and his whereabouts, but she denied it. Once she had outlined the details, she acted like the rest was a big secret. Maybe someone had come into the room, someone who was hoping I would stay out of the picture. When we hung up, I started calling local hospitals, and eventually I learned that he was at UNM, the university hospital.

The nurse I finally got on the phone told me that he'd been awake for a short while when he'd first come in and then he'd had surgery and he hadn't woken up since. His condition was quite serious. He'd lost a lot of blood, and even as they were pumping him full of new blood, he was still losing more.

I lived on the phone for the next two days. If I was not talking to the nurses, I was talking to Ralph's sisters, begging them for more information. The nurses confirmed that there were a lot of people there in the waiting rooms, and as I knew these people were all my enemies, all people who did not consider my re-marriage to Ralph to be legitimate, including Karla and her brother-in-law and other drug-dealing relatives, I could not bring myself to go down. Ralph's sisters confirmed that I was wise to stay away. Besides, no one was being allowed into the room with Ralph yet.

And of course I called Richard and Tony. "Where the hell were you, you son of a bitch?" I screamed at each of them. "Who got to you? Who paid you not to show up? To ignore me after all your promises?" Their excuses were too inane for me to even listen to. I called the newspaper too and learned that a reporter had, in fact, gone out to the ranch, but since none of the promised authorities showed up, he wasn't able to go in and he left without a story.

According to one of Ralph's sisters, the police were looking for Chava. He'd gone back to his house with the horse trailer after hitting Ralph, and his son helped him to get the horses out and clean up the blood. Then Chava got into his car and left. The rumor was that he'd picked up Karla's sister, who, apparently, he'd been seeing behind his wife's back for some time, before leaving town. He had a cabin somewhere in the mountains. No one seemed to know where exactly, but everyone was pretty sure that was where he'd gone.

While Karla's sister was busy hiding away with Chava in the mountains, Karla, so one of the nurses informed me, was wringing her hands in the waiting room, asking anyone who would listen what would happen to her if something happened to Ralph? Where would she live? How would she get money for herself and the baby?

Five or six days passed and Ralph did not come out of his coma. Sr. Josephine got special permission to leave the convent, and she and Mother Superior traveled together to pray at Ralph's side. She reported to me that while he never awoke during their visit, he did squeeze her hand when she spoke to him, and I hoped with all my heart that this was a sign that he would recover and not a manifestation of her great desire for his recovery.

When I was not on the phone, I was on my knees praying. I prayed at home and at church and at the gym. I had it in my mind that when Ralph was released, he would be in a wheelchair for a long time, and I promised myself that I would be ready to take care of him for as long as it took, even if he were paralyzed. That was what our vows were all about, after all. And so I lifted weights until I was on the verge of collapse, until every cell in my body was oozing sweat. I ran on the treadmill, more feverishly than I had ever run before, and I imagined that my strength was his strength, that if I ran hard enough, fast enough, long enough, some of my vigor would find its way from my body into his, even as he lay motionless in a bed at the university hospital on the other side of town. I focused on the treadmill's timer, on the minutes clicking by, minutes turning into hours, hours into days. When he awoke, I knew, he would ask for me. And then I would go to him, even if it meant that I would be ripped apart by his brothers and nephews and Karla and her relatives. I would go to my husband the minute he called.

I prayed at San Felipe Church too. I couldn't bring myself to ask that God's will be done, because I didn't know what His will was and I didn't want to take the chance that it was not the same as mine. So I prayed — pleaded — instead simply for Ralph to heal. Wherever I went, I prayed. I prayed even when I didn't realize I was praying. One night I got out of the bathtub and collapsed on the floor, naked. I stayed there for a long time, sobbing, and even then I realized I was simultaneously lost in prayer.

The nurses told me he had ten percent chance of recovering, and that was good enough for me. Ralph and I had bet against horses with worse odds and they had come in to win or place or show. "Yolie," he would have said, "we can do it. Together we can do anything."

There was a political event going on that week, and I decided that I was going to go to it, because that's what Ralph and I would have done if things had been right in our world. Ralph loved politics as much as I did. I called Mother and asked her to accompany me. She was only to glad to drive up. She had been worried sick about me and wanted to be with me. The event, a congressional debate between Philip Maloof and Heather Wilson for the first district, was at the Hyatt Regency. No sooner had we walked in than Jennifer Romer, a woman who knew Ralph's family, came rushing up to me. "I just heard from Ralph's daughter-in-law Denise that they're taking him off life supports," she said. "They're having Judge Brennan take care of the paperwork."

I realized then I think that all the resolve in the world was not going to bring Ralph back to me. I broke down crying on the spot. Judge Brennan had married us, the first time at least. Now he would be helping to end Ralph's life. "No, no," my mother cried as she held me to her. "He's not going to die. We'll pray. We'll pray and he'll be okay." Later I called Ernesto Gomez, my friend at work, and he said the same thing. But I knew this time that no amount of praying would change the outcome. A few days before, I had hired a woman to help me clean up my apartment, because I couldn't stand the disorder it had fallen into, but yet I couldn't seem to organize myself well enough to do anything about it. As it happened, she had a daughter who worked at the hospital, right on the floor where Ralph lay dying, and so I had yet one more source for information. The cleaner's daughter confirmed that there had been talk of removing the life support.

Now when I prayed, I prayed that God would let know when he passed on. That was the most I could hope for. That night I took a sleeping pill because I was in dire need of a decent night's rest. Ralph had been in a comma for 13 days by then.

In spite of the pill I woke up a few hours after going to bed. I looked at the digital clock. It was 12:12. Strangely, I heard a bird cooing, and my first thought was that I must be dreaming because birds don't coo in the middle of the night, and moreover, even if one did, I would never hear it as I lived in a brick building and all the windows were closed and the cooling system was running. I never heard anything going on outside. Nevertheless the bird was cooing, emphatically, and I was not dreaming. Beyond the cooing I could sense Ralph saying, "Yolie, ya mi voy." *Yolie, I am leaving*. I held my breath and cherished the moment for what I knew it signified. I held myself so still that when I said "Adios, mi amor," the words barely moved my lips. Then the clock changed to 12:13.

I woke up Mother, who had insisted on staying with me. "Ralph's dead," I said. "No, no, you're wrong," she cried. But I told her about the bird and she was quickly convinced. When the housekeeper called at six in the morning, I saved her the trouble of breaking the bad news. "I know," I said. "He's gone."

"How could you know?" she exclaimed.

"God let me know," I answered. She told me he had died at 11:35 p.m. which was very interesting to me, because I had driven past the hospital many times over the last several days, and I knew for a fact that the drive took between 30 and 40 minutes, depending on traffic.

Do souls travel at the average speed of a car? Or does it simply take a half hour for the soul to fully separate itself from the body? I can't answer those questions, but I know what I know in my heart — that Ralph came to say goodbye to me 12 minutes after midnight.

Later in the day I spoke to Sr. Josephine and she confirmed the time of death. She had been there with him, along with his son Mark. She said that Ralph, who had weighed about 190 before the accident, looked to be over 300 pounds by the time he died because he was bloated with gases his body wasn't able to release and he was swollen from all his injuries. Septic body, it was called; his kidney and liver had ceased to function and his pelvic area was crushed into a million pieces. And still Mark had not been able to bring himself to agree to the removal of life support. Sister Josephine pleaded with him. She held onto Mark as Mark held onto his father. She said liquids from Ralph's body were oozing from his eyes, his ears, and from every wound, right through his bandages. She looked down and saw that Ralph's fluids were splattering onto Mark's boots. Finally Mark let go of his father, and just at that moment, the heart monitor lit up, and Ralph's spirit seemed to separate from his body.

There was a song that Ralph wanted sung at his funeral, "Cruz de Cemento" by Los Huracanes Del Norte. It went something like: *"When I die, dress my horse in black and dance him right to my grave. Have all my friends raise a shot glass in my name."*

That was typical Ralph, and if I had been there, I would have had a horse dressed in black to follow his casket right to his grave and dance there while Los Huracanes sang their song. But I wasn't there when he died, and I didn't go to the funeral either. I would not have been welcomed by anyone. Karla and her cronies were still around, awaiting their next move. And my conversations with Ralph's sisters had been getting increasingly more awkward, so I was quite sure that the family in general, or at least those who had accepted me at one time, had turned against me now. I took comfort in the fact that Ralph and I had had our own private moment the night of his death.

While it wasn't handled exactly the way Ralph would have wanted it, Sister Josephine did report that an effort was made to bury Ralph properly. He had about 60 employees at the time, and Sister Josephine said they arrived in spanking clean trucks which they lined up outside the cemetery gates. When the funeral procession began, they beeped their horns. Ralph would have liked that. When it was over, when the trucks were gone and all the visitors had retreated, I went to the gravesite to say a final farewell. While I sobbed over his freshly dug grave, I could not help but think of how we had laughed over how much like Liz and Richard we were. Liz too had gone to her husband's gravesite alone, after all his family had gone.

As soon as the funeral was over, I called Mickey Barnett and told him that I wanted to file a wrongful death lawsuit. Before we could even really sit down to discuss it, I learned that Ralph's kids had found their own lawyer and were planning to have my marriage to their father annulled. The cheerleader behind their decision was none other than Ken W, their father's lawyer and so-called friend.

This was one thing I would not stand for. Ralph and I had decided to remarry because we had no choice, because, in spite of his behavior and my mistakes, we loved each other and we wanted to make a commitment to sharing our lives together. If he hadn't died, eventually we would have figured out a way for him to shake himself free of Karla and I would have moved back in with him and we would have begun the task of putting the past behind us. I had already been denied the opportunity to be with my husband on his deathbed and even to attend his funeral. There was no way anyone was going to deny our marriage. After all, Ralph had died defending our marriage.

Knowing what we would be up against, Mickey Barnett brought on Paul Kennedy, another lawyer whom he trusted, to work with us. And as we would be fighting in both Albuquerque and Las Vegas, the latter being where Ralph and I had married the second time, Mickey and Paul engaged Ed Kainen, yet another attorney, to represent me in Nevada.

After everything that had happened, I was full of venom. Going to battle, with Mickey and Paul and Ed at my side, would give me a channel for some of it. Otherwise I don't know what would have become of me during those months following Ralph's death.

My only other solace was the memory of the day that Ralph had come into my office to tell me that he had accepted Jesus as his personal savior. Had I not been adamant that Ralph do this before we married, neither Ralph's soul nor my heart would have found any peace. And peace was the best I could hope for for now.

Chapter Twelve

The Path to Peace

Oscar had negotiated yet another contract; this time he had landed a position as a pitching coach for a New York Yankees minor team, and he and his family would be making their ball season home in Tampa, Florida. He had met with Don Zimmer and George Steinbrenner. Steinbrenner had said to him, "Either you improve the staff at Triple A or your butt is gone." Oscar liked that kind of straight talk. It was a philosophy he understood. As for Zimmer, Oscar didn't describe the conversation, but it must have gone well because he did say that Zimmer was his baseball hero.

In the months before he left for Tampa, while he was still in Elida and Portales working cattle (and only a few months after Ralph's death), an incident happened out on someone's ranch that introduced me to a new level of apprehension. Oscar had committed to caring for some 500 head of cattle, and as long as Ryan didn't have school, he took him along each morning to teach him the ropes. One January morning when they were out near a canyon bringing feed to the cattle by truck, Oscar's legs suddenly buckled and he fell to his knees in incredible pain. The pain was radiating, so he didn't know where it began, but it seemed to him that it might have been his chest. He thought he was having a heart attack.

Ryan, who was ten at the time, thought his father was having a heart attack too. "Let's go," he cried when he saw his father on the ground. But Oscar grit his teeth against the pain and got to his feet and told Ryan that the cattle had to eat, that it was their job to feed them, and there was no way they were going to leave until the job was done. And moreover, there was a blizzard expected within hours, and they would have to make sure the cattle all got out of the canyon before that or they'd get trapped and some would die. Since Oscar was in too much pain to drive, he had Ryan, who hadn't driven anything since the kiddy car that looked like a baseball cap in Oklahoma, get up in the driver's seat while he sat in the passenger seat and shouted instructions and shifted the gears. At each stop he put the truck in neutral so that Ryan could get out with the feed. In this way, Oscar and a very frightened Ryan made their way around the whole field and got the job done.

Somehow Oscar managed to drive to the hospital in Portales. The attending nurses could see that he was in pain right away, but he told them all to get away, that no one was to touch him except Dr Dixon, who was Mother's doctor. Even Carol, who worked at the hospital at that time, was sent away. "You people will kill me," he told her. "Just get me Dr Dixon." Dr Dixon was found, but after examining Oscar, he admitted that he didn't know what was wrong either. It wasn't his heart; he was certain of that. He made arrangements for Oscar to see another doctor, at the hospital in Lubbock. That was where Oscar learned that he had a slipped disk. Oscar had been born with curvature of the spine, and he thought that might have led the way for the disk slippage.

The apple doesn't fall far from the tree, and just as Mother never wanted Oscar to know when she was suffering, Oscar didn't want her, or any of us for that matter, knowing that he was preparing to have surgery in Dallas. He was in Portales with his family the weekend before he went, and he called Mother to ask if he could borrow the Cadillac that Carol had recently bought her, for a trip he wanted to make. Mother assumed it was a business trip. Actually he wanted the Caddy because even though it was older than his own car, it rode like a dream and he couldn't endure any bouncing with the pain he was in. Without even telling Kathy where he was off to, he drove himself to

Dallas and admitted himself into the hospital and had his surgery. When it was over and he was deemed as healthy as a horse, he called us, one by one beginning with Mother, to let us know the truth. When he got to me I cried, "Oscar, why would you keep this from us? If we had known, we would have been right by your side." But when we hung up I pictured that, Mother and me and Carol and Kathy, all crying and praying over him, and I figured he just didn't want that much feminine drama permeating the ordeal.

Oscar whipped back into shape in no time, and before we knew it, the season had started and he was in Florida coaching. His work was as exciting for us as it was for him. Oscar was not one to talk much about it on the phone, but we read the accounts of his activities in the papers. We learned about Hideki Irabu, for instance, a player who had signed with the Yankees majors but would be breaking in with Oscar in Tampa.

Irabu had an interesting story, and the part that Oscar played in it exemplifies who Oscar was as a coach, as well as who he was as a person. Hideki Irabu was a top player in Japan before coming to the U.S. to play ball. He started with a contract to play with the Padres, but he insisted that he wouldn't play with anyone but the Yankees. The news reached Steinbrenner's ears, and sight unseen (unless you count TV), Steinbrenner offered him a $12 million four-year contract, the most lucrative rookie contract in history up to that time. (Steinbrenner also had to pay the Padres with Rafael Medina, Ruben Rivera, and $3 million in cash.)

All of New York City welcomed Irabu with open arms. As if he were an astronaut returning from the moon, there was a parade for him in Manhattan. And Rudy Giuliani, who was mayor then, presented him with a Tiffany crystal apple as a token of the Big Apple's love and admiration. In spite of all this recognition though, Irabu turned out not to be the person everyone hoped he would be. First of all, he drank a lot. Secondly, he was rude, especially to reporters. And moreover, his pitching skills seemed to be getting worse instead of better. By the end of the first season, everyone had taken a turn trying to talk to him, including managers Brian Cashman and Joe Torre. Yet neither his personality nor his pitching improved.

Irabu didn't speak English, and on one particular day during spring training, some reporters came at him with cameras and he wasn't in the mood to talk and he had his interpreter confirm that. But one of the reporters thought he could sneak in a picture at least, and when he lifted his camera, Irabu grabbed it and threw it on the ground and stomped on it for good measure. The managers tried to talk to him about the incident, but Oscar felt that they were tiptoeing around him, afraid, because of his temper, that confrontation would only make things worse.

One day Oscar just couldn't take it anymore. Irabu had completed a fielding drill for pitchers in a slothful manner. And Oscar, who had conducted the drill, called over both Irabu and his interpreter. In front of a dozen other pitchers, Oscar berated him, saying his behavior was embarrassing the organization and that he was overweight and overrated and weak in the belly and he had better get into shape. (Later, when Brian Cashman learned about the incident, his only comment was, "If Oscar did it, I agree.")

After that, Irabu began to make an effort, and Oscar acknowledged it and began working with him. In fact, in his first exhibition outing after the event, Irabu had his best performance to date with the Yankees, dominating the Atlanta Braves at Kissimmee during a 14-2 Yankee victory. Eventually Irabu lost weight and got into shape, well on his way, thanks to Oscar, to a turnaround with the majors that history would prove to be nothing less than amazing.

Oscar was relentless, especially with the talented players who just needed to be harder on themselves in order to play to the best of their ability. He didn't care if they were major leaguers with big contracts or minor leaguers with their futures up in the air. His job was to get them ready to play ball. Orlando Hernandez was a good pitcher but his fielding skills were less than perfect. Oscar got him out on the field and started fielding balls to him one after the other, in quick succession, until Fernandez was on the verge of exhaustion…until he "got it."

Oscar firmly believed in the team; the team stuck together; he wanted everyone to be a well-rounded player. "No man is an island," he liked to say. One reporter told the story of how Oscar reacted when his pitchers had lost a game because their fielding was so poor. At the next day's practice, the reporter said, Oscar first went around asking everyone if they had had a good breakfast and if they were feeling okay. Once he had ascertained that everyone was in tiptop shape and that there couldn't be any excuses for a poor performance, he marched them all out and lined them up and stared batting balls at them. This was a story we had heard before.

We may not have been perfect, but this fighting spirit, this ability to be fearless when it counted, was something that ran in our family. We had all been tested in different ways, and we had all proved to have backbone. While Oscar was out there hammering his players, I remained busy with my lawyers, working to ensure that the sanctity of my marriage would not be obliterated. My challengers, Ralph's kids (with the exception of Mark, his oldest son, and of course Karla's baby), got feistier and feistier by the day. Not only were they determined to prove that I was not Ralph's wife, but they insisted that there was inadequate proof that Ralph was the father of Karla's baby. They wanted us both out of the picture for the simple reason that legally all his children and I were equal partners in his inheritance. Ralph's children and their attorneys forced Karla to have a paternity test. The test came back 99.9 percent positive. Sometime after the testing, I heard that the foolish girl thought it was me who had requested it.

The Bible says, "My people will perish for lack of knowledge."

That wasn't about to happen to me. If I was going to perish, it wasn't going to be because I hadn't done my homework. I read up on the judges who would be overseeing my cases in both New Mexico and Nevada. I read everything I could about the attorneys for the other side.

Final result: we kicked their asses in court in Albuquerque and then we were on our way to Las Vegas for part two, which would be the harder round.

There are not that many flights from Albuquerque to Las Vegas, and sure enough, we were all on the same flight on Southwest Airlines that day — Ralph's kids, along with Ken W and some others. It was disconcerting, especially as my attorneys were already in Las Vegas and, with the exception of Robert, who, in his mind, had become my protector over the months since Ralph's death, I was all alone. I kept my backbone and my beliefs, because what else did I have?

That night in my hotel room I awoke at four in the morning, and since it was clear that I wasn't going to get back to sleep any time soon, I got out my Bible and started praying. But I was soon distracted by the wind, which had been nonexistent moments ago and now was blowing incredibly hard. The feeling of standing on the cliffs in the wind, with my arms stretched out and Ralph at my side, the sound of our combined laughter blowing back on us, came back to me in a flash, and I had such a strong feeling that Ralph was there with me, and that everything was going to be okay. When the sun came up I called housekeeping to see about getting an iron. Before I let the attendant go, I asked her about the windstorm during the night. She said, "We get them from time to time, but that one wasn't expected. That one came up out of nowhere." "Yes, it did," I agreed.

Before I left for court, I read from the Book of Isaiah: "In righteousness you shall be established; you shall be far from oppression, for you shall not fear; and from terror, for it shall not come near you.

"No weapon that is formed against you will prosper; And every tongue that accuses you in judgment you will condemn. This is the heritage of the servants of the Lord, And their vindication is from Me."

The court scene that day was very hard to digest. One after the other, Ralph's kids got up and portrayed their father in the worst possible light; so as to explain how he had come to remarry me, they made him out to be a lunatic. Ralph had some problems, I can vouch for that, but he was not crazy. Even the infamous Ken W, who had helped to arrange the illegal event that resulted in Ralph's death, portrayed his dear friend as a crazy, drunken nut. But when asked under oath if Ralph loved me, Ken W broke down and began to cry. "Yes," he said, and he hung his head all the way down to his chest.

When it was my turn, I got on the stand and told everyone in the courtroom the truth about Ralph. "Ralph was a proud man," I said. I told them I couldn't believe that his loved ones would drag his name through the mud for the sake of putting a little bit more money into their pockets when all was said and done. I said a lot of other things too, including what everyone there knew in their hearts: that Ralph and I loved each other; that he was going through a period of confusion and withering confidence; and that, yes, he made some mistakes, but he had never stopped loving me and I had never stopped loving him.

When I returned to Albuquerque, I went directly to the home of Augustine, the oldest of Ralph's brothers and the only family member who had stood by my side throughout. He was a man of character and I had come to love him like a father. I found him sitting in his favorite chair, wearing the same huge sunglasses he always wore indoors, to ward off the pain in his eyes that resulted from his diabetes and other health problems. I knelt down beside him and rested my head on his knees and cried my heart out, releasing all the emotion that I had had to hold back in the courtroom in order to be able to remember all that I needed to say to the judge. Augustine ran his hand over my head while I told him all of the awful things Ralph's kids had said about their father. "Little coyotes," he whispered. "I'm glad my brother is not here to know this."

I was at work when the calls came, first from Paul Kennedy and then from Ed Kainen. The court had ruled in my favor; my marriage to Ralph would not be annulled. I broke down and cried so hard that my supervisor came over and held me for a while before she sent me home.

Ralph's gravesite is just a couple of blocks from my job. I stopped there on my way home and knelt on the ground. The site was marked by a black marble headstone featuring a picture of Ralph. Behind the headstone was a tree. "Even in death, they can't separate us," I told Ralph.

Later I called Mark, Ralph's oldest son, and told him about the ruling, and he congratulated me. "My father loved you," Mark said. "It might have made everyone angry, but that's a fact; he did love you."

When my portion of Ralph's inheritance arrived, I went immediately to meet with the administrators of UNM Hospital, where Ralph had died. I wanted to work with them to refurbish the reception room in the trauma area and also the Chapel. I wanted the new altar to include a carving of a dove in memory of Ralph S. Villegas. This was my way of thanking the hospital for doing their best to save my husband, and also ensuring that other people who were waiting to find out the condition of loved ones would be able to do it in a beautiful environment. But it was also my way of asserting my presence into places where I would have spent my every moment while Ralph lay dying, had I not been spurned. The hospital was only too glad to have the donation.

It would take about a year to complete the remodeling project. In addition to fresh paint and new carpeting and a new altar and other basics, I presented the hospital with a replica of the San Damiano Cross of St Francis. The story goes that St Francis was out walking alone in the countryside one day not long after his conversion when he came across a rundown church known as San Damiano. He went in to pray, and while he was staring at the crucifix within, he thought he saw the lips of Jesus move and he heard the words, "Francis, go repair my house, which is falling to ruin." And so he did.

In addition to the cross, I also presented the hospital with two beautiful glass goblets for the chapel, one with the initial V and the other A. The V was for vino and the A was for agua, but it could have just as easily been for Villegas and Acosta.

While I was busy ensuring that my marriage would not be annulled, prosecutors for the state were preparing to put Chava, who had long since returned from the mountains, away for a good long time for killing Ralph. Their prosecution was based on the witnesses who had been there at the ranch the evening Ralph was injured. Now that I had won my case and could turn my attention to other matters, I sought out the sergeant who had been at the hospital when Ralph first came in, one of the last people to be with Ralph before he went into a coma. "Did he say anything about Chava?" I asked him. The officer said that Ralph was unable to talk and he seemed not to be able to hear. So the officer wrote on a lined yellow pad, "Do you want to prosecute?" And Ralph shook his head no. The lawyers already knew this, and they didn't think it was enough to get Chava off the hook. For all that Chava had done everything he could over a period of many years to make Ralph see me through his eyes, I knew in my heart that he loved Ralph and would never have hurt him on purpose.

I moved out of New Mexico about this time. It seemed that everywhere I went, I was reminded of Ralph, and I felt as if I would wither and drift away, like dandelion fluff, if I didn't save myself. So I went to Nevada, which I had become familiar with during my court case, and I got a job working in a dress shop in the mall. I worked two shifts, from the time they opened until they closed at night. I thought all this time spent in a place where I knew no one would keep me from thinking, but of course I was thinking all the time. Then 9/11 happened, and I was overcome with the need to be near my family, so I returned to Albuquerque. And one of the first things I did was call Billy Marchiondo, Chava's attorney. "How can I help Chava?" I asked.

Billy said, "You can go talk to his kids."

I laughed. "They won't talk to me," I responded.

Pete Ross was the prosecuting attorney on the case. I had met him before, after Ralph's death. He was wheelchair bound. At the time of our first meeting he had asked me who Ralph was working with dealing drugs. I answered that he was mistaken, that Ralph had never been involved in drugs. "Ralph was like Mr Gotti," he said. "They keep these things away from the family."

After talking to Billy I went to meet with Pete again. It became clear back during our first conversation that he was a pit bull of a man, and the neck he wanted most to bite into was Chava's. I joked with him during the meeting. I called him "Old Ironsides." I figured a man that tough could take that kind of joking, and he could. Nevertheless, he was upset to hear that I had changed my position regarding Chava. I shrugged. Justice is indifferent. She doesn't care about who's a nice person and who's not. Justice only cares about the truth. And the truth was, Ralph didn't think Chava had done it on purpose, so why should anyone else?

Of course when Chava learned that I had decided to take his side, he wasn't happy. But Billy told him point blank, "Chava, you have no friends here. Yolanda is the only one willing to go to bat for you." When the big day came, Billy put me on the stand and I took my oath. Then I straightened my back and looked out at all the faces of Ralph's friends and family and proceeded to tell them how much Ralph had loved Chava and his brother Henry, how much they had loved him. I told them too all about the day of the race, how I had called the authorities and the authorities had failed to take me seriously. I told everyone in the courtroom how I had prayed all during the time that Ralph lay in bed dying — 13 days; 312 hours, 18,720 minutes, 1,123,300 seconds.... I had nothing to gain by standing up for Chava, I said. Everything was lost to me, so for my part it didn't matter. But the man I loved had loved the accused, and acknowledging his innocence was just about his last act. And that had to be taken into account.

When I was dismissed from the stand, I walked straight out of the courtroom and closed the door behind me without looking back. Then I waited in the hall to hear the news.

Chava got probation.

He hesitated before me as he was leaving the courtroom and I gave him a quick awkward hug. "It's going to be okay," I whispered. But his family was on his heels, and before I could say more, they whisked him away.

I joined Pete Ross in the elevator. I could see that he was furious, but I laughed and said, "Come on, Ironsides, it's time to go home." The doors to the elevator hadn't closed yet, and just before they did I saw that Chava and his family had assembled in the elevator directly opposite ours. Everyone was hugging him and I saw him choke up and heard him say, "I've got my family back," before the doors slid closed. Yes, he had his family back, minus his beloved Uncle Ralph.

Later that day I went to Ralph's grave. The site was always a bit of a surprise to me. Ralph, the cement entrepreneur, had liked to joke that his grave would have a cement cross bearing the words, Guaranteed To Get Hard. Instead, it had the picture of Ralph in a suit that I had bought him when he had decided to serve on the board of the Hispano Chamber of Commerce. I'd bought him a white shirt to go with it, with his initials embroidered on the sleeve cuffs. The day he'd worn it, I'd shined his shoes for him. I remember looking at him and giving him a thumbs up and saying, "Go and look like the Chairman of the Board." "Chairman of the Board" was a nickname that Frank

Sinatra acquired after founding Reprise Records in 1961. Ralph and I had loved Sinatra's music. "I Did It My Way" had always been one of our favorites; it seemed to define us as individuals as well as as a couple.

Suddenly I found myself drunk on memories of all the good years. I told Ralph that everything was going to be all right in his family, that Chava was going to be all right. And I realized then that I was going to be all right too. I saw in my mind's eye that living with anger and bitterness would have destroyed me ultimately. In the one act of forgiving Chava, I had thrown off my own self-imposed manacles.

I began to spend more time with Robert. I had been through a lot and it was good not to be alone. And he had been so good to me, throughout all the trials. He had been kind and supportive. It still upset me that no one in Ralph's family, with the exception of Augustine, seemed to want to have anything to do with me, but even that changed as time passed. One day one of Ralph's sisters called me to say that her husband was dying of cancer and that the only thing he wanted before he died was to see their son, David, one more time. But David was in prison in Hobbs. "You know how to get things done," she said. "Please try to bring our boy home before my husband dies." I told her I would try, but in my mind I knew in fact that I would try until I succeeded, because I never wanted anyone to go through what I had, not being able to see my loved one on his deathbed.

I called the warden at Hobbs. When he told me that it could not be arranged in the short time we believed we had until David's father died, I called the then-governor, Governor Johnson. He said that the only way it could be done was if the dying man was actually in hospice. I explained that David's father was in hospice at home, where his wife could be with him. A day or so later I received a call from the warden. They had relented; the prisoner could be brought home to say goodbye even though his father was not officially in hospice — as long as someone could pay for the guards he would need and the car that would bring him from Hobbs to Albuquerque, and other miscellaneous expenses. I said, "How much and where do I send it?" The warden seemed surprised that the $600 he needed for David's transportation hadn't deterred me. "You are really serious about this," he marveled. When we hung up I called Western Union and wired the money.

The next day David spent five hours in chains, in a car with two guards, en route to his father's deathbed. But the strange (and wonderful) thing was that David's father didn't die, at least not then. Seeing his son's face, which he never thought to see again, completely rejuvenated him and brought him the kind of hope he needed to last another six months. And his wife, Ralph's sister, thought that maybe seeing me had helped too, because he got the idea in his head that I might be able to get clemency for his son. That was beyond my range, but his family let him think it, and he got out of bed the next week and went on living with some hope.

Not long after I got a call from another of Ralph's sisters. Her son was in jail because of a domestic violence incident with his wife. She swore he was a good boy and that the circumstances in this one incident had been unusual. I told her I would not help unless her daughter-in-law, the victim, said the exact same thing. So she gave me her number and I called and she confirmed her mother-in-law's words. "He's my husband," she said. "He's the father of my children. We can work it out." I made some calls and helped to get his sentence reduced.

Little by little, Ralph's family came around and began to see that I wasn't the terror that Chava had made me out to be so many years ago. Even Chava's mother, I heard through the grapevine, stood up at a family gathering and said to the others, "I don't want anyone to say anything bad about Yolanda ever again." And Ralph's sisters, who had all begun to call me, began to lament that they hadn't gotten to know me better when Ralph was alive. "We're sorry we turned our backs on you," they said. "Now we know why he loved you."

This metamorphosis was all important to me, for his family was all that was left of Ralph, and no matter how much time passed — in fact, it had been almost three years by then — I could not seem to stop longing for him. In the meantime, Robert was still there. And after everything that had happened, he still wanted to marry me. One day I went to Augustine, and I asked him for advice.

I had been visiting Augustine regularly to talk about the dialysis he needed to stay alive. He had given up on life at one point, but those of us who loved him encouraged him to hang on and accept treatment. When he saw me at his knee, he assumed that I had come to talk again about his health. But I surprised him by telling him about Robert.

I said that if he did not feel inclined to give me his full blessing, I would tell Robert no. But he said I should marry Robert, that he seemed to want to protect me, that it would be good for me to have someone to look after me. Not long after, Robert and I got in the car and drove to Laughlin, Nevada and had the small ceremony that we had almost had years earlier.

I wish I could report that marriage to Robert did me a world of good, but that was not the case. I needed a friend, someone who could make me laugh and help me to forget the past. In return I was willing to offer the love and loyalty I knew myself to be capable of. But once we exchanged vows, Robert, who had followed me around like a puppy for so long, begging me to see how supportive he was willing to be, decided it was his time to release his pent-up anger. He took to saying bad things about Ralph. He called him a fat Mexican. Every chance he got he told me that he hated New Mexico and all the Mexican politicos who ran the state. He hated Speaker of the House Raymond Sanchez, and Senate pro tem Manny Aragon, both of whom were my friends.

In fact, he said bad things about Mexicans in general. He called us greasers. When he got angry over even the smallest hitch, he would say vile things, like, "You should have died along with that fat Mexican of yours."

And his house remained his god. If I put a glass down on a table, he would run and bring it to the sink before it soiled something. My mother and children and friends couldn't stand to visit for fear that they would put something in the wrong place and bring about his wrath. Even though I was sharing his home with him, as his wife, he still wouldn't let me cook in it. He brought home TV dinners frequently. Half the time I would say I wasn't hungry so as not to have to eat them. Then when we were out at a restaurant and I was able to order real food, he would throw my words back at me, saying, "I thought you didn't get hungry anymore."

He hated the Mexican music I enjoyed. "You live in the United States," he would growl. "You're not a Mexican." He couldn't stand it when I watched Christian programs on the TV. "Turn that shit off," he would demand.

Having never had children himself, Robert could not understand a parent's love. He thought it was a waste of money to buy gifts for my kids, or even wedding or shower gifts for friends and relatives. And he didn't understand buying Christmas gifts at all. In fact, he didn't get the concept of family. Robert's family never came to New Mexico from Tennessee to visit us. We didn't visit them either. For him, life was his home, his job and his stocks and bonds. He could spend hours and hours staring at stock indexes on the computer.

Once I told Robert a story from the Bible about a wealthy man who buried his gold and who for years would go daily to the hiding place to look at it. Over time people in the community began to take note of his routine, and sure enough, one day he went as usual to the secret place and found that his gold had been stolen. He was beside himself after that, utterly inconsolable. "Why do you cry about it?" his wife asked. "For all the blessings that the gold brought you and your loved ones, you could just as easily have had stones buried there."

I was back working for the Department of Labor by then, and my habit was to get up early, put on the coffee pot, take a shower, and then sit down and have a cup of coffee before getting dressed for work. One morning I came out of the shower to find that the coffee maker had gone crazy, spitting grains and liquid all over the stove and the white tile counter and backsplash. I immediately removed the towel from my head and began wiping everything up. Once I felt certain that the kitchen looked just as it had before the coffee pot had exploded, I threw the dirty towel in the washing machine. Since Robert wasn't due to get up for another hour, I figured I was safe. But unbeknownst to me, some of the coffee had leaked down into the stove, causing the electric pilot to click until it dried out a bit, and from the other end of the house, Robert, who should have been happily dreaming about floating-rate bonds and stock certificates, heard the clicking before it stopped.

He came into the kitchen and lifted the stove top and peered in...and saw the coffee and grinds that had slipped down there. He immediately went ballistic. His eyes turned as red as those of the devil himself. "You can't do anything right, can you?" he screamed. I rushed back into the bathroom and finished dressing, and with him still fuming in the kitchen, I ran out the front door and went to work. But that was it for me, the last straw. He knew from the start that I would never love him the way I had loved Ralph, and he swore that whatever I could give him would be enough. But he was wrong. It wasn't enough. And it was clear to me that I was only beginning to see the tip of the iceberg that his anger had become.

I stopped talking to him after that. I volunteered to work extra hours and stayed at the office as long as possible while I set about trying to figure out a plan to get out of the house. One day he told me that he was going to the casino and hang out by himself. And I said, fine, that suited me. But I got to thinking about what a mess my life had become, and I had a drink or two, and somehow my gaze settled on twin vases — peach-colored — that had belonged to his wife before she died. The house was full of trinkets that had belonged to Bonnie. I was not allowed to move them and I was not allowed to add to her collection of do-das with do-das of my own. I was not allowed to change anything in the house, not even move a teaspoon. On that day, just days after the episode with the coffee pot, I felt a strong impulse to do what I was not allowed. So I put down my drink and got up from the chair and crossed the room and took up the twin vases, one in each hand, and threw them on the floor.

When Robert came home he went crazy. He called my mother and then my kids and told them I was losing my mind. They all came to the house as quickly as they could travel there to see for themselves. It was the off season, so Oscar came too. I'm sure it was not a pretty sight: me tipsy, even hours later, wearing a smug smile, and shattered glass all over the floor. I think Robert's hope was that he would turn my family against me, that if I didn't have them, I would have no one to run to and I would love him by default. But my family only wanted to help me to leave without getting hurt. I said to Robert, "You can never turn one of us on our own," and I left the house.

Our marriage ended shortly after. I put a restraining order on Robert so that I could return to the house long enough to get my clothes and personal items. But Robert, who was so afraid I would destroy yet another trinket, showed up during the time we had agreed on. So I did what I had to do: I called the police and had him arrested.

Chapter Thirteen

They Live the American Dream

During the three years that I was working to dignify my marriage to Ralph and then to ensure that Chava stayed out of jail and that others in Ralph's family who were in trouble got special privileges and minimum sentences, Oscar's life was changing in ways he could not have imagined.

It all began around Thanksgiving in 1998. I was in my apartment in Albuquerque one evening, still hurting badly some five months after Ralph's death, when I got a call from Oscar, an event that always cheered me up no matter how dark things were. "What are you doing, Sis?" he asked. I told him I wasn't doing much of anything and asked him what he was up to. In a flat tone that belied the excitement he must have been feeling, he responded, "Well, I just got a new job." "Where?" I asked, my pulse quickening. "Well, with the Chicago Cubs again, but this time with the majors." "Praise God!" I exclaimed. I was thrilled, elated. I nearly fell out of my chair. "Praise God! Praise Jesus!" I couldn't stop exclaiming. "Thank you," Oscar said, his emotion somewhat evident now. "Thank you so much for all your prayers over all the years, for all your support."

Mother was scheduled to visit me that weekend, and I couldn't wait for her to come walking through the door. As soon as we saw each other, we collapsed into each other's arms, crying with joy because Oscar's dream had finally come true. We were utterly giddy, unable to talk about anything else. For me, in the hard times I was living through, this answer to our prayers was proof that joy is always right around the corner. And I intended to focus on it. I called everyone that weekend. I called friends, relatives, all of the attorneys I was working with, and told them all, "Guess what! My brother is going to coach for the majors!" When I went to work on Monday, I told everyone in the Department of Labor. But it wasn't enough. I wanted to shout it from rooftops. So I called all the local newspapers and TV and radio stations. "My brother Oscar," I told them all, "is going to be the pitching coach for the Chicago Cubs."

And the local media was glad to hear the story. Several papers and stations mentioned it in the days to come. But I needn't have bothered to tell them. Oscar was going to be in the majors now, and that kind of news didn't require a big sister's sideline cheering to spread.

The story was everywhere in no time, told mostly by reporters for Chicago papers and then picked up by the newswire and repeated in local city papers all over the country. Outside of diehard sports fans in the cities where Oscar had played or coached for minor teams, no one had ever heard of Oscar Acosta before. Now everyone wanted to know who he was and where he had come from. And while the media previously had been put off by his tough demeanor, now they fell in love with the story of how the son of Mexican immigrants who had grown up in a small border town learning to be a rugged and unflinching cowhand had found himself out on the ball field; overnight he became a media darling. But as one reporter confirmed (writing for the *Chicago Tribune* in a story that went across the country via the *Knight Ridder*), even though Oscar's name might have been known previously only by folks who "sold hay in Portales," everyone who was a baseball fan had seen his work, whether they realized it or not: Kevin Brown, Robb Nen, Orlando Hernandez, Hideki Irabu, Ruben Rivera and Corey Patterson were only a few of the baseball greats who had learned their skills at Oscar's side back when they started in the minor leagues. And the people at the top had been keeping an eye on him as well; it was Joe Torre, Stump Merrill and Don Zimmer of the Yankees who had recommended him for the position with the Cubs.

That year the Cubs owners had hired not one but three minorities to run their team, breaking a 130-year streak in baseball at large for excluding minorities from coaching staff. Don Baylor, the new manager who had chosen Oscar, was black, and Sandy Alomar Sr., another coach, hailed from Puerto Rico. With so many minorities playing baseball, this fact seemed to slip by unnoticed. Nevertheless, and whether anyone realized or not, it was a big moment in baseball history.

Oscar and his family moved back to Portales from Tampa to get ready to move to Chicago with the Cubs. In the meantime, the kids were still all registered to attend school in Portales. That school season Oscar was honored during Elida's homecoming, along with a doctor who was also an Elida alumni. With no disrespect to the doctor, the nominating committee wanted to honor Oscar all by himself, but the school board president would not permit it. We all went to the event. And our hearts were bursting with pride when Oscar got up to talk. He thanked everyone in Elida, all the people who had been there for him as a kid and who had had a part in making him who he was now. He was gracious and sincere. And he was irresistibly handsome in a black turtleneck and khaki pants. On his finger he wore one of the two Yankees World Series rings he now possessed.

After the event he had a talk with me. I was still running around telling anyone who would listen that my brother was a superstar. "Knock it off, Yolie," he said. "It's enough." He said I was like Paulie, in the Rocky movies, the overly enthusiastic brother-in-law who was always talking to the media. "You really have to calm down," he reprimanded.

The Cubs had their annual convention in Chicago in February, a chance for fans to meet the staff. Oscar was interviewed multiple times, for print and on the radio. In one interview, he was joined by Kerry Wood, who had been Rookie of the Year in 1998 and with whom Oscar had worked with when Kerry was in the minors. Kerry was a real celebrity now. He had been on TV lots of times, including high profile entertainment shows like Letterman and Leno. In the interview they talked about the fact that his arm had been injured, and that Oscar planned to rehab him during spring training.

(Though Kerry didn't say it to the interviewer at that time, we would later learn that what stood out in his mind from his work with Oscar in the minors was a day when Oscar had turned to another player, someone who wasn't giving it his all, and said, "You're a cancer. Don't ever reproduce and have kids." Kerry was only 18 at the time and Oscar's words scared him to death.)

Oscar told reporters that he would probably be "more crass" than the Cubs players were used to. Don Baylor backed him up, saying that the guy from the New Mexico outback and Wrigley Field would be a good match. In one interview Oscar said that in this day and time, it was so important to get guys to believe that you were on their side. If they knew you were going to be in their corner through thick and thin, that was half the battle. "The biggest thing I bring as a pitching coach is a work ethic. It's being able to work smart, being able to answer the question of 'why should I do this on the mound? Why is this happening?' I've seen a lot of gimmicks, a lot of theories and philosophies, but what I've always worked on is stressing basic fundamentals."

He went on to say, "My reputation is being brutally honest. That's how I've always coached and it's how I've raised my children. You have to know that as great as the game is, as great as this life is, it can be yanked away from us in a heartbeat. If you have been blessed with God-given ability, you're not to let it slip away. It is our responsibility to get the most out of our ability as we can."

If possible, the media's preoccupation with Oscar became even more intense post conference. Barry Rozner of the *Chicago Daily Herald* wrote that Oscar was "as tough as nails" and "as loving as your mother." He'd hit the nail right on the head; that was the Oscar we knew in our family. Rozer said that Oscar had "picked himself out of the dust of poverty" to become "the most important man on the coaching staff of the most beloved team in the world." He ended his story by saying that no matter what happened, Oscar was already a success. Some reporters wanted to know how Oscar, a relative unknown, had so impressed Baylor to get him to hire him. Oscar was quoted as saying that he'd told Baylor he was brutally honest, and Baylor was pleased because honesty was what he was looking for. When we heard him on radio interviews or saw him on TV, we swelled with pride. Oscar had always been articulate, but now he was more than that. He was witty; he was prepared; he was smooth. He had truly come into his own in every possible way. He had not only made himself into a great coach, but he had become a great spokesperson for the game itself.

Spring training took place in Mesa, Arizona. Randy Harrison, a reporter for the *Albuquerque Journal,* drove out there to interview Oscar, and then drove to Elida to interview folks who had known him when he was growing up. The resulting story was a wonderful, lengthy piece entitled, "A Cowboy in Chicago." While the Chicago papers were more interested Oscar's "climb out of the dust of poverty," Harrison highlighted Oscar's devotion to his wife and kids. While Oscar was in Mesa for spring training, Harrison noted, Oscar's daughters, Amanda and Melissa, were still in Portales and they were both on the basketball team. Since there was no way that Oscar was going to miss any of their games, he was making the 22-hour round trip from Mesa to Portales and back again constantly. "My children come before everything else," Oscar told Randy. "Daddy didn't have much time for us when I was a kid, so when I brought these kids into this world, I promised my wife that they would get everything I didn't get." He would watch his girls play and then hop in the car and rush back to work with Wood on his arm. He felt that Wood had "Michael Jordan talent" but he threw across his body, and when his arm healed, Oscar wanted to get him to throw differently. He also wanted to get him to stop beating himself up mentally because of his injury. Oscar felt that he was dealing with adversity for the first time and at the highest level of baseball, that he would have to find a balance between the emotional side and the physical side of the equation, just as Oscar had done. There was no one better equipped to show players how to build character through the game.

The Cubs would be a challenge, which was another reason why Oscar was getting so much press. He had been turning pitchers around for years, and now people were finally beginning to talk about that fact and wonder if he could do for a major team what he had done for the minors. And it wasn't just the pitchers that were having a hard time. The Cubs hadn't won a series in over 90 years. Yet their fans remained loyal and hopeful, and as a result the team had come to be known as the "Lovable Losers."

Another problem in Chicago might have been the "curse," which many fans took very seriously. The story is that a Greek immigrant named William Sianis purchased a pub in Chicago in 1934. One day a goat fell out of a passing truck and wandered into the pub. Sianis decided to keep him, and soon after Sianis became known as "Billy Goat" Sianis, and to take advantage of all the attention he and his goat were getting, he changed the name of the pub to the Billy Goat Tavern.

The Cubs won two World Series back to back in 1907 and 1908, and they won several pennants thereafter, the final one in 1945. That same season they found themselves in the series again, and by game four, they were leading the Detroit Tigers two to one and needed only to win two of the next four games at Wrigley Field to become the champs. Billy Goat Sianis had two tickets for Game Four. He was a great Cubs fan, and hoping to bring them good luck, he brought his pet goat with him to the game. But the ushers would not allow the goat into the park. Worse, when Sianis went over their heads and challenged PK Wrigley directly, demanding an explanation, Wrigley told him that the goat stunk.

Legend has it that Sianis threw his hands up in the air and said, "The Cubs ain't going to win no more." And thus began the curse.

The deaths of both Sianis and original goat seem to have done little to rid the Cubs of the curse. Sianis' nephew, Sam Sianis, even brought a descendant goat onto the field years later — with the full permission of the management this time — to see if that would lift the curse, but it still didn't happen.

Whether based on fact or fiction, Cub stories like this abound. In Chicago, baseball operates at a higher level, captivating the imaginations even of those who don't think of themselves as sports fans. Hall of Fame sportscaster Harry Caray began singing "Take Me Out To The Ballgame" at Wrigley Field for the Chicago Cubs in 1982, beginning a great tradition which clearly honors all that is good and beautiful about the game. Now Oscar would be incorporated into the Cubs history as well. The legend was already building. A few of the reporters found themselves writing that while some of the new players might be afraid of the Chicago wind, they had better keep it to themselves because Oscar Acosta was not afraid of the wind — nor anything else. That would be their opening to talk about some of the challenges Oscar undertook when ranching in Elida, where you don't let even the worst of weather stop you from doing what needs to be done.

Mother and I drove to Scottsdale, where Kathy and Oscar had rented a place, in March, to celebrate Oscar's birthday. I bought him a golf shirt and his kids bought him a new set of clubs. Everywhere I went I told people about him, ignoring the little voice in my head that reminded me constantly that Oscar had asked me to calm down. I simply couldn't help myself. Oscar's good fortune belonged to our entire family, and beyond.

We went to see the Cubs play the Mariners before we returned home. Oscar brought us into the clubhouse before the game started and we met Sammy Sosa. "Oh, qué hombre más agradable, tan agradable," Mother said. *Oh, what a nice man, what a nice man.* We met Lou Piniella, the Mariners' manager. We took pictures with him. We met Oscar's colleague Sandy Alomar. By the time we walked out of the clubhouse, the bleachers were full. I started waving and the crowds, who had no idea who I was, responded, looking for any excuse to begin cheering. I pointed to my mother and yelled up to them, "This is Oscar's mom!" They cheered louder. And in that way, Mother and I got a little taste of what it must have been like for Oscar to experience his new-found celebrity.

Kerry Wood and Oscar seemed destined to become friends from the very beginning. Oscar spoke a lot about him. Until Wood was completely recovered from the surgery he'd had on his elbow (following a torn ligament), Oscar didn't want him throwing sliders, which would put a strain on his arm. He believed that Wood's curveball was better than that of any pitcher he had seen, and he didn't think he needed the slider anyway. Once, during a practice in which he was throwing curveballs in the batting cage, Wood dropped his elbow and Oscar jumped all over him. Wood took it well. He told interviewers later that if Oscar was going to bark at him like that every time, he would break the habit pretty quickly.

Another guy who Oscar liked a lot was Todd Van Poppel. Van Poppel, who was from Texas, had started out with the White Sox in 1991, but he'd had a mediocre year and got sent back to the AAA teams. After that he bounced around between minor and major leagues from Oakland to Detroit to Texas to Pittsburgh. In the two years before he found himself in spring training with Oscar, he'd been through 11 different coaches. In spite of all the moving around he had done, and in spite of the fact that he had some kind of a back problem, Oscar picked him out as being a guy whose determination did not waver. Oscar told us that he was a blessing to him.

By the end of March, we had read so many stories about Oscar in the sports sections of newspapers that between our reading and our conversations with him, we could pretty much piece together his entire life away from us. From a *Chicago Sun Times* story we learned that while he was designating most players as his "blessings," he was still the same old Oscar regarding those who were not. He singled out Carlos Zambrano and Will Ohman for their lack of focus. "I need to see more of a to-hell-with-you attitude from them," Oscar said. Closer Tom "Flash" Gordon looked promising, but Oscar was concerned because he was recovering from elbow surgery too and would have to be used cautiously. He also had concerns about whether right-handed relievers Kyle Farnsworth, Van Poppel and Zambrano would be able to handle left-handed hitters. "I like Zambrano," Oscar said, "but I don't trust him." On one occasion Oscar criticized him for having his cap pulled up when he came to the mound, as if to say, "Here I am, world. Look at me." He was just a little too relaxed for Oscar's tastes. Someone suggested that Oscar cut him some slack because he was only 19 and Oscar hit the roof, saying that Zambrano had been 19 since he'd had him years before in the minors. "What, in Venezuela they have three years for every one of ours? All I'm looking at is a big kid with a good arm. I want to see him hungry. Not that happy-go-lucky stuff," my brother said. "I want to see Duncan in him," he continued, referring to Courtney Duncan. "I want to see Duncan in all of them." Courtney Duncan was relatively unknown at the time, but my brother felt he had all the right stuff. He kept his mouth shut and did his job. And he didn't whine about the mechanics. "He has no fear," Oscar said. Fear was something Oscar kept a lookout for. It was the antithesis to what was needed in the game of baseball (or in life) in his mind. Ohman, he felt, was fearful, and it affected his game. Oscar thought he might have faked a sore shoulder at one point early on so as to have an excuse for why he wasn't doing what he was supposed to do. "You think you are going to make the club because you have a little flash, a little charisma to you? We don't need that. You got to do it between the white lines," Oscar said.

Before Oscar came on board, the Cubs had had pitching coach changes for three seasons in a row. They had Phil Regan in 1998, Marty DeMerritt in 1999 and Oscar in 2000. By the middle of July of 2000 it was clear that Oscar's pitchers were beginning to respond to his no-nonsense philosophy and his incredible understanding of the mechanics of the game. The word among sportscasters everywhere was that maybe the turnover streak was finally over. Baylor couldn't say enough good things about Oscar's work ethic. In one interview with the *Sun Times* Baylor said, "He pretty much wears his heart on his sleeve every single day. He can be tough, but he's not unfair at all." He added, "He doesn't let things slide. He changes every single pitch. He goes over it every half an inning with the pitchers. Sometimes guys get caught up in throwing too many breaking balls and he has it right there to tell them they have to mix it up better."

Some might have thought that Oscar purposely tried to intimidate his players into pitching better, but Oscar really meant everything he said. In another *Sun Times* piece, sports writer Mike Kiley noted that in one game (against the Giants), Ruben Quevedo took a beating not only on the field but also afterwards, from Oscar. "If you don't have your heart and mind into it, to hell with it. Let us know before the game starts and we'll get somebody else," Oscar said. On the other hand, Oscar pointed out that there were players like Kevin Tapani, who would sometimes have to pull over in his car on the way home from a game because his knee was hurting so bad. Oscar was a fighter, and if you had any fight in you, Oscar was the one who could find it and help you to show it to the rest of the world.

We tried never to miss a Cubs game on TV that season. When I could, I drove to Portales to watch the games at Mother's side. She was a wreck watching Oscar on the screen. And to tell the truth, so was I. In one game, someone hit a ball into the outfield and two Cubs collided trying to catch it. Neither had even yelled out, "I've got it." Even in high school everyone knew to yell out when you knew you had the ball. The two outfielders somersaulted in opposite directions after their collision, and the other team scored in the interim. But Mother and I were more intent on Oscar in the dugout than the incident itself. We could see in his expression that he was really upset. "Oh dear," I said, "he's really mad now." Mother was muttering the same thing, but in Spanish. We chewed our nails and hoped none of the other Cubs would mess up. By mid-season the sportswriters were already beginning to talk about how the Cubs' pitchers were piling up the strikeouts. We didn't want anything to go wrong. We didn't want the media to turn on Oscar again.

We seemed always to be praying, for whatever Cubs' player was up at the time, and always for whoever was pitching. And each pitcher was as important to Oscar as the next. While he knew their individual weaknesses inside and out, when they got up to play ball, they were all winners, he liked to tell reporters. Oscar might not have wanted us bragging to the media, but when it came to prayers, he was happy to have our support. He would even call before some games and tell Mother specifically who we were to pray the hardest for, usually a player who was suffering with some ache or pain. "Oh, Lord, you are the great physician," we would begin. We prayed so much for Kerry Wood and his injured arm that I finally wrote out a prayer just for him and placed it under Mother's candle on her altar in the spare bedroom. Poor Mother got to the point where she blamed herself when the Cubs lost a game, or when a particular pitcher let the opponents capture a base, or worse, make a run. My memories of the games I watched with Mother seem to consist of watching Oscar in the dugout eating sunflower seeds and spitting out the shells while Mother mumbled a stream of prayers in Spanish in the background.

Oscar's reputation for being a tough coach persisted all

through the first season, but Kathy told us not to worry, that the players, especially his pitchers, loved him for it. He had told them on day one that they could leave their egos at the door because there was no place for them in practice or in games, and they all went along with that. They also went along with his belief that both the game and the uniform they wore to play it warranted their utmost respect. "I'm not a dictator," Oscar said, "but I am not going to change my standards or expectations of people being paid to play a very simple game."

But what appealed most to many of the players was that Oscar was a coach who liked to talk baseball. As Kerry Wood said in an interview with Mike Kiley towards the end of the season, "Oscar has had confidence in me all year when I didn't have confidence in myself. We have done a lot of talking and I'm sure we are going to do a lot of talking this off season and work on a lot of stuff. Oscar's great." Kiley reported in the same article that bullpen coach Sandy Alomar hoped that Corey Patterson was paying attention to how much talking Wood and Oscar did. Corey, a quiet guy, didn't ask enough questions about the game, and Alomar was afraid it would hurt him. "Talking baseball is a time-honored tradition that has linked generations of players," Alomar said, and I began to see that this was true.

While the players wanted only to please Oscar, Kathy hinted that there might be some personality conflict going on with Baylor, the manager. "Are you sure?" I asked, my stomach doing flips. "Well, I'm not sure," Kathy said. "I think there's something wrong, but maybe I'm wrong, because Oscar hasn't said anything."

As always, we all gathered together at my mother's for Thanksgiving that year. After the meal, Oscar and Kathy and their kids left to prepare yet another big meal at their house. Oscar had invited James Gibson, an elderly man who had no family, to eat with them. He could have brought James to Mother's house, but I guess he wanted to make sure that the example he intended to set for his children was not overlooked by virtue of too much commotion. I stopped over too to see James, after they had eaten. "Do you still play the piano, James?" I asked. Years ago he had played at our church. He said he still played now and then. Oscar poked his head in from the kitchen, where he was helping Kathy and the girls with the clean up. "Have some more pumpkin pie," he said to James. Little Ryan sat at the table with James and me, asking him all kinds of questions about his past. You could see that James, sitting there in his overalls and work boots, was only too happy to have people making such a fuss over him.

Oscar's children were growing up to be fine individuals. He kept after all of them all the time. He wanted them to work as hard as they could at whatever they did. He made sure they got their exercise. If the girls ran one mile, he would tell them that meant they could easily run two. If they ran two, he would tell them to run three. As for Ryan, he was already involved in basketball, soccer, and baseball; and on top of his school sports, he was the Cubs' bat boy, which meant that he got to wear the Cubs' uniform. Oscar made sure he always said "Yes, Sir" and "No, Sir" when he spoke to any of the players. There were times when Ryan was asked to get some of the players a cup of coffee in the clubhouse. They always wanted to tip him for his efforts. Oscar sat him down early on and told him he was never, under any circumstances, to take a tip or to think that he could speak out or take liberties with any of the players. Since the players had to wear suits when they flew to an away game, Oscar had taken Ryan out shopping that first season for a suit of his own. They found something a dark purplish color with pinstripes. Ryan said he felt like a gangster in it, but they had been limited by both time and lack of selection in Ryan's size. When Ryan boarded the plane in his gangster suit, all the players started clapping.

Ryan was good on the field. He was alert. It gave us so much pleasure to see him run out onto our TV screens.

During that same off season, Kerry Wood and his fiancé came out to spend some time in Portales with Oscar and his family. A pitcher from the Yankees came out too. Oscar took the men out quail hunting during the days, along with his old Elida friends, Dan Howard, Jim Bob Nuchols and Jimmy Dale Ward, and of course his son. In the evenings they sat outside and talked baseball. While he was in Portales, we took Kerry over to Mother's and showed him the prayer that I had written out for him. His arm had since healed. We had no doubt that the praying had been responsible for his recovery.

The first year had been bumpy but it certainly turned heads. Oscar's pitchers had played hard for him, but they still had more work to do. The second year began with a Cubs' trip to Japan. John Lieber, one of the Cubs' star pitchers, and another man who Oscar regarded as a blessing, said his dream came true when he got to open the game there. Oscar and Kathy, who had made the trip without the kids, had a great time. But again, after their return, Kathy mentioned on the phone that Baylor, who had gone too, just didn't seem as warm as he had previously. I told myself that Kathy was imagining things and that nothing bad could happen.

In the meantime, Mother and Carol and I, along with a cousin, prepared to make the trip to Fresnio, Zacatecas, Mexico to give our thanksgiving, as we had promised we would if Oscar made it to the majors. There is a beautiful church there, built in the 1690s in commemoration of a miraculous silver crucifix that Spanish miners once found on the site. Thereafter, it was said those who came to pray experienced miracles, including women praying for husbands trapped in the mines. Now people come from all over the world to pray to El Santo Niño de Atocha, or the Holy Child of Atocha. People bring gifts, often shoes for the baby Jesus, who is said to walk at night to places where His miracles are needed — and they leave behind crutches and wheelchairs and other evidence of their healings.

There is a rock outside the church that has its own story. Years ago, it is said, a mother, father and daughter walked for miles and miles to pay thanks for a miracle that had occurred in their lives. But the girl got tired of walking, and not too far from their destination, she sat down for once and for all and pulled her big sombrero over her head. When her parents went to pull her up, they found that she had turned to stone. In terror, they began to run the rest of the way to the church, thinking the priest there would know what to do. But when they looked over their shoulders, they saw that their daughter was a kid again. They ran back to her, but before they reached her, she turned to stone again. Back and forth they went, with always the same results. Finally they went for the priest, and when they told him their story, the priest made arrangements to have the stone that had once been a girl moved to the front of the church where he could keep an eye on it. But the girl never did reemerge.

We took buses from Portales to Fresnio. The moment we arrived at the great ornate door of this church rich with stories both strange and miraculous, Mother dropped to her knees. And although her legs bothered her all the time and she often had to go to the doctor to have fluids drained from them, she went down the long aisle from the door to the altar on her knees, praying with each step.

We returned to New Mexico and resumed our game-watching vigil. At a game with the Reds, there was a rain delay at the bottom of the fourth and Oscar didn't want the same pitcher, Jon Lieber, to go back on the field when it was over. But Baylor sent him out anyway. Oscar walked out of the dugout and into the clubhouse, and he did not reappear the rest of the game. I understood his position: he was the pitching coach, and if he couldn't set the rules for the pitchers, why was he there? But it made me nervous to think that Oscar would do anything that might ruffle Baylor's feathers.

In the games that followed, I thought I could "see" some tension between Oscar and Baylor on their faces, but I could never be sure if I was just imagining it or if it was really there. I am quite certain there was less communication between the two over time.

Once Oscar was ejected for arguing balls and strikes with the umpire. This had happened a time or two when he was coaching for the minor teams, but I had only heard about it after the fact. It was different to see it for myself. I hoped with all my heart that it would not somehow upset the applecart.

In the meantime, Oscar's bond with his pitchers was only getting stronger. He couldn't say enough good things about them. His pride was almost paternal at times. He told Mike Kiley at the *Sun Times* that Kerry Wood "doesn't waste a moment that his eyes are open. He is going to enjoy every moment of his life and live the way he wants to. God love him for it. If I was somebody his age, I would want him to be my friend. He is a fun-loving human being. He can go home at night and lay his head in bed and say he didn't waste whatever God gave him today." He spoke that way about the others as well, alluding not only to their prowess on the field but also to the way they lived their lives.

At some point Kathy mentioned to us that Baylor had hired an exercise guru, one Mack Newton, who was going to fly in from his headquarters in Arizona on a regular basis and help the Cubs to get in shape through stretching. Oscar had gone with Baylor to meet with Newton. I was impressed that they had made the trip together, and I felt more hopeful that things would be okay between them after all. Then I read that during a game in Pittsburgh Oscar had had a clash with Zambrano, refusing to visit him on the mound. Apparently Zambrano had celebrated the three Mark McGwire strikeouts he had thrown by pumping his fist in the air. I wondered what ramifications — if any — that that would have. But a few games later, Zambrano had his first major league victory, and it came after a visit from Oscar out on the mound. Zambrano had just walked one hitter (Lance Berkman) when Oscar appeared and said, "You're smart. You stay focused on what you're doing." And Zambrano did just that, striking out the next two players to finish the inning.

As if the sports writers were as worried as I was about my brother staying with the team, Mike Kiley wrote that since coming on board as team president in 1995, Andy MacPhail had not kept a pitching coach for more than two years. Still, Kiley, who clearly admired Oscar, predicted that Oscar would be the man to break the pattern. "Passion alone can't win," Kiley wrote. "But mix Oscar's fiery dedication and devotion to duty with some actual talent, and look what happens." There was no denying that Oscar was doing his job. "Oscar may have ruffled some feathers in spring training with his raw honesty," Kiley continued, "but he has gotten results from a bullpen he challenged in March to start paying attention to business and quit dawdling."

By late May, after winning a game against the Cincinnati Reds and not much before a shoulder injury would disable him for the season, Tom "Flash" Gordon told Mike Kiley that it was Oscar who was responsible for his success. "Oscar has a great plan," he said. "He quieted down my delivery and it showed tonight. It made me feel like I was in a rhythm.... I'm letting my stuff take care of itself." Oscar turned the compliment around, saying of Gordon, "As journeyman as he is and the wars he's been through, you look at him out on the mound, he does anything you want him to do. He's got ice in his veins. Nothing affects him." Perhaps Kerry Wood summed up progress the best, saying, "I honestly can say that there is no one who is pitching here who doesn't respect Oscar and give him full attention when he's talking."

Reflecting on Oscar's time in Chicago, Kiley wrote, "Oscar initially figured he could mold and bully pitchers in the same manner he learned to punch cows and people as a youth. He grew up in a border area and crossed over to Juarez, Mexico in the summer to live with his half-brother John, 13 years his senior, and act out some of his rebellious nature in an environment rife with temptation. John still lives there, a proud and rich owner of a city block." Kiley went on to say that Oscar got into boxing because of John, that he knew he wasn't a great fighter but fought with Spinks anyway to get Daddy's attention. Likewise, it was to get Daddy's attention that he got involved in rodeo competitions. "Daddy thought you needed to wake up working," Oscar told Kiley. "He worked other people's ranches and sometimes would stay out all night plowing. I never could work for him. You were damned if you did and damned if you didn't and I said after a while, to hell with this."

It was a strange thing to know that Oscar had become so comfortable with the media that he was able to discuss aspects of his childhood. He seemed to be especially open with Mike Kiley. "My parents taught me you are always going to have to work with your hands for a living," he went on in the same interview. "I worked on ranches all my life — cattle, horses, fences — all the detail. I escaped to go to my brother's place in Juarez in the summer because I didn't have to work. I worked all winter and sure didn't want to work all summer, because it got hot as hell. I would rather be a little hoodlum."

He even told Kiley about Jerry Stroud, the guy who had the scar on his cheek who forgave his most despised enemy on his deathbed, thereby teaching Oscar a life lesson that he would never forget. "Jerry explained to me at the end that we can't live that kind of life, that any moron can live like that. It takes a bigger man to conduct himself the right way."

The *New York Times* wrote a story around this time, noting that Jon Lieber had pitched a one hitter to beat the Reds 3-0 one day, and then the next day Kerry Wood pitched a one hitter, beating the Brewers 1-0. Kevin Tapani was scheduled to pitch the following day. He was quoted as having said, "Don't expect me to pitch a one hitter too." Tapani allowed six hits in seven innings and beat the Brewers 4-1. Oscar told the interviewer, "We keep raising the bar on each other." Tapani spoke for the team in the interview, saying, "Oscar makes us concentrate all the time."

Dan Rather put together a piece for *Parade Magazine*, the title for which was "They Live the American Dream." The piece featured people who had made it from the bottom to the top in their respective fields. Oscar was one of them. His picture, in his Cubs uniform, appeared on the cover. Dan Rather quoted Oscar as saying that pitching for the majors had been his dream, and that he had neglected everything else, his homework when he was a student and then later his wife and children, trying to get there. He talked about how he then lost everything; a torn rotator cuff ended his prospects for a pitching career, and his wife and kids leaving ended his prospects of having the family life he had dreamed of. He gave up, he said, but then when he got the offer to coach for the Rangers, and when Kathy took him back, he knew he was getting a second chance.

Mid-season brought with it the All-Star game at Shea Stadium. Oscar was concerned that National League manager Bobby Valentine would overlook some of the most deserving Cubs players. Not only did Valentine have a history of conflicts with Baylor, but he had let it be known, back in the days when Oscar coached for the Rangers AAA leagues, that he didn't much care for Oscar either. One of the problems Valentine seemed to have was Oscar's inability, back then at least, to kowtow to the media. He had said he would never have a guy like that on any team he managed. I couldn't help but wonder what someone like Valentine thought now that Oscar had become a media darling, and he hadn't had to kowtow to anyone to achieve that status; he had just gone on being himself and the rest of the world had finally caught on to his genius. In fact, Jon Lieber and Sammy Sosa did get to play, but the National League lost again anyway.

Like the first half of the season, the second continued with

Oscar dishing it out and his pitchers happily taking it. Writing for the *Arlington Heights Daily Herald*, Bruce Miles noted that Oscar was not always politically correct and that "the faint of heart and weak of knee shouldn't waste his time." He talked in his story about how Oscar's respect and passion for the game came first over anything else. "When Julian Tavarez doesn't run out groundballs, he hears about it until his ears blister," Miles said. But even after he suffered a 14-5 loss to the Rockies in early August and Oscar got upset with him, all Tavarez said is, "Oscar is one of the best that I've had as a pitching coach. You have to have somebody like Oscar."

By the second week of August, the Cubs had an ERA of 3.68, the second best in the National League. If they hung onto it, professed Miles, most of the credit would go to the pitching staff, which had succeeded in keeping the offense afloat. "It has all been done with Acosta riding herd — cajoling here, needling there, and yes, providing the much-needed pat on the back when it's merited." He quotes my brother in his story as saying, "These pitchers are my family members, my brothers. There are a lot of times when we had disagreements, a lot times I've raised my voice, they've raised their voices. That's part of it."

What drove Oscar crazy, he admitted to Miles, was "when you watch guys coming to the plate, making fashion statements, wearing earrings, not running balls out, not running to their positions, not going from first to third, not being competitive, that's what turns my stomach. If you want to wear jewelry, there's only one jewelry you need to wear and that's that ring that says 'World Champions.'" (Oscar didn't wear his wedding ring to the games. Once while he was out working with Rod Lambirth on the Lambirth's ranch, Oscar lost the tip of his finger baling hay. Rod found it some days later, putrefying in the glove that had also come off during the accident. Whether in construction or ranching or sports, there was always the chance that a ring could get caught on something and the skin around it would get pulled off.) Flash Gordon was quoted as well, saying, "It's not that he's a pitching coach. He's established that he's also a friend. Tough love is sometimes the best love. His approach is that this is the game and you should understand where you are and what you have to do and what you should be ready for each and every day. That's a great thing. Somebody's in your corner every day." Miles summed it all up saying that Oscar might rub some people the wrong way, but as long as he had the respect of his pitchers and could look his family in the eye, he was okay with whatever happened. "He'd just as soon go back to ranching in New Mexico than be somebody he's not," Miles concluded.

Oscar was doing just what he had been hired to do; he was turning his pitchers around. But his methodology was catching everyone's attention and imagination. One enthusiastic freelance reporter named Rany Jazayerli wrote, "Acosta created a huge stir in the Cubs spring training camp by questioning the manhood of some of the young pitchers, particularly Will Ohman and Carlos Zambrano. At the time, we all thought Acosta was nuts. It appeared for all the world that Acosta was going to make men out of his young charges by working their arms like a galley master. The fact is, Acosta has taken a staff of boys and turned them into men. He has turned a pitching staff that struck out 1,143 men last season (fourth in the NL) and posted a 5.25 ERA (15th in the NL) into the most overpowering collection of flame-throwing, gas-cooking, cheese-chucking, deuce-bending, bat-sawing fireballs the world has ever seen."

In fact, more and more often, people began to say that it was the pitchers who were now carrying the team. Between them and Sammy Sosa, who was making the runs, they managed 12 straight wins. One night Carlos Zambrano got up and didn't pitch well and I could see Oscar's frustration on the TV screen. The harder Zambrano tried, it seemed, the worse he did. Maybe he was intimidated by Oscar. After the game, Oscar was interviewed on TV. I held my breath when the interviewer asked him what went wrong. Oscar said, "What I think is if you don't keep to the mechanics of pitching, you're going to have your ass handed to you every time." The camera glided from Oscar's angry face to the interviewer's cheerful one. "Well, folks," he said, "that's Oscar Acosta, and he tells it like it is." And all I could think is, Oh, dear, he's going to be called into the front office for this one.

By early October, end-of-the-season wrap-up reports were asserting that the Cubs had already improved by 23 games over their disastrous record of 65-97 in 2000, the biggest forward leap in the major leagues. The team had held first place in the Central division for almost three months because of its starting rotation and the late inning work of left-handed pitcher Jeff Fassero and right-handed pitchers Kyle Farnsworth and Tom Gordon. The right-handed rotation of Kerry Wood, Jon Lieber, Kevin Tapani, Julian Taverez and Jason Bere missed only one start until August, when Wood suffered tendonitis in his shoulder. Even MacPhail praised Oscar saying, "I don't know much about pitching. I just know people get people out. It's hard for me to understand the nuances, but what I have seen is the pitchers have gotten better."

It looked more and more likely that the Cubs would make it to the series. But it also seemed more evident that Oscar and Baylor's "personality conflict" was not a figment of my imagination. The *Chicago Sun Times* announced one day that they had an altercation in the dugout, that Oscar had become offended by Baylor's tone when Baylor told him to get someone out from the bullpen at a game in San Diego. Apparently, Baylor did not address Oscar by name; instead he addressed Oscar as "You." "You treat me with respect," Oscar countered, and after the game, when they went into the front office to continue their "discussion," things got explosive and they almost came to blows. Then later there was another incident, in Florida, when Oscar told a reporter that the Cubs offense had failed to support Jon Lieber during a game, which would have been his 18th win if he had won it. "I'd like for him to pitch one damn time with a big, damn lead, so he wouldn't have to grind it out every damn time," Oscar declared. "He's the best thing that has ever happened to the Cubs as far as a pitcher is concerned. Every fifth day he has been there, and I guarantee you one thing — he's not going to blame anybody. That's why he's Jon Lieber. He's going to take it upon himself. He's a man." Baylor was furious, and he made Oscar apologize to the entire team for his remarks.

Another problem between them seemed to be that Mack Newton, the stretching guru who Baylor had hired, was not doing his job. Newton, a Viet Nam vet and a black belt in Karate, was full of himself, and although he was just a freelance consultant who showed up only occasionally, he seemed to feel he could talk to the players the way a coach might. When they played poorly, he would tell them they were nothing, they were losers. When they played well, he would take the credit, saying it was his stretching instruction that made all the difference. And he didn't just toot his horn with the players. He loved to get in front of the media and tell them too that he was the one responsible for any and all team successes. At one game Newton walked in the stands and signed autographs. Even the players who didn't mind him so much agreed that that was out of line.

Hitter Ron Coomer might have expressed the problem best in a newspaper interview: "I just don't like someone to say they are responsible for how I did or how anybody did when you never see the people. I don't buy that, there's no room for that in baseball. For a guy who hasn't been here for more than a handful of times this season, if he thinks he's responsible for the success we've had, he's barking up the wrong tree." Tapani agreed, saying, "Not one time did he ask the question of what can I do for you or how can I help you. It was, 'Here's my thing, give me my money and I'm checking out.' He didn't follow up." Others complained that half the time Newton came unprepared; that his lectures hadn't been thought out and that he lost a lot of listeners as a result.

Oscar's pitchers disliked Newton intensely and across the board. Kerry Wood was quoted as saying, "I don't know how many bases he saved, but he comes in and flies in and out and thinks he made us? I don't think so." Once, when Newton was lecturing the pitchers about what losers they were, they got up collectively and walked out. It doesn't take a wild imagination to guess how Oscar felt about him. Newton's contract was ultimately suspended. But Baylor, a total Newton advocate, was fuming over it. It seems that when Newton was hired, MacPhail approved his services at a fee of $200,000. But as Newton was more expensive than that, Baylor dug into his own pockets to make up the difference. Perhaps that was part of the reason he was so upset.

In the meantime the games went on, and Oscar continued to call home to ask for prayers for his pitchers. I took almost no pleasure in the games anymore; I was too intent on watching Oscar and Baylor in the dugout, trying to read their minds. Sometimes I would call Oscar's apartment while he was at a game and leave short messages. "Oscar, you are so handsome," I would say, "but maybe you should trim your hair a little." Or, "Oscar, you're looking so good, but I bet you'd look even better if you shaved." It was all I could think to do to help.

One night Oscar called Mother and asked her to pray specifically for Jon Lieber. He said it was really important and she should pray very hard. Lieber needed to break Greg Maddux's 1992 record of 19 wins in a season.

Mother prayed for all she was worth that night, and sure enough, Lieber got his 20th win and broke the Maddux record. The crowds went wild. Oscar ran to the pitching mound and shook Lieber's hand and gave him a hug. Only later we would learn from the papers that Oscar had tears in his eyes at that moment, and that his words at the time were, "If you're done, I'm done,"— because that very same night, knowing that Baylor planned to fire him that weekend, Oscar resigned. Jon Lieber and Oscar walked away in lock step, the pitcher who was one of the best things to happen to the Cubs, and the pitching coach who had led him to victory. They went down to the clubhouse and had a couple of farewell beers while the game finished up.

When the game ended, the TV reporters made a mad dash for the clubhouse. A very upset Lieber told them that Oscar was the reason for his victory. "This is bullshit," an equally upset Wood cried when he found out. All the pitchers were upset. The reporters turned to Oscar, but he claimed to have nothing to say in the matter. He said the day belonged to "Lieb" and he wasn't about to take it away from him. Baylor, meanwhile, told reporters he couldn't see it continuing, and that ultimately he thought it would be best for the Cubs. "This was something I agonized over," he said.

I couldn't sleep that night. I was devastated for Oscar. I called Mother and we wailed together over the phone, both of us utterly broken-hearted. Over the next few days the papers were full of stories, all of them attesting to what a great coach Oscar had been. Kerry Wood said he attributed everything he'd done to Oscar, that Oscar was the first pitching coach who had really showed him what professional baseball was all about. He even refused at first to play at the next night's game, but the coaches ultimately convinced him that he couldn't do that to the team. Wood told writer Bruce Miles, "He was the first pitching coach I had (in 1995 at Fort Myers) and really showed me what professional baseball was all about. You've got a kid coming out of high school making a million-dollar signing bonus and that's the first guy you run across, he put me on course pretty quick." Tapani said that the whole thing made no sense, adding, "It's okay when you can see why decisions are made. Something like this is kind of outside the bounds.... Everybody has a lot of respect for Oscar. He is one of the best people I've ever had the privilege to be around in baseball.... It sounds like a personality thing where he was honest with Baylor, and Don didn't like hearing it.... You can say as a manager he has the right to do this. But I guess we also have the right to disagree with it and look for an upfront and honest answer as to why you would want to take the guy who is...getting results and having his group of players either meet or exceed the expectations set out before the year." Catcher Joe Girardi said simply that he loved Oscar; Jon Lieber continued to say that Oscar was the one reason he was where he was in his career. Jason Bere said, "We want to win. Winning was made easier with Oscar here." He added, "What makes him such a good pitching coach is maybe what some people don't like. He preaches mental toughness and being mentally prepared for the game." *Chicago Sun Times* Carlo Slezaqk summed it up: "If Baylor and Acosta didn't like each other, one of them had to go. But the players feel the wrong guy left."

Baylor could not be made to say why he fired Oscar, which left a lot of room for the media to conclude that the fact was that Oscar was respected so much by the pitchers and was given so much credit for what the Cubs had accomplished that Baylor felt threatened — a case of jealously, pure and simple. What Baylor did say was that he was going to bring back Newton, who, because of the team's animosity, hadn't been around for a while. Hell no, the pitchers said. He'd been a wedge in the team and none of them wanted to see his face again.

Baylor seemed oblivious to the fact that the very notion of rehiring Newton was causing division in the team. Speaking to writer Bruce Miles, Wood disagreed. "Yeah, I would say that there is," stated Wood, "especially with the pitching staff." He went on to say about Oscar's firing generally, "I can't find a reason to justify the decision. If it's stuff that's happening off the field, there has to be some other way to handle that. The man showed what he could do with a pitching staff. In two years, we went from what we did last year to turning around and breaking the strikeout record that was set by the best pitching staff (the

Braves) in baseball. If that's not teaching aggressiveness in the strike zone, I don't know what else a man can do." The other thing Baylor said — a little joke that would ultimately prove to be ironic — was that he hoped the Cubs would react the way they had when they lost Oscar if *he* ever got fired.

Before Oscar came home, his pitchers took him out to the famed Harry Caray's Italian Steakhouse for a private retirement party. They had all chipped in and bought him a gift to remember them by: a Harley Davidson. The papers said of that night, "I bet Don Baylor's ears were burning." They continued to call Baylor's decision "inexplicable."

Oscar and his family came home and assumed their off season lives in Portales, except this time it was not yet the off season. Oscar got jobs right away working with cattle. He had gotten his commercial driver's license some years back, and now he would be hauling cattle in an 18-wheeler. When we saw him, he said nothing about what had gone down, and we knew enough not to ask. Kathy said nothing either (though she would later concede that losing the job with the Cubs took the air out of him, that he was never quite the same after that). But we could tell by the way she talked to him about other things, domestic issues, that she was totally supportive.

When he wasn't running cattle back and forth, Oscar was on his motorcycle, and if it was after school, Ryan was with him. They were a picture of wild masculinity, speeding by with their leather jackets and matching bandanas on their heads. Ryan helped him with the ranching too as much as he could. One weekend Oscar was supposed to go out to a ranch in Santa Rosa to do some work, and Ryan, thinking that his father had left without him, got on the Harley and drove over to Mother's to see what she knew. He had carried an extra gallon of gas, in a plastic container, over with him on the bike. He smelled of gas. "Where's my dad?" he wanted to know. Oscar arrived shortly after and Mother gave him a scolding for teaching Ryan how to ride a

Harley in the first place, and for letting him carrying around a container of gas in the second. Ryan was too young, she felt, but Oscar disagreed. He wanted to teach him everything, and fast. He had already taught him to rope, to ride horses, to ranch, and to play baseball.

Now and then Oscar would drive out to visit me in Albuquerque. We would take a picnic lunch and go out into the Sandias. The Sandias offer not only incredible beauty, but also exquisite quiet. Sometimes Oscar would say, "I wouldn't mind living out here away from it all." And in the calm of the moment I could well imagine that for all that he loved baseball, the constant crowds, the constant interaction, the pavement and the airports and planes must have taken their toll on him. I knew from interviews I'd read that Oscar was utterly devastated since leaving the Cubs, but I knew from sitting beside him looking out over the city from a still mountain perch that Oscar was okay. He was very much a man of two worlds, and when one abandoned him, he could be comfortable, at the very least, in the other.

The Daily Herald's Barry Rozner wrote a story about Oscar in November of 2001; it was called "Acosta mending fences, but not the kind you think." It began, "Just when you think you couldn't respect Oscar Acosta more than you already do, he forces you to rethink your position." The article went on to talk about a post-Cubs interview Rozner had done with my brother, when he learned that Oscar was building and repairing fences and barns for local ranchers. Rozner noted that while Oscar was mending fences, Baylor was making $1.5 per year and the Cubs execs were living in North Shore homes never having to worry about a paycheck.

Rozner was most impressed with the fact that Oscar refused to complain about the way things had turned out. "This is America, and what makes it great is people who stand up and say what's right and fight for their loved ones," Oscar replied when Rozner asked if he regretted anything he had done in defense of his pitchers or his ideas. "If you regret that," Oscar said, "there's no point in being an American." When Rozner asked him about being fired, he said, "It's hard to swallow, but I have to swallow it and move on."

Chapter Fourteen

Tough Love

Perhaps because Oscar seemed so impervious to Baylor's actions, I felt them all the more acutely. In my own life I was still reeling from – among other things – the failure of state agencies to respond to my call for help regarding Ralph. I had become indignant to waste, fraud and laziness in government. I was hyper aware of moral apathy and incompetence. I felt like fighting everyone.

At the time, Clinton Harden was our state Labor Secretary, and he hired a woman from Elida, JI, to head our department. I knew her family very well. They were big landowners. I can still remember when I was a kid and the hired hands would stop by to visit after working at their ranch, branding cattle all day. I recall one woman crying her heart out in my mother's kitchen about the working conditions that her husband and sons had to endure. JI's family kept the Mexican workers and the Anglo workers separated: their wages were different, their housing was different, their treatment was different, and the amount of respect they received was different. The woman in my mother's kitchen cried because she felt so utterly disgraced.

JI was the ex-wife of a state senator, and that was her main "qualification" for the job with the Department of Labor. She was a tall, well-dressed woman, and she carried herself just the way you would expect a woman from a powerful, wealthy family to carry herself. Her heading the agency was a major breach of competence, and the department suffered dearly for it. For one thing, she made the decision to purchase inferior software that made it almost impossible for the rest of us to do our jobs. She also spent money on things we didn't need and thus depleted our budget when it came time for things we did need. Moreover, she hired Hispanics for clerical positions and Anglos for management positions time after time after time, without regard for individual qualifications.

I was not alone in my conclusions about her. My co-workers were equally upset, and when I talked about discussing the situation with Clint Harden, they stood behind me 100 percent. But when I made the appointment to actually meet with him, they suddenly didn't know whether it was such a good idea. So I went to see Harden alone, and I told him just what I thought. As part of a Republican administration, I said, I expected he would be a better manager. The management we were getting was terrible. The software that JI had purchased was costly and ultimately worthless and had made it impossible for us to serve our clients properly. And nobody was doing anything to rectify the situation. How did Harden respond to these charges?

He said he had just flown in from Washington D.C., where, ironically, he had been the recipient of a "manager of the year" award. I didn't care what he had received; the department was going to hell in a hand-basket, and I told him that. He looked at his watch and said thoughtfully, "You know what, I have to go now." I said, "Fine, go."

Since Harden had refused to have a conversation with me, I called Conroy Chino, an investigative reporter for various local TV networks. I told him that our work was being outsourced to India, and that the management had never come forth to speak to us foot soldiers regarding their ideas before they carried them out. Chino was intrigued and said he would come and talk to us, but about the same time we all received emails saying that we were not permitted to speak to reporters about internal affairs. In truth, I didn't want to lose my job any more than anyone else.

This of course is a familiar story. It happens all the time in all sorts of industries. People get hired for political reasons. People get fired for political reasons. Meanwhile, who is looking after the people who are to be served?

When Bill Richardson came in as the new governor, I contacted him to say we needed a good secretary of labor to replace Harden now that there had been a change of parties. No one wanted the position. Conroy Chino applied for the job and was hired. And even though he knew better than anyone about her ongoing blunders, he kept JI on as head of our department. And she in turn kept the heads rolling. Every Hispanic male was a target for her, even our bureau chief. I told my co-workers, "Hold on to your britches; she's used to running illegals on her ranch."

Eventually they put her in charge of the TANF (Temporary Assistance to Needy Families) program. Without any warning (which is in violation of state law), several Hispanics who had been working for years in that program were fired. Collectively, the pink slip recipients drafted a letter, compiling incriminating instances and explaining point blank that JI didn't like Hispanics and requesting that the governor overhaul the department before it was too late. I delivered the letter (which was signed by "Veteran Employees of the New Mexico Department of Labor" because the individuals who had written it were too intimidated to use their actual names) to Governor Richardson. But no one at the governor's office read it. When I took the story to the *Albuquerque Journal* and they in turn talked to the governor's office, they were told there was no record that the letter had been received, though they acknowledged that that didn't eliminate the possibility that it *had* been received. Finally it was agreed that an investigation into the allegations in the letter might be worthwhile. But in the meantime, the TANF program was lost because it did not meet performance goals.

Incompetence. Moral apathy.

While I was trying to right the wrongs of the world, Oscar was finding his way back to baseball. Only three months after Don Baylor fired him for reasons he never did make clear to the press or the players or anyone else, Oscar got a call from the Texas Rangers. A few years earlier, recognizing that they had a problem (they had fallen to last place in their division) they had hired Alex Rodriguez. The contract he signed was the most lucrative in sports history: a ten-year deal worth $252 million. Still, and in spite of the fact that A-Rod was breaking records left and right, the Rangers finished last in the American League Western division. So, Oscar was called to work with their pitchers. Jerry Narron was the manager at the time, and John Hart was the owner. Back in Chicago, an enthusiastic Barry Rozner was one of several reporters who wrote to let the sports world know that Oscar was back in the game. Everyone had been rooting for him, Rozner and the other reporters confirmed.

Back in Chicago, Don Baylor was still dealing with disgruntled pitchers. Sammy Sosa was campaigning to bring back Mack Newton, the stretching guru, and Baylor was backing him on it. Sosa said he didn't understand why Newton's contract had been terminated in the first place. The pitchers didn't want any part of Newton. Jason Bere, Kevin Tapani and Kerry Wood were especially vocal on the subject, but the others were adamant as well. And it wasn't just the pitchers; so many of the other players got behind this issue that the papers referred to it a time or two as "a mutiny." Oscar's supporters were so clearly in opposition to Newton that the issue became emblematic on how one felt about Oscar generally.

I had no use for Sammy Sosa once I knew that he was fighting the rest of the team to get Newton back. I had two baseballs with his signature on them. I called my old friend former State Senator Manny Aragon, who had so kindly helped Oscar to get the support he needed to build a baseball field at Eastern New Mexico University some years back. I told him I had a gift for him, a potentially valuable one, and if he ever needed money, he should sell Sammy's balls for whatever he could get for them.

When I was in Portales visiting Mother, I told her about

Sammy Sosa's support of Newton, and she immediately ran to her bedroom and ripped the photo of her and Sammy off the wall and, after a moment's hesitation in which she looked around for a place to dispose of it, threw it under the bed.

In the end, the voices of Sammy Sosa and Don Baylor were not loud enough to drown out all the others and Newton was not brought back. The players didn't want him and the fans didn't want him either. No moral apathy for those Cubs!

As for the Rangers, they were psyched to know that Oscar would be working with them. Writing for the *Fort Worth Star-Telegram*, Randy Galloway might have said it best: "We all know what's wrong with the Rangers. The pitching is broke. Can Oscar fix it?" He answered his own question by saying that it depended on who you asked. "Some swear by Oscar and others swear when his name is mentioned." But he conceded that if you asked the pitchers who worked with him in the past, you got a unanimous answer. With few exceptions, pitchers loved him.

Oscar was interviewed for the same story. "A lot of people don't necessarily like me," he said. "I've been told I'm a bit rough around the edges. But if a pitcher will give me his full attention and his full effort, I will crawl out there on any limb for him."

When asked about being fired from the Cubs, Oscar said that Groove (a nickname for Baylor) was his friend, someone to go out to eat with, play golf with. "But you put the two of us in the dugout for three hours, and there's going to be a clash. Two strong-headed SOBs. We couldn't live together once the game started. We were a wreck fixing to happen." He added, "He's the boss. Even in disagreement, I respect that. I had to go. I told Groove that. I have learned to accept political correctness whether I particularly like it or not."

The article noted that Oscar had worked with the Rangers years ago, when he'd first started coaching. Sandy Johnson, then the director of Rangers' minor leagues, had hired him for the Butte, Montana team based on the recommendation of Doug

Gassaway. Johnson said, "Doug had warned me he was about as unpolished as it gets. But you could see even then he was something special. He was working with a bunch of 17- and 18-year-old kids in Butte. To this day, I can run into one of those pitchers and the first thing they say is, Hey, tell Oscar hello for me. Pitchers will climb into a foxhole for Oscar. He's tough, but with him, it's all about tough love. And he knows his stuff."

The consensus was that the Rangers pitchers were a bunch of misfits. But Oscar was confident he could turn them around. So was everyone else in sports, now that they had seen the magnificent job he had done with the Cubs. Todd Van Poppel liked working with Oscar so much that he followed him to the Rangers team. "I had my two best seasons under him," Van Poppel admitted. "He keeps me consistent. He keeps me rolling."

Oscar and owner Hart lobbied to get John Rocker, who had been with the Cleveland Indians (and before that the Atlanta Braves) on the team. Oscar thought Rocker had a good arm and wanted to take him on as his personal project. Over the years, Rocker had been heavily criticized for making statements that were viewed as racist, anti-gay, and sexist. For instance, in a 2000 *Sports Illustrated* interview in which he wanted to explain that New York was "the most hectic, nerve-racking city" he'd ever seen, he said, "Imagine having to take the 7 Train to the ballpark, looking like you're riding through Beirut next to some kid with purple hair, next to some queer with AIDS, right next to some dude who just got out of jail for the fourth time, right next to some 20-year-old mom with four kids. It's depressing." During this same interview, he also managed to mock Asian women and call his then-teammate Randall Simon a "fat monkey." He made such a reputation for himself with this interview and other off-color remarks that fans began to boo him consistently, and in a "Tonight Show" segment, Jay Leno was inclined to encourage guests to beat a John Rocker dummy with a baseball bat.

Oscar knew all this, of course, but he said he didn't plan to judge Rocker for anything other than that arm of his. In fact, Rocker, who had apologized for his remarks, came to the Rangers in a state of humility. "Whatever you want, I'll do; I'll work with you," he told Oscar. Anyone who professed to want to work hard was someone my brother could get behind.

On the other hand, if someone didn't want to work, Oscar had no use for them. The season had just gotten started when one of his pitchers, Doug Davis, showed himself to be less capable than Oscar had hoped. During a post-game interview, Oscar was asked what he thought Davis needed to get his stuff up to par. Oscar didn't hesitate in his answer. "A heartbeat," he said flatly, and of course the media jumped on this assessment and in short order it became fodder for those who were intent on confirming that Oscar was just too tough.

Oscar worked with Francisco Cordero, the slider, helping him become of one of the majors' top closers. He worked with Dave Burba, who had signed as a free agent from Cleveland, helping him rebound from a tough 2001 season during which he was dropped from the rotation and had pitched only one inning in the post season. Burba said he knew he had a mechanical problem, but he couldn't quite put his finger on what it was, until he started working with Oscar. And Oscar worked with Hideki Irabu, who of course he had worked with years before. Now Oscar took him from being a starter to being a closer, and he made nine of the Rangers' 11 saves at the beginning of the season.

Oscar remained supportive of Rocker. In one game in June, Rocker gave up a two-out, run-scoring single to Craig Biggio in the ninth against Houston. Oscar said, "He's not going to be my whipping boy. You don't want him getting beat on his second best pitch. He rolled the dice and went with what he believed in."

Whatever Oscar did, management was on his side, and I thanked God every day for that. During one game, Oscar got ejected for going out to talk to an umpire who was making bad calls. He got right in his face and spoke to him in Spanish.

Narron's comment afterwards was, "I don't know what he said, but whatever he said, it's working." By mid-May reporters were saying that the Rangers pitching staff was the surprise of the league, ranking fourth and reflecting brightly on new coach.

But then came the game at Wrigley Field.

The game at Wrigley fell midway in the season. All the Chicago sportscasters and sportswriters were buzzing with the news that the Cubs' beloved former pitching coach was to oppose them with his new team. Everyone was speculating on what it would be like when the Cubs pitchers reunited with him. Kathy and Ryan flew out with Oscar for the event. While Oscar naturally stayed in the hotel with the other Rangers, Kathy and Ryan accepted an invitation to stay at the home of Kerry Wood and his fiancée, Sarah.

In the clubhouse, before the game started, there was a lot of excitement. Bere, Wood, Girardi, Tapani and Lieber and the others were all thrilled to see Oscar. And he was thrilled to see them too. In interviews before the game Oscar was asked once again about relationship with Baylor. Oscar responded by saying that he didn't know why people were making an issue of Baylor and himself. "I'm grateful for Don giving me the opportunity," he said. He added, "Don's the boss in the clubhouse. If he wants to make a change, that's his privilege." When Don Baylor was asked if he was concerned about the obvious pleasure the Cubs were taking in having Oscar back in town, he said he didn't care, that what concerned him was Alex Rodriquez.

Out on the field that day Oscar did what he was hired to do: he poured all of his experience and expertise into his players, and the Rangers won 7–4. After the game, however, Oscar was asked how it felt to be back in Chicago. Of course he spoke from his heart, enthusiastically admitting that he loved Chicago, that it was great to be back at Wrigley Field, that what happened there was what baseball was all about.

Regrettably, he also mentioned that back in Texas there was

really no one to "talk" baseball with. I assume he was referring to his pitchers but I can't be sure. I do believe that by "talk" he meant the Sandy Alomar sense of the word, as in, "Talking baseball is a time-honored tradition that has linked generations of players."

"It's pretty sad," Oscar told the cameras broadcasting his words to sports fans all over the country, "when the only ones I can talk to about baseball are my wife and my son."

As I said, it was only midway through the season, and already the Rangers' pitchers were showing signs of turning around. But Narron couldn't deal with what he called the "differences in philosophy and problems in communication" that he and Oscar had. So he went to Hart, and Hart told him that he was the one who had to make the decision, and once again, Oscar was fired.

When Baylor had pushed him into resigning the year before, Oscar never made any comments to the media about why he thought it had happened. It was Baylor's doing, and as far as he was concerned, it was Baylor who had to explain himself. It was the same with Narron. Oscar didn't have anything to say on the matter. But everyone else threw their two cents in, including Baylor, who said he was sorry to hear the news, and sorry for Oscar's family. Orel Hershiser stepped up to take Oscar's place, telling interested media reps that he felt responsible for the whole mess, because he in fact had recommended Oscar for the job in the first place. (I do believe he gave himself a little too much credit there.) According to the a *Knight Ridder* article, Hershiser called Oscar to ask for help in his new duties, and Oscar told him he was happy to help as much as he could.

Interestingly, not long after Oscar was fired from the Rangers, Don Baylor was fired from the Cubs. Everyone knew his job would be in jeopardy after he suffered through a nine-game losing streak in May of 2002. Even MacPhail acknowledged that the Cubs lacked enthusiasm. Baylor was still rallying to bring Newton back when he got the axe. Naturally he blamed his failure on Oscar, saying that Oscar undermined him when he didn't stop the revolt against Mack Newton.

I followed the story with great interest. Apparently right after he got the news, Baylor went to the clubhouse, thinking that, like Oscar, he would momentarily be surrounded by bitter players swearing they would never go out on the field again without their beloved manager. But that is not what happened. Baylor sat alone, reflecting, most certainly, on his aloneness. *The Daily Herald* wrote that "the end of Don Baylor was carved in stone the day he ran Oscar Acosta out of town."

Whereas Oscar had seen Baylor coming, Narron's actions had stunned him. We were all stunned. Narron, Oscar remarked when we spoke of it alone, presented himself as a Christian, but while he talked the talk, he had no idea how to walk the walk. That was about all he had to say on the matter.

And so, once again, Oscar came home to Portales and, with no time to dwell on what wasn't, immediately found work hauling cattle, building fences, whatever he could find to do. He also rented a building and started a kids' gym in town. This was very important to him. He wanted to get kids early, when they were just beginning to discover their talents, and teach them how to be athletes.

Oscar seemed determined now to make a life away from baseball.

It was clear early on that he would not be able to get the gym to be profitable; the money just wasn't there in that community. And while the ranching continued to be a labor of love, he felt there must be some way that he could put his years of coaching and managing expertise to work. He came to visit me one day in Albuquerque and we talked about his job prospects. I suggested we go see Governor Richardson and that he apply for a position with the New Mexico Sports Authority. He agreed that it was worth a try and we found a professional resume writer and put a new resume together for him. We forwarded it on to the governor's office. In the meantime, I called my friend Guy Riordan, who, at that time, was a boxing promoter and the director of Rancho de La Joya Game Preserve. He was also a long-time Democratic Party contributor, and he had contributed to the governor's campaign. As Governor Richardson was a big fan of boxing, Guy and I made arrangements for Oscar and me to attend a match at the Sandia Casino, in Albuquerque, on the same night the governor was going. Oscar came up with Kathy, and when the time was right, Guy motioned for the three of us to come up to the governor's private box. We went in and Oscar and the governor shook hands and spoke a bit about sports.

We followed up with the governor's office, but in the end Oscar wasn't hired. Nor had I ever received a response to the letter I'd sent regarding the problems at the Department of Labor. But shortly thereafter I found myself at another boxing match that the governor was also attending, and with the support of a well-made martini and a welcoming wave from Guy Riordan, I marched into the VIP box and pointed a finger at Bill Richardson and said, "You didn't give my brother a job; that's fine. But what about the letter I sent you about the Department of Labor? You can't keep bad people in powerful positions just because you owe favors. That's not right." Bill hunched his shoulders like a turtle trying to retract its head into its shell and said to whoever was listening, "She's telling me off," and as I looked aside, I saw that his security people were on their feet and heading toward me, so I turned and walked out on my own.

Mother was still cleaning for a living after all these years, and around the time that Oscar returned to Portales she started some volunteer work, cleaning the rectory and the Catholic Church over which one Father Tobin presided. She was immediately impressed with him. Unlike many Catholics, he avoided grandeur like the plague. He slept on a board on the floor and had very little furniture. Likewise, and to the disappointment of some of his parishioners, he kept his statuary in the church to a minimum, believing that Christ should be the focus and the presence of various saints was only a distraction. When he had to go somewhere, he rode his bike. His sermons were beautiful but simplistic as well, in that he got right down to brass tacks. "Drinking is wrong; don't do it," he would tell his parishioners. And, "If your kids won't sit down and be still on their own, then it is your responsibility to get them to sit still. We're in the house of the Lord here." And everyone listened to him, even the kids.

Daddy used to say that he could break a herd of cows sooner than he could get his kids to listen to him. Oscar felt the same way, though he might have changed kids for "pitchers."

"How does he do it?" Oscar asked mother. She didn't know the answer, so Oscar went to find out for himself. And before long he and Father Tobin had become friends. Not only did Oscar and Kathy and Ryan convert to Catholicism, but Oscar and Father Tobin began spending time together away from the church, talking about their views and their experience of the world.

During this time, Oscar, who had always been so intense in all his pursuits, began to relax. You could see it on his face and hear it in his laughter. Perhaps part of it was his friendship with Father Tobin. Perhaps another part was being away from the media, not having to worry about speaking his mind and being who he was. All of his energy — and he had such a vast amount of it — was focused now on finding a good high school for Ryan, a place where he could play baseball. Previously, he had wanted only that his kids should attend Elida and Portales schools, and they had, but it was clear now that Ryan had the gift, and Oscar wanted to make sure that it was developed. He called me and asked what I thought of the schools in Albuquerque, and I told him about one, the Academy, that I thought might work. He said he would check into it.

Needless to say, since leaving the Rangers Oscar was spending more and more time with his family, and loving it. He had all the time for Ryan now that our father had never really had for him.

Kathy likes to tell a story about how the whole family took a trip to California and somehow the girls got mad at the boys and left them on the beach. Oscar and Ryan had to walk back to their hotel room, and in order to do that in a respectable fashion, they had to first go into a shop and buy T-shirts. They were deciding which shirts they wanted when Oscar turned to Ryan and said, "I bet you you'd be afraid to kiss me, right here in the store." Ryan responded, "I'm not afraid to kiss you, Dad." "Well, then go ahead and kiss me right now," Oscar said, and Ryan got on his toes and gave his dad a peck on the cheek.

Mother was also the beneficiary of Oscar's additional time and outpouring of love. Just about every morning he would call her and say he was coming over for coffee before he started his day. Both of them earlier risers, they would eat breakfast together and talk about everything.

Baseball was far away from my mind by then, though I don't think any of us missed hearing about (or lost any sleep over) Sammy Sosa getting caught using a corked bat. (One could not help but wonder if he had been cheating when he hit any of his 500 plus home runs before his faux pas.) We had plenty of other things to focus on. Carol's son Danny, one of her twins, had joined the army right after high school. He had been stationed in North Carolina for a while and had gone to Kosovo for a time. Danny was a parachuter, responsible not only for jumping from planes into danger but also for making sure the parachutes were safe for other jumpers. Still, he wasn't sure what he wanted from life, and when the time came for him to reenlist, he turned to his Uncle Oscar.

Oscar told him that by reenlisting he had a real chance to learn what it meant to be a man. Danny came to agree, and at about the same time, the Iraq war began in earnest. When Danny got word that he was likely to be called to go to Iraq, Mother nearly lost her mind. She had a bad feeling about it and she didn't want him there. She began crying the day she heard, and she cried every day after that. I tried to comfort her. "Let's pray," I would say, and we would. We promised to go to Chimayo to give thanksgiving if only Danny's fortunes would reverse themselves.

This was the first time I couldn't think of any political connections that I could call on to help move things along in our favor.

Mother prayed not only for Danny but for all the soldiers waiting for their orders. Danny insisted that he would be fine, but she wouldn't hear of it. And she wouldn't stop crying. Then one day while Mother and I were on our knees, Danny walked in and announced that his orders had come through, not to go to Iraq but to head up the National Guard right there in Portales. Oscar was there at the time. He leaped up from his chair and hugged Danny, the tears pooling in his eyes. When he released him we all hugged Danny and danced around the kitchen with him. Later Oscar told Mother that she had no idea how bad he felt, that it would have been his fault if Danny wound up in Iraq. Once again, our prayers had been answered.

One day Oscar walked into Mother's for their breakfast meeting and announced that he had been offered a job with the Yankees, with one of their minor teams. He had negotiated his deal with Steinbrenner himself. As one reporter, Barry Lewis, noted, it wasn't surprising that Oscar thrived with the Yankees because "his traits were the type that George Steinbrenner embraces." They were sending him to Tampa, and he was glad because his research had confirmed that Clearwater Catholic School, being both Catholic and big on baseball, was the perfect school for Ryan. The Yankees had always respected Oscar and they knew what a great coach he was. Billy Connors, the VP, and manager Joe Torre, were happy to welcome him on board.

Oscar and Kathy sold the house in Portales and bought Billy Connors' house in Tampa. They hoped to be in one place long enough for Ryan to graduate from high school and they wanted to have their own home. We didn't see many announcements regarding the fact that Oscar was back in the game, but then that was never what was important to him, and as history had already proven, publicity never did him a lick of good anyway. Oscar liked working hard and seeing results. And he worked hard for the Yankees, and he saw results — not only accolades from everyone but also a "manager of the year" award his first year out.

Oscar and Kathy came back to Portales every chance they got. And Oscar always brought with him a huge box filled with baseballs and jackets and T-shirts and hats, all signed by baseball greats, which he would give away to all the young people in our extended family. His first year with the Yankees he came home for Thanksgiving and stayed through Christmas and announced during that time that he was being sent to the Dominican to manage the Gulf Coast team. My heart clenched when he said that; it seemed so far away. But it was more than that. Looking back, I guess it was a premonition, though at the time I only recognized it as a selfish response to the fact that my brother would be working off the continent.

Kathy stayed based in Tampa of course, so that Ryan could stay in school. Kathy would video tape all of Ryan's games and when Oscar could get away, he would fly home and watch the tapes at his son's side. If he was home long enough, he would fly to Portales and spend time with Mother and the rest of us.

It was clear after his first trip back from the Dominican that Oscar was happier than he had ever been. He had found his element. He was being paid to help talented young men who had nothing to polish their skills and, in the case of the best of them, fulfill a dream that would eventually take them to the most famous ball fields in America.

"I thought people in Mexico were poor," Oscar told Mother. "These people have nothing, nothing at all." He said some were so poor that the only decent meals they had in the course of a week were the ones that the Yankee organization provided for them. But hungry or not, they would play ball with all their hearts and souls.

Oscar taught them not only the mechanics of the game but also about grooming, about how to take care of the clubhouse. They hung on his every word. And Oscar, who had never been one to talk much about his work, seemed to want to talk about it all the time now. He loved these young men, and they loved him.

Oscar told us that he would bring his players and their families to the beach on the weekends and make sure they were all well fed. He seemed to want to touch as many lives as possible. And he certainly wanted his boys to be healthy. "The Dominican supplies more players to major league baseball than any other country outside the U.S.," he liked to remind us. José Garcia and Ricardo Rodriguez. Pedro Martinez and Raul Mondesi, and like it or not, Sammy Sosa. And so many others. In the Dominican, Oscar said, the players lived, breathed and ate baseball. And that was all he ever really wanted from his players. Barry Rozner, one of the few reporters still closely following Oscar's career, wrote that Oscar cared more about what kind of men he was sending from rookie ball up the ladder than what kind of players they were.

"Kids grow up and they push the boundaries to see how far they can go," Oscar told Rozner in an interview, referring to players in the States, "and if there's no discipline, then they keep going and pushing. These young players today, it's mind-boggling the things they say and do. Everything's about the money, and morals and ethics and integrity go out the windows."

In the Dominican, Oscar had found the integrity he had been searching for all along.

Oscar brought the Gulf Coast League rookie team to the pennants two years in a row. As noted by sportswriter Craig Mertz, "He was a ball of fire. He was very adamant and very in love with the mechanics and the mental aspects of pitching. He challenged pitchers all of the time."

That same year, Oscar started talking about wanting to have a family reunion. He wanted all the relatives from Colorado, from all over New Mexico, from Mexico, as well as all his friends from around the country, to come together for a huge party. This obsession, I believe, was a symbol of how good he felt about his life. He and Kathy, who had had their share of hard times, were happier than ever together; Ryan was getting great grades and showing himself to be an excellent ball player; his daughters were both happily married; and Oscar had found his own personal happiness working with the poorest of the poor in the sport he so loved. He wanted this reunion to take place in Tampa, in his new house. To that purpose, he started making changes, improvements, when he was home.

Most of the time we knew well in advance when Oscar was coming to Portales, especially now that he was working in the Dominican, but one day Mother called and said, "Guess what! Your little brother is here." I could hear in her voice that he had surprised her too and that she was thrilled. I said I would be there as soon as I could, but before I could even call in at work to ask for some time off, Oscar called back and said he would come up to see me, and he would bring everyone with him — Mother, Carol, her kids, their spouses, whoever could get some time. Either that, or I could come down and then we would all go to Juarez to see John. "Whatever you want," I told him. "Whatever you decide, I'll make it work on my end." Albuquerque was better, he decided in the end, and he asked me to reserve a few hotel rooms as too many people would be coming for everyone to stay in my apartment.

On the ride up to Albuquerque, Mother later told me, he never stopped reminiscing. As they passed Fort Sumner, he talked about how much he enjoyed the company of Tom Drake, whose family lived there. He talked about how he and Tom would drive out into the fields and drink beer and listen to music by Ray Price and George Strait. He said that once he mentioned the great Goose Gossage to Tom, and Tom cried, "You know him?" Oscar said, "Hell yeah. You want to talk to him?" And he pulled out his cell phone and got Goose on the line and handed the cell to Tom and said, "Here, say hello to Goose." And he even told Mother a story about how once he and Tom and another baseball friend went to the Prince Lounge in Clovis, a place patronized by Mexican laborers, most of them from the slaughter house in Friona, Texas and some of them dairy workers. The owner went right up to Oscar and his friends the moment they walked in and said they'd have to pay a $20 cover charge. "Is there a live band or something going on?" Oscar asked. She looked him straight in the eye and said there was nothing like that. I guess she thought she would scare him and Tom and the other gentlemen away before any trouble broke out. But Oscar surprised her by taking out his wallet and giving her three twenties. Then he marched up to a table in the front and sat down. Tom and the other guy followed, but they were looking around like they thought they might be jumped at any moment. The place had gone quiet, and all the other patrons were all regarding Oscar and his friends with suspicion. Oscar looked around at all their faces. Then he laughed and started talking in Spanish, asking everyone there how they were doing and what was going on, and all the patrons started laughing, and everything was good.

We met at a pizza place, where Carol's grandchildren, Noel and his wife Kim's kids, could play. We sat for hours talking, and then Carol offered to take the babies back to the hotel so that the rest of us could go out to a club. Oscar said he wanted to listen to Spanish music, so we went to the Sunset Grill, where Los Bohemios play. We had a great time there, listening to music and watching Noel and Kim dance. I could not help but notice how relaxed Oscar was, how satisfied he seemed.

We were tiring, but no one wanted to bring the night to a

close. After we left the Grill, we went to the Village Inn for breakfast. Noel, who is very funny, had us in stitches telling us his version of how some woman had tried to steal him away from Kim out on the dance floor back at the Grill. Oscar laughed so hard I thought he was going to fall out of his chair.

We all went back to my apartment or the hotel to sleep for a few hours, but by late morning we were at it again, this time at the Marriott, at a restaurant that features a Mariachi trio. Oscar ran in ahead of everyone and told the band he wanted them to play "Las Mananitas," a traditional Spanish birthday song, because Mother's birthday was only a few weeks away. Then in we went and the band started up and Oscar said, "Mother, this is for you," and he bent to give her a kiss. She was touched to the core.

When the song was over, I got up and asked the Mariachis if they would play "No Me Sé Rajar," (a song by Vicente Fernandez) if I sang to it. I had learned to do this back during my years with Ralph. I did not feel shy at all about singing my heart out in this song about a brother who doesn't give in and doesn't run away.

I saw Oscar again a few weeks later, at our big annual Thanksgiving at Mother's house. He called from Portales to find out when I was leaving Albuquerque and I explained that I was running late and they might have to start without me. He said they would wait for me but that I had better hurry. Leah Dawn, who was now living in Albuquerque (as was Brandon), was the one who was holding things up; she had to bring her motorcycle to her friend's before we could leave. Oscar called again before we ever got out of the house. "Did Thanksgiving kind of slip up on you this year?" he joked.

We had a lovely dinner, and after the meal Oscar brought out a CD of Dominican music, which he had fallen in love with. As soon as he put it on, Naomi, Carol's oldest, got up and began to dance with her uncle. I tried to dance to it, but as much as I loved the music, I found it hard to dance to. Carol loved the CD, and after it was over, Oscar gave it to her to keep.

We put on other music, and Naomi continued to dance, teasing some of us good-naturedly about the way we looked when we were dancing. Then Mother got up and began to dance with the little ones. Amanda was there with her new husband, Kyle, who was also from Portales. God knows what he must have thought of us, as none of us seemed to be able to sit still. Leah Dawn and I had gone to Juarez a week or so earlier, and we had bought a CD there. I ran and got it out of the car and brought it in for the others to dance to. I totally forgot that it began with some cuss words. "Oh, mi Dios," Mother cried. "What is that?" "Are you crazy, Sis?" Oscar asked. "Take that off, take it off right now." So I took it off and we put others on and everyone began to dance again. Somehow it was two in the morning when we finally stopped.

The next day Oscar, who was staying at Carol's son Danny's house, came over for breakfast, and before long it was time for me to head back to Albuquerque. I didn't want to say "goodbye." Ever since I had the premonition I tried to avoid using that word with him. Maybe he felt the same way. He said, "Have a good trip back," and I said, "You too; have a good trip home and I'll see you soon."

I didn't call Mother the next day or the day after that. On Tuesday, when I knew he should have arrived back in the Dominican, I called Mother and she said, "Oh yes, he just called. He got there safe and sound." While I was breathing a sigh of relief, she went on to say that she hadn't seen him off. One of twins had taken him to the airport at three in the morning. Usually Mother would give him her blessing right before he left, but as he knew he would be getting up in the middle of the night, he had her do it the night before.

Oscar stayed in Tampa for the Christmas holiday. Then back he went to the Dominican. His house was getting closer to being ready for the huge reunion that he wanted to have, and sometime in February he called Noel, who worked in construction, and asked him if he would come out and tile all his floors. Leah Dawn came up with the idea that Noel should FedEx all his tools, so that he could fly there. They made arrangements for him to go in April.

At Easter time, Mother went to Mexico to see her sister. With all my family scattered and no plan to get together for Easter dinner, I crawled into bed and pretty much stayed there for three days, watching the Christian stations on TV and thinking about all the ups and downs our family had undergone over the years. I wasn't depressed really; I was calm. I just didn't feel like doing anything. Mother called at the end of the week to say that she didn't feel like being alone so she was bringing her sister back with her from Mexico. She said she had talked to Oscar in the Dominican and that he sounded really happy. Carol had talked to him too. He'd called her to say what a great job Noel was doing tiling the floors in his home. A few days later, Noel, having finished the tiling job at Oscar's house, got on a plane to fly home.

In the short time between Noel's departure in Tampa and his arrival at the airport in Albuquerque, the news came in. His wife, who had gone to pick him up, had to tell him that Oscar was dead.

The next several days were a jumble. I can't remember what I was told or by whom. I know that Ryan played baseball the day after Oscar died. (How could he not have? He had seen his father doubled over in pain, refusing to leave someone else's ranch until the cattle were tended to. You make a commitment, you keep it, Oscar would have said.) And during that game, Ryan hit a home run, and as he ran from base to base, one hand pointing to the sky, yelling, "Daddy, this is for you," the crowd rose collectively and cheered him on. I know too that the Dominican boys who flew over for the memorial in Tampa beat their fists on their hearts over and over again in grief. Flags flew at half mast at stadiums across the country. Yankees and Cubs and other baseball people flew to Tampa and were part of the big memorial that Mother and Carol and I did not attend. The mourners included current and former All Stars, Hall-of-Famers, and executives from teams across the nation. Those who couldn't come called. Reggie Jackson called. George Steinbrenner called. Kathy said to Steinbrenner, "You lost your most valuable employee." Steinbrenner answered, "He was a valuable employee, but a more valuable person." Cashman said about Oscar, and Humberto Trejo, with whom he had died, "Their dedication and passion to improving young lives far exceeded the boundaries of a baseball field."

Then there was the Rosary service that we had in Portales. Kerry Wood and George Steinbrenner would not let Kathy and Ryan fly from Florida to New Mexico on commercial jets. They hired a private charter for them. When Ryan walked in the door, Mother and Carol and I nearly lost our minds, he looked so like Oscar. He showed us the tattoo he'd gotten, "En memoria a mi Papa," on his shoulder with a Yankee emblem. (Leah Dawn and Donny and Danny and Noel would all get tattoos bearing Oscar's name and the Yankee emblem too). Some Yankees came to Portales as well. Melissa and Amanda and their husbands were there. Relatives from Colorado came down. More relatives from Mexico came up. Family, teachers, friends, and friends of friends from all over the state joined us.

One man, and to this day I don't remember who he was or what baseball organization he represented, told us he admired Oscar so much that he gave his son "Acosta" as a middle name. Arkie Kiehney, Oscar's next door neighbor from when he still had his house in Portales, said that Oscar had called him right before he died, just to say hello. Arkie, a tall cowboy with a beautiful wife, had tears streaming down both cheeks. "We were joking on the phone," he sobbed, "like we always do. He said, 'Hey, Gringo Pendejo, what are you doing?' And then he said,

'You know, I'm ready to come home to Portales and run some cattle.'"

Father Tobin presided over the service. He spoke for a while about the suffering that is generated when the good die young, comparing Oscar, maybe because he was so handsome, to James Dean. Then Ryan got up to talk about his father. Watching him standing there, totally in control in spite of the fact that his heart was breaking, I saw my brother, and also my father. He said what he had to say in both English and Spanish, because that is the way Oscar would have wanted it. He had worked with Carol before the event to make sure he had all the Spanish down correctly. He said, "My Daddy died in pinstripes, Yankee pinstripes," and we all knew that was as it should have been.

While Ryan went on talking about how proud his father had been to be a New York Yankee, I saw in my mind's eye my baby brother stretched out on the floor as a kid again, in front of our small black and white TV, asking Carol or me go outside and adjust the antenna so he could get a good picture to watch the baseball game, his baseball cards all lined up in front of him, as if the people on them — Mickey Mantle, Babe Ruth, Willie Mays — were watching the game along with him.

After Ryan finished speaking, we played a George Strait song called "Love Without End, Amen." The song talks about the love between father and son and the love between God and the Son. I had always thought my brother resembled George Strait, especially when he was dressed as a cowboy. They had met; when Oscar was with the Texas Rangers in 1988 and 89, George Strait had come to spring training to see the team.

At one point during the ceremony Mother turned to me and said, "He got what he wanted. All the family is here."

The day after the Rosary, there was another service at Wheeler Mortuary. Kathy wanted it to be private, and as we didn't know ourselves where it would be until the last minute, we were not able to tell others, and many of Oscar's friends were upset that they had been excluded.

When Mother and Carol and I and our children went into the funeral home, we found Ryan holding a small wooden box on which baseball bats and gloves had been carefully engraved. There was a photo of Oscar, tanned and smiling, on the lid. It was hard for me to come to terms with the fact that all that remained of my brother could now fit in that box. Mother looked so small and ashen when she took it from Ryan. "Mi hijo, tu mamá aquí está, mi niño, chiquito mío," she cried as she caressed it.

After the service at Wheeler Mortuary, there was a reception at the Baptist Church. Mother was too weak to attend. She went home to begin her Novenas, praying for, among other thing, the chance that Kathy would allow us to bury what little was left of Oscar in Portales. It didn't happen immediately; but Carol continued to talk to Kathy, and eventually she gave in.

Most of Oscar's ashes were buried at the foot of Daddy's grave on a Thursday afternoon, just after a rainstorm, and before the beautiful rainbow that had appeared began to fade. Father Tobin was there to say the blessings, and afterward, Carol and Naomi played the Dominican CD that Oscar had had us all dancing to the previous Thanksgiving. Amanda went to one of the ranches that Oscar loved and spread some of ashes there too.

Often my mind wonders back to an article that Barry Rozner wrote just after Oscar was fired from the Rangers. Basically it said that it was easy to take shots at Oscar, who, by Rozner's math, had lost two jobs in nine months. But if you understood baseball, then you knew there was no place in today's game for an Oscar Acosta, that "these old school types are an endangered species in baseball," that they try to teach players to be men and play the game with "a fire, devotion, respect and intelligence almost nonexistent today;" that they don't coddle their players or lie to them, that what they offer is "tough love."

I'd have to agree with this assessment heart and soul, not only for Oscar but also for our family.

For all the mistakes that we have made individually and collectively, we have tried to live with fire, devotion, respect, intelligence and love, tough and otherwise. And of course, prayer.

ACKNOWLEDGMENTS

All glory and honor to my Lord Jesus Christ. May those who have read my book come to the foot of the Cross and ask Jesus Christ to become their Lord and Savior. It is only through Him that our sins are forgiven and we will have everlasting life. The Bible says, "You do not know what your life will be like tomorrow. You are just a vapor that appears for a little while and then vanishes away" (James 4:14). Our purpose in life is to love and praise our Lord Jesus Christ and to love one another. One day we will be joined with our loved ones who died in the salvation of our Lord.

Thanks to my beloved mother Concha (Connie) Acosta, who gave me backbone and prayed that this book would tell the story of her baby boy, Oscar. The Bible says, "Her children arise up, and call her blessed; her husband also and he praiseth her" (Proverbs 31:28). And YES we have. The love and devotion my Mom has for God and her family is what has helped us cope with the fiery arrows that have been sent our way. It is the memories she shared with me that helped me write this book.

Thanks to my children, Leah Dawn and Brandon Scott Montoya. It is a blessing from God to be their mom. The joy and happiness they have brought into my life is immeasurable.